C000245871

'A compelling story of marriage, passion and betrayal that reads like a richly textured novel. With skill, wit, and empathy, Parry takes readers on a compelling journey to find the truth of her grandfather's love affair with a famous novelist. Gripping, poignant, and fascinating.'

Charlotte Gordon, author of *Romantic Outlaws: The Extraordinary Lives of Mary Wollstonecraft and Mary Shelley*

'I have always taken a particular interest in other people's lives. It is the life of 'the shadowy third', the betrayed wife, that interests me as much as those of the lovers. Even if you have never read Elizabeth Bowen's novels and have never heard of Humphry House, his grand-daughter's quest will hold your attention as it held mine.'

Ann Thwaite, award-wining author of *AA Milne: His Life* (Whitbread Biography of the Year)

'While V.C. Andrews wrote of flowers in the attic, author Julia Parry investigated letters in an attic that uncovered the illicit affair of her grandfather and the acclaimed author, Elizabeth Bowen. In order to come to grips with her family's secrets, Parry traveled to the lovers' haunts of Oxford, Ireland, and India. *The Shadowy Third* reveals the secret life of the author of *The Death of the Heart*, a title that applies to the man and women whose sepia-covered correspondence led to this riveting memoir.'

Marlene Wagman Geller author of *Women of Means: Fascinating Biographies of Royals, Heiresses, Eccentrics and Other Poor Little Rich Girls*

'A captivating mélange of memoir, biography, social history and literary evaluation… Parry's meticulous investigations expose the extraordinary way in which Elizabeth Bowen "haunted the third chair at the table" of her grandparents' unorthodox marriage. Her palpable excitement at what she uncovers is bright and infectious. Parry offers us rich, rewarding new insights… what distinguishes Parry's book from more conventional biographies is her unique ability to empathise with her grandmother, who shared her husband with a rival. Parry describes her research as akin to reading over her grandmother's shoulder. She channels Madeline's voice in a way that no dispassionate biographer could.'

Eleanor Fitzsimons, author of *Wilde's Women* and *The Life and Loves of E. Nesbit*

'What a gorgeous book Julia Parry has written. It seemed to me a book all about ghosts and the way that they inhabit the present with their enigmatic absent-presence. The power of traces ran throughout the book – both the idea of dusty letters retrieved from an attic, and then the poignant remains of Bowens Court half-hidden in the grass… This is a magnificent debut.'

Gail Crowther, author of *Three-Martini Afternoons at the Ritz: The Rebellion of Sylvia Plath & Anne Sexton*

'Julia Parry's prose debut is a triumph… this masterful work tells the story of the author's grandfather's affair and friendship with the Anglo-Irish writer, Elizabeth Bowen. Parry, a former photographer, writes with a keen cinematic sensibility. Here, her beautiful, visual prose is crystal clear, deeply erudite, poetic in exactly the right places. *The Shadowy Third* is not just a brilliant new addition to critical studies of Elizabeth Bowen (in particular the chapters on Bowen Court, where Bowen, 'chatelaine' of the house in a post-Independence and rapidly changing Ireland, is vividly rendered by Parry), but it is a completely moving, thoroughly researched account of a family, and the effect an outside literary force (one of the foremost writers of the 20th Century) had upon it – and it upon her and her work.'

Jaki McCarrick, playwright of Belfast Girls

The Shadowy Third

Love, Letters, and Elizabeth Bowen

Best wishes,
Julia Parry

JULIA PARRY

This edition first published in the United Kingdom
by Duckworth in 2021

Duckworth, an imprint of Duckworth Books Ltd
1 Golden Court, Richmond, TW9 1EU, United Kingdom
www.duckworthbooks.co.uk
For bulk and special sales please contact info@duckworthbooks.com

A catalogue record for this book is available from the British Library.

Printed and bound in Great Britain by Clays.

9780715653579

For my beloved mother

BOWEN'S COURT,
KILDORRERY,
Co. CORK

Sunday June 15

Dear Elizabeth

Ireland

H. House, Esq

BOWEN'S COURT,
KILDORRERY,
Co. CORK.

Saturday

Elizabeth my dear, you have now played th[e] … on me. For moments this morning I did … the address on your letter at all. … Shaya Berlin's — inside however all … Elizabethan. I do not understand … do not know metaphorically whether … "concentrated" there is the whiskey … hymn in which God's love a grace … distilled in the dew and the rain … two sorts of letter, and often think … the mood rather than the mood … makes me have black depress… centre. This not is one of the … between the two kinds, and … to make it write at all. … me simple & solid, a present … indeed become difficult, … I have become one.

Your letter was not the … the course of it which … worked into its late… physical. I have very … and have no place, and being … They are in order: but this time they …

KENSINGTON 5722.

45 MARKHAM SQUARE, S.W.3.

Wednesday

My dear Humphry
I came here yesterday afternoon and found your letter, ...

Wednesday

Yes, I should like …

Contents

Wadham College, Oxford

Chapter 1

Oxford: *Encounters*

The linen is crisp, the light abundant through high stained-glass windows. There is a clink of glasses, innuendo, and clever chatter. A luncheon party in Oxford in 1933. The host, thick-necked and tipping into portliness, eyes the table with satisfaction. His chosen men, bright young fellows of the college, are acquitting themselves well. The woman on his right, intelligent and bold-featured, is a superb addition to the group – all the better for not being part of the university.

She, for her part, loves a good meal, particularly if served with wine and virility. There is nothing quite like being the one clever woman in the room. Deftly she slips impressions of the table up her imaginative sleeve. She's already written a version of her host, with his air of cultured complacency, into an earlier novel of hers.

Further down the table sits a young man. Square-faced, taciturn. Here is the Oxford he has been aiming for, yet one he now fears he might lose. Here too a woman unlike any he has met – spirited, older, other. It is essential to catch her eye, pique her curiosity, be memorable.

2011

This was the start of the affair between the brilliant novelist and short story writer Elizabeth Bowen, and my grandfather, Humphry House. A story contained in a box of letters that for years had lain, largely forgotten, in my uncle John's attic – a heart left to beat unheard.

Opening the cardboard box one afternoon at his house, I was greeted by a chaos of paper of various weights and sizes. Large manila envelopes, the texture of old skin, bore simply the information: 'E. B. to H. H.' and 'H. H. to E. B.' Some envelopes had a visible date in the postmark: others merely a year added tentatively in pencil near a peeling green stamp of George V. I took all the letters and sorted them loosely into piles. 1933: first six months, 1933: second six months, 1934, 1935, after 1935, dateless.

The letters from Elizabeth to Humphry sat on one side of the sofa, his to her on the other. Only then, when I saw them all laid out, did I fully realise our family's good fortune. Unusually, we had ended up with both sides of the correspondence. The whole relationship was there at my fingertips.

Elizabeth leapt off the page immediately – her energy, her breathless handwriting, her imperatives: 'Stop worrying about your heart and try and have a better brain.' I heard the dynamic voice not just of one of my favourite novelists, but of one of the great writers of the twentieth century. I was plunged into new worlds – of the Anglo-Irish big house, of bohemian London in the 1930s, of the last days of Empire in India. Beyond the personal dramas, the correspondence gave me a fascinating glimpse of the interwar period. There was much discussion of women's roles, in an era that afforded them greater freedoms whilst still keeping them harnessed to societal expectations.

I devoured the letters, gripped by their brilliance and slightly starstruck by Elizabeth herself. My grandfather, whom I never met, was a tangible presence for the first time in my life. And yet I could not help thinking of my grandmother, the unscripted third player in this vivid tale of love and betrayal.

Five hours flew by, and then there was John again, asking if I was ready for a drink.

I had tried, albeit inexpertly, to line up the letters on the sofa so that the back and forth element of the correspondence could be appreciated by the next reader, whoever that might be. My suggestion for reorganisation was rejected, kindly but firmly. Back in their separate crepey manila envelopes they went, into the box, and off into the recesses of the house.

What impact did the affair have on my family? Why had my grandmother preserved the love letters another woman had written to her husband? Did the relationship spill over into the work of Elizabeth Bowen, as family folklore told?

All those questions remain unanswered. Six months later my dear uncle died quite unexpectedly, and the tattered old box came to me.

Elizabeth Bowen is a writer obsessed with letters. Her belief that a letter could establish a psychic affinity between sender and recipient is everywhere in her fiction. Indeed, the grip a passionate correspondence can exert on a person dominates an entire novel, *A World of Love* (1955). In it, a collection of love letters from the past springs out of a trunk, into the mind of a young woman, and into the fire. The missives are repeatedly referred to as 'husks' – vessels emptied of life, but not of emotion. Their violent immediacy remains: 'The ink, sharp in the candlelight, had not faded.' For the protagonist, Jane, the letters inspire 'reluctant awe, and some misgiving'.

Several elements of this novel are, for me, eerily prescient. The first is the way in which the letters arrive in Jane's life: 'They fell at her feet, having found her rather than she them.' After my uncle's death, I went over to his house for the last time with my mother. Just six months earlier, I had spent that thrilling afternoon there reading the correspondence between Humphry and Elizabeth. That day had been rounded off with wine and laughter in John's garden, an overdue catch-up with my favourite uncle. What I did not know then was that I would never see him alive again.

When I entered the house on an overcast February day, the place was cold. Books were still lining every wall. The Japanese print hung over the fireplace. His collection of stuffed hippos snuffled about by the window as usual. But the life of the place had gone. I remember very little about the visit itself except the shock of seeing the novel *The Sense of an Ending* by Julian Barnes at John's bedside. The title seemed such an awful irony for a person who had no inkling of his own untimely death.

We put all the family papers, including the letters, into the boot and headed home. During the journey, I felt viscerally the power of objects to choose their human hosts. This was more than a question of timing and my own literary interest. The correspondence grasped me.

A second essential component of *A World of Love* is the power of the letters to let loose their spirits, enabling them to seep into the present. In the novel, the dead writer exerts the 'extraordinary power of his illusion' over impressionable Jane and the other characters, and continues 'affecting them, working on them,' throughout the story. The link with the past is tangible: 'A thread lay dropped on the grass, for Jane to pick up.' The thread, once gripped, is a live wire and sets off an 'electric connection' between the living and the dead. For me, it is not simply that through their letters Elizabeth Bowen and my grandparents can be seen more fully than before. Rather, it is that their charged presences can be felt.

Not long after taking possession of the box of letters, I was in Oxford for the unveiling of a blue plaque at Elizabeth's home in

Headington, which lies about ten minutes from the centre of town. I took the opportunity of spending a few hours in the Bodleian Library reading about Elizabeth's association with the city. I turned to typing up a few notes. I plugged in my tablet which started, randomly and furiously, to spit out letters. The keys changed colour as though hit by a ghostly hand.

When the burst of energy had passed and my computer breathed again, I tried to decipher what was on the screen. Among a gobbledegook of symbols, only three words were discernible: 'ghost', 'get', and 'out'. I felt a chill on my arms. My mouth was dry. I feared I was transgressing. My rational self told me that it was a computer bug. These things happen, though never to me before or since. My spooked self told me this had nothing to do with malfunctioning technology or a sudden surge on the National Grid. It was, without doubt, a Bowenesque 'electric connection'.

I left the library glad to be meeting a friend for lunch. She, I knew, would enjoy my account of what had just happened. Eyes wide, she listened, shuddered, and then laughed. 'Well, what do you expect? You're a ghost hunter. You are chasing after people and their pasts. Best be ready!'

Waldencote, Headington, Oxford. Elizabeth Bowen's marital home, 1925–1935

Chapter 2

Headington: *The New House*

I shiver slightly. I am standing in Elizabeth Bowen's study in Headington. The lozenge-shaped room is heavy with books, inhabited. A large desk in the window casts a quiet eye over proceedings outside. A giggle of children run round the sunken garden. People drift out from the house, glasses and cakes in hand, to have a good look round.

On the blind front of the sandstone house, called Waldencote, is a new decoration: a blue plaque to commemorate the years that Elizabeth lived here, from 1925 to 1935. Today's ceremony, attended by neighbours, fans, academics, the large-chained mayor, is over. Sunday afternoon quiet closes up the lane once again.

The air of the house is filled with Elizabeth. She hums through every conversation. A man in the kitchen tells me she had an open relationship, sniggers, and scuttles off with a Bakewell tart. Another gives me the name of the scholar responsible for the return, to my uncle, of Humphry's letters to Elizabeth.

And then I find myself speaking to a professor, divulging my possession of the correspondence. Unseen, scholarly hands stretch forth. 'We should get together sometime. It would surely be better to work with someone else. This could be mutually beneficial. You will get in touch, won't you?'

I retreat, get another cup of tea, and return to the side of the Irish lecturer I had met during the unveiling of the plaque. I tell him of the encounter, of being caught cold by a real expert. And of my desire to hoard this treasure, to keep the letters to myself.

He lets me finish. 'It's your family,' he says. 'Safeguard your heritage.'

1923

Elizabeth Bowen was in her early twenties when she published her first book of short stories. This marked the start of a long and varied career – novels, short stories, autobiography, reviews, plays and letters all flowed from her pen. She would go on to write one of the great wartime novels, *The Heat of the Day* (1948). She is a writer of wit sliced through with cruelty. Her work is described memorably by a pair of critics: 'Bowen's novels are like Jane Austen on drugs.'

Born in Dublin in 1899, Elizabeth was the only child of Henry and Florence Bowen. The family was of the Anglo-Irish gentry, grown in the claggy soil and conflicted past of rural Ireland. Henry Bowen was a barrister in Dublin and Elizabeth's earliest years were spent there with trips down to the family home, Bowen's Court, in County Cork. Elizabeth was a treasured only child, but her parents' love alone could not ensure a cloudless childhood. Instead, her early years were fractured and peripatetic. When she was seven, her father, who struggled with mental illness, suffered a breakdown and required residential care. Mother and daughter went to live in Kent close to several of Elizabeth's relations.

A few years later, Elizabeth suffered a devastating loss – the death, from cancer, of her mother. Elizabeth was thirteen years old.

The darkness of this misfortune was lessened by no-nonsense aunts who took charge of her, arranging schools and giving her a home. Nevertheless, the taste of the bereavement was ever in Elizabeth's mouth – throughout her life, the word 'mother' sharpened her stammer. Her father, now improved, was back at Bowen's Court and Elizabeth spent her summers there, often with her cousin Audrey Fiennes as a companion. She was, in her own words, a 'tough child, strong as a horse – or colt', responding to the vicissitudes of life with resilience, not self-pity.

Elizabeth finished her secondary education at Downe House, a private school in Kent. In the account of her last school years, *The Mulberry Tree*, Elizabeth discusses a topic central to the futures of young women of the day – marriage: 'I and my friends all intended to marry early, partly because this appeared an achievement or way of making one's mark, also from a feeling it would be difficult to settle to anything else until this was done. (Like passing the School Certificate.) […] Not one of us intended to be L.O.P.H. (Left On Pa's Hands).' Elizabeth was not, it seems, a great romantic when it came to marriage.

The step into higher education, even for women educated privately, was far from certain in the early part of the twentieth century. As the only child of a landed Anglo-Irish family, Elizabeth would not have been expected to go to university. On leaving school, she spent more time at Bowen's Court with her father, who had remarried. There was also a spell in Italy with one of her aunts, an unsuccessful stint at art college, and a course in journalism.

In her early twenties, Elizabeth made two life-changing decisions. The first was her determination to become a writer. This required a move to London, where a great-aunt living in Westminster gave her not just a roof, but a desirable address. In an interview later in life, she recalled those days: '[I] was extremely keen to meet and mingle with other authors because maybe I thought authorship was something infectious. If you could catch measles, why couldn't you catch a sort of genius or gift?' Some early short stories were sent, without success, to periodicals. The change in her fortunes came when her old headmistress put her in touch with the novelist and critic Rose Macaulay. Quiet words were said to key people on Elizabeth's behalf. Shortly afterwards, her first story was published in the journal *Saturday Westminster*. Her first book of short stories, *Encounters*, followed in 1923.

The year was auspicious for another reason – Elizabeth married Alan Cameron. Several years older than her, he was a decorated veteran of the First World War. He had a slightly heavy face and, later in life, the moustache of a cavalryman from a bygone era. There had been an earlier, unwise engagement to an army officer which the family had managed to head off at the pass. Solvent, solid, devoted, Alan was good husband material. He was, at the time, employed as Assistant Secretary for Education for Northamptonshire. For their wedding, Elizabeth wore a droopy hat and a home-made dress with an uneven hem, much to the horror of her aunts. Alan was aware that she needed to look the part, to have the appearance of somebody's wife. He helped to smarten up this slightly gauche young woman, recommending more fashionable clothes and shoes. Elizabeth's stated aim, to marry early in order to allow herself a degree of flexibility, was accomplished.

By all accounts, Elizabeth's marriage to Alan Cameron was not one of thrilling romance and sexual passion. Like other respectable couples of their day, they slept in separate beds. Sexual relations were more a matter of choice – each of them could maintain a degree of separateness if they so wished. For all couples, there was also the important issue of securing an heir.

Books written about sex and relationships in the interwar period cast an interesting light on the Cameron marriage. In *A Marriage Manual* published in 1936, the authors (a Mr and Mrs Stone) deal with the issue of a wife's sexual coolness: 'The fears and inhibitions accumulated by a woman during a lifetime cannot be thrown off by her on the very day she is united in wedlock, and the husband must understand her behaviour.' If sexual relations still do not shortly commence, there arises the possibility of frigidity: 'In cases of frigidity the husband's sexual capacity and behaviour, as well as that of the wife, must be taken into consideration, and that in many cases the frigidity is not a quality inherent in the woman but rather a problem of a particular marriage.' The man's role in helping his wife develop her 'latent sexual capacities' is emphasised; fashioning a sex life within marriage is part of the husband's role. In the Camerons' case, this responsibility can, perhaps, be laid at the foot of Alan's single bed.

A Marriage Manual does highlight other requirements of a successful partnership, ones that were evident in the relationship between Alan and Elizabeth. The Stones stress the 'importance of social and economic security to happiness in marriage'. The popular 1930s columnist Mrs Miniver goes further: 'The most important thing about marriage was not a home or children or a remedy against sin, but simply there being always an eye to catch.' Sex and physical attraction were not seen as indispensable ingredients of a successful, lasting marriage.

The Camerons enjoyed a contented, mutually supportive union which lasted until Alan's death nearly thirty years later. What Elizabeth needed in Alan was more than simply a man at her side – she craved the permanence he offered. The early loss of her mother, and the sporadic presence of her father, left these two roles as mere sketches in her life. She later reflected in a letter to a friend that Alan was, to a certain extent, like a parent. This need for familial structure was compounded by her being an only child, which she described as engendering a 'sort of childish dependence on attachment'. What Alan gave her was, according to Elizabeth, 'the feeling of being located, fixed, held by someone else not only in affection but in their sense of reality'.

In 1923, the year she married, Elizabeth published a short story entitled 'The Evil that Men Do –' which brilliantly and humorously explores the particular emotional terrain of a married woman. A couple, each married to someone else, meet at a poetry reading. The woman writes to her new lover: 'Of course my husband has never entered into my inner life.' She adds a P.P.S. to the letter: 'You must not think that I do not love my husband. There are moments when he touches very closely my *exterior life*.' Here Elizabeth draws a crucial distinction, between 'exterior' and 'inner' lives; there is an understanding that a wife's passionate self, her core, is often beyond the scope of her husband, outside the reach of their relationship. Marriage to Alan provided Elizabeth with security – in her phrase, 'the bricks and wallpaper of a home'. But deep in the viscera of the house, Elizabeth had a room of her own.

The photograph of my grandfather that sits on my mother's desk has him on one knee in a garden. He is solidly built, in his thirties, with small round glasses. His clothes seem bulky. He has a slightly brooding countenance – but more in a Home Counties than a Heathcliff sort of way. At the back of her study, a shelf guards editions of his literary criticism. The beautiful, fox-logo Hart-Davis editions of his books on Coleridge and Hopkins, a first edition of *The Dickens World*, his great success, and a posthumous volume of his lectures and broadcasts entitled *All in Due Time*.

His early death meant that, for me, he lived only in photographs and hardbacks. When my mother and aunt talk of him they use his nickname, 'Did'. I don't. For me, he is Humphry, that oddly spelt, fusty name he preferred to his first, Arthur. He and his elder brother Lancelot were named for characters in Tennyson's *Idylls of the King*, a favourite poem of their parents. Given names steeped in the legend and poetry of the British Isles, they were, in fact, the children of a Sevenoaks solicitor.

Born in 1908, Humphry went as a scholarship pupil to Repton School. He was tireless in his study – not many teenagers wish to be excused from cricket in order to read John Henry Newman's *Apologia Pro Vita Sua*. His afternoon immersed in this book beside the River Trent was to be far more significant than he realised. He read hungrily of a clergyman's crisis of faith, a foreshadowing of events to come in his own life.

Just as Humphry's schooling was coming to an end, at the age of seventeen, he suffered a major blow. His mother, who was only fifty-three and had a history of high blood pressure, died suddenly. The two of them had been close. With his father he had a far more abrasive relationship, one choked by their shared desire for conspicuous success and financial stability. Though Humphry lost his mother later than Elizabeth, both became, at a tender age, motherless children.

Humphry's casting about for anchors and answers following his mother's death took a number of forms. One saw him approach a spirit medium, a Mrs Howarth-Scaling from Devon. Her business card reads: 'Lessons given. Questions answered ethical or mundane.' Hedging her bets with admirable aplomb, she envisaged any number of future professions for Humphry – scientist, mathematician, teacher, preacher, masseur. His past life she conjured as more exotic still, with spells as a snake-charmer in India, a vivisectionist in seventeenth-century France, and a number of lives in Egypt: 'You have at one time in a female body been the slave girl in a Temple devoted to Atlantis, to the worship and cult of the Sacred Cats.'

Leaving his colourful incarnation in Egyptian temples behind him, Humphry entered other hallowed halls in the autumn of 1926. He won a scholarship to Hertford College, Oxford, to read Classics ('Greats'), taking with him the fresh wound of his mother's death. This first degree was followed by a second in Modern History completed in 1930. He was not a teddy-clutching undergraduate of the *Brideshead Revisited* model, all cucumber sandwiches and old-family privilege. Nor was he a 'hearty' – described by Isaiah Berlin, the philosopher and a friend of Humphry's at university, as the type of student who 'wore huge woollen scarves and had enormous muscles and rowed and went about in groups and drank beer'. Humphry's engagement with the university was shaped by background and personality as well as the uncertainties of the age.

At Hertford, Humphry met Arthur Calder-Marshall, the future biographer and novelist, who would become a lifelong friend. In his unpublished autobiography, Calder-Marshall describes the particular feel of Oxford at that time: 'We were caught between the gaiety of the post-war twenties and the earnestness of the pre-war thirties. While we were up, news came of the Wall Street Crash, of stockbrokers defenestrating out of sky-scraper windows, of businesses folding overnight. Even in the City of Dreaming Spires I realised that we were going down to a world of Dwindling Hopes.'

Dubbed 'the morbid age' by one historian, the interwar years saw an economy in tatters and a crisis of faith in civilisation itself. Books such as Gilbert Murray's *The Ordeal of this Generation* (1929) spelt out the fear that Western civilisation was irrevocably degenerating. The First World War and the manner in which it had been fought heightened this sense of doom. The writing of Beatrice and Sidney Webb further contributed to the public perception that capitalism was diseased, and that politicians did not have the cure. This was the age of T. S. Eliot's *The Waste Land*.

Money, inevitably, had a heavy bearing both on how undergraduates lived and on their prospects. The poet Stephen Spender, who was a friend of both Humphry and Calder-Marshall, writes in his memoir, *World Within World*: 'Money played a decisive part in fixing the boundaries of one's Oxford career. To have an income of three hundred pounds a year meant that one could take part in most University activities.'

Taking part in student life was one thing, being able to support yourself on leaving university quite another. Calder-Marshall observes drily that 'the future was all right for Stephen Spender' who 'had a poetic gift as certain as his private income'. He continues: 'But to leave Oxford with nothing coming in and a number of unpaid bills was an alarming prospect in 1930.' This was the reality for both Calder-Marshall and Humphry, who did not come from deep-pocketed families.

Later in life, Humphry reflected on how Oxford made him feel: 'I felt very strongly how meagre and uncivilized my family background had been.' His desperate urge to escape his own feelings of inadequacy and insecurity took many forms – it was evident in his studiousness, his ambition, his choice of friends, and his relationships with women. He tended to set his sights on women of a slightly higher class than his own.

Humphry House, photographed by his father Harold House

Arthur and Humphry wasted no time in attaching themselves to two friends from a women's college, Lady Margaret Hall. Humphry's flirtation was with a woman called Katherine, a wealthy daughter from the shires. At Oxford she and Humphry were on a more equal social footing and could enjoy their attraction to one another. Beyond the dreaming spires their lives did not converge. Katherine's world, one of hunting, fishing, and opulence, put paid to their emotional attachment.

Calder-Marshall's opinion of these 'undergraduettes' at Oxford is revealing. He felt that pretty female students were, 'so thin on the ground that they would have been hard put to muster a netball team. Conscious of being for the first, and perhaps the only, time in their lives, in a seller's market, these highly desired young ladies bestowed their favours sparingly. […] Attractive young ladies of good standing expected proposals of marriage: those of lesser demanded money'. Though Calder-Marshall's view of female students is faintly amusing, it also speaks of a sexism that was ingrained and unquestioned among the young men of the day.

Where Humphry was on safe ground was intellectually, and in the cultivation of his male friendships. The more gregarious of the two, Calder-Marshall describes Humphry's engagement with his peers: 'But while he despised me for going to every party to which I was invited and others which I gate crashed, he was very shrewd in winnowing the grain from my chaff. Stephen Spender, Isaiah Berlin, Louis MacNeice, Bernard Spencer and Martin Cooper, he had time for. Dozens of others he dismissed as waste of his time. He was far more certain of where he was going than I.'

These clever young men, all destined for distinction in their chosen fields of literature, criticism, or philosophy, were those Humphry sought out. He selected his friends where he imagined his future. Spender writes gratefully about being swept along in 'this great wave of the talent of my time'. He knew, as did Humphry, that they were a peacock generation.

Isaiah Berlin, in a later letter to Elizabeth, describes Humphry as 'my kind of prig which is why I like him I think. I am sure that is what I originally fell for in Humphry: the splendid reactionary violence, a sort of Fascist sternness which contrasted with the surréaliste undergraduates of my first year at Oxford'.

My relationship with Elizabeth Bowen is a curious one. Despite reading English at St Andrews, I did not come across her work. Only one female writer of the twentieth century, Virginia Woolf, was deemed worthy of attention. Yet learning of the family association with Elizabeth, I read much of her fiction in the following years. I loved her writing: its biting wit, rich description, and emotional acuity. I was also intrigued by her as a person – not every family has a brilliant writer hidden in the closet of its past.

When I later became an English teacher, I couldn't help using her work in my lessons. Her ghost stories have always proved a huge success, gripping successive classes with their chilly brilliance, the menace of the ordinary. Many a bloody end has been inked in for characters lost in the gloaming hinterland of a Bowen narrative. My literary appreciation of her inevitably became entangled with my received family history – one in which Elizabeth had not been cast in a favourable light. The uneasy overlap between her affair with my grandfather, and Humphry's own marriage to my grandmother, Madeline Church, had ensured a version that wrote her as domineering and predatory.

Another version of the affair, albeit a slightly curious one, appears in the biography of Elizabeth Bowen written by Victoria Glendinning and published in 1975, just a couple of years after Elizabeth's death. Details of the relationship between Humphry and Elizabeth are given, and a description of a young man who is clearly my grandfather. Yet his name is never mentioned. When I first read the biography, I didn't think of the possible reasons why his name was not used – that came later. Instead my reaction to Humphry's shadowy presence in this account was emotional. I had wanted to encounter him there and I had failed to do so.

As for the letters themselves, I had known of their existence for years but given them little thought. Only when I moved to Spain to teach did something shift in my relationship with my family and its history. I made a point of reading the correspondence during a trip back to London – the geographical distance from home acted as some sort of psychological spur. Knowing my family's past seemed more urgent now that I was missing elements of its present. That afternoon at my uncle John's house, deep in drama, was to have far-reaching consequences. I did not know then all the meanings of possession.

On John's death, I had the uncanny feeling that the letters required me not merely to house them, but to engage with them imaginatively. And it was not just the story in the letters but the characters themselves that were so gripping. Elizabeth writes of how fictional characters arrive in her life: 'From the moment they hove into view, they were inevitable.' These newcomers, who seem more real to her than the living, she invokes; a character's coming is a visitation. I found myself bewitched by the Elizabeth I saw in the correspondence. Spontaneous, wholehearted, occasionally overbearing – her character, eerily, had echoes of my own. I knew I had to tell the story the letters contained, to accept the visitations of all these characters. After twenty years of teaching I was ready for a new challenge and it had arrived, as things do in Elizabeth's world, at 'the hour arranged'.

Elizabeth delineates this type of encounter: 'Fate has worked, as in a falling in love – the writer, in fact, first knows he has found his subject by finding himself already obsessed by it.' For me, the falling in love was the easy bit; more complicated was how to negotiate the archive's in-laws. Firstly, there was the importance of Elizabeth's unpublished letters in terms of literary history. These particular letters could not sit in a box for another eighty years. Then there was a strange tug of duty to my grandparents – even to a grandfather I had never known. Finally, there was the debt I owed to my aunt and my mother who had entrusted the letters to me.

Soon after deciding to reveal the stories contained in the letters, I had a conversation with one of my dynamic A level English Literature pupils. Our discussion of her homework at an end, she asked about my embryonic literary project. I told her of my feelings of responsibility both to my family and to the material, of the challenges of weaving all the elements of the story together.

'But Miss,' she smiled, 'this is just like that Atwood lesson – it's what you made us do. We had all those bits of text from *The Handmaid's Tale* and we had to put them in the 'right' order. Now you have to do it. That's karma, Miss.'

By the early 1930s, Elizabeth was an established name in the literary world. She had three volumes of short stories and four novels behind her. A distinct voice was emerging, and her leitmotifs – stifled people, sinister houses, dislocation – were already in evidence. As was her obsession with time: the way the past beds down with the present, affecting both the narrative and structure of the writing.

Elizabeth was friendly with, but not a member of, the Bloomsbury Group. She was just beginning her career when Virginia Woolf was publishing some of her best work, such as *Mrs Dalloway* (1925), and *To the Lighthouse* (1927). An innovative writer throughout her life, Elizabeth's modernism, though of a different flavour from Woolf's, is no less striking.

While Virginia Woolf held court in Bloomsbury squares, it was left to Elizabeth to charm the quadrangles of Oxford colleges.

Alan Cameron's job had dictated a move there several years earlier and Elizabeth happily settled into life in the soft-stoned city. The years in Oxford were to be both extremely productive and pleasingly social. Elizabeth loved being 'in company with the articulate and the learned', especially as it required smartness, both intellectual and sartorial. Elizabeth was a meticulous dresser, fond of a well-cut outfit. This she complemented with heavy bracelets, and clip-on earrings visible under her neatly waving hair. A generous layer of make-up, a bag full of cigarettes, and Elizabeth was ready to go down the hill from Headington into Oxford for any social occasion. Her married self and her husband she often left at home.

At the head of Oxford's erudite table in 1933 sat Maurice Bowra, a Fellow in Classics at Wadham College, where he would later become warden. Bon viveur, homosexual, writer of dirty verse, he basked in his reputation as the most celebrated Oxford don of his day.

Bowra describes Elizabeth in his memoirs:

> She was handsome in an unusual way, with a face that indicated both mind and character. Unlike some Irish, she did not talk for effect but kept conversation at a high level and gave her full attention to it. She had a slight stutter which added force to her remarks. She had the fine style of a great lady, who on rare occasions was not shy of slapping down impertinence, but she came from a society where the decorum of the nineteenth century had been tempered by an Irish frankness. With all her sensibility and imagination, she had a masculine intelligence which was fully at home in large subjects and general ideas, and when she sometimes gave a lecture, it was delivered with a force and control of which most University teachers would be envious.

Despite Elizabeth's comfortable home life with Alan and the pleasures of being a personality in Oxford, it seemed something was missing. She was in an unconsummated marriage (something her relationship with Humphry would soon reveal) and of an age when most women would have been having children. Surrounding herself with clever, mostly unmarried men, rather than broody women, must have eased this situation for her. It is perhaps no coincidence that Elizabeth's most fertile years creatively were when she was of child-bearing age. Her professional and exterior lives were full. It seems, however, that the dissatisfactions of her inner life chafed increasingly. And then she crossed paths with Humphry, a striking man nine years younger than herself.

For Humphry, the years before Elizabeth strode into his life were peppered with disappointment and difficulty. Wishing to stay on in Oxford, Humphry took the highly competitive exam for a fellowship at All Souls College in 1930. This would guarantee him prestigious academic jobs for life. He would, once and for all, be able to leave behind his feelings of inadequacy and insecurity. When unsuccessful in his bid, he fell back on the idea of the Anglican priesthood. His family was not religious, but the Church was still seen as offering a decent, stable living for young men in the 1930s. Humphry trained for only a year and then was ordained a deacon in the Church of England.

In the autumn of 1931, he secured a highly desirable job, as English lecturer and chaplain at Wadham College, Oxford. The promise of the post was such that, a couple of months later, he proposed to the young woman he had been seeing. She was not an Oxford 'undergraduette' but a woman called Madeline Church whom he had met a couple of years earlier in their shared hometown of Sevenoaks. A job, a fiancée, a future – everything seemed to be falling into place.

However, soon after he became a deacon, it became apparent that Humphry was not cut from priestly cloth. He found he had different ideas from most clergymen about what constituted sin – fornication, in his eyes, was no worse than a failure to read Virgil. In his spare time he read Havelock Ellis's writings about birth control rather than the Book of Job. His appetites for tobacco, rich food, and alcohol proved difficult to rein in. 'I am not', he wrote, 'stream-lined for asceticism'.

More worryingly, his certainty about his faith began to fray. Services were dreary. He found himself swearing rather than praying under his ornate tunicle. Asked by a keen young student what he had done for Jesus, Humphry had no reply. As 1932 dawned, Humphry suffered a massive crisis of faith. He railed against 'a puny pseudo-Christus who was never my God', and wrote that 'moods wheel, thicken, multiply, take hideous forms and I want death'. He besought Madeline not to write to him all term. In the few letters he wrote her, even his beautiful handwriting is broken.

At this point in his life, Humphry was beginning his first major academic work, on the papers and notebooks of the poet Gerard Manley Hopkins. The mirrored circumstances of their lives would not have been lost on him. Both men were creative undergraduates at Oxford. In their early twenties both were looking for spiritual direction. Hopkins found his calling, becoming a Jesuit priest at the age of twenty-four in 1868. Humphry, by contrast, lost his way. 'Oh thou lord of life, send my roots rain', Hopkins prays in one of his best known sonnets. For Humphry, it was a dry spring; his belief in God was over.

Humphry informed Wadham that he could no longer continue as chaplain. He hoped he could be reappointed as simply a fellow in English. The slow wheels of Oxford bureaucracy meant that it was a full year before a decision was reached about his position. It was not good news – there was no role in the English faculty for him. He felt this failure keenly. It seemed all his hard work had come to nothing. Maybe he was, after all, destined to be a small town solicitor like his father.

Humphry's uncertain months took their toll on his relationship with Madeline. She found him increasingly unsympathetic and was unsure whether she wanted to continue seeing him, let alone marry him. In November 1932, he went up to London to renew his proposal of marriage. The encounter did not go well – Humphry later confessed to being 'foul'. Nevertheless, he wrote immediately afterwards pressing Madeline to 'marry at Christmas or not at all'.

This letter has accretions in the margin, scribbled in frail pencil. Written years later by my grandmother, is the following: 'On receiving this, I decided this was the end. I collected together all H's [Humphry's] letters and every scrap of his I'd got, meaning to burn them!'

In the end, Madeline did not burn the letters, though she did decide against a hasty marriage. A couple of months later, Humphry met Elizabeth Bowen.

Appleton, Oxfordshire

Chapter 3

Appleton: *The Shadowy Third*

I turn my back on the Oxfordshire village, on the war memorial shielded by an oak, the thatched cottages, the trees heavy with apples. I have walked all the lanes, talked to every villager I could find, asked in the church and shop (the pub was closed) but without success. I have failed to find the cottage a few miles from Oxford where Humphry lived; where he and Elizabeth chose to meet in the early days of their affair.

As I walk back to the main road to pick up the bus, the downpour begins. My spirits, already low, descend further. I think of sticking out a thumb for a lift but there are no vehicles and who halts, these days, for hitch-hikers? Hood up against the deluge, I do not hear the engine of the car. Then there it is, bright as a lemon, stopping at my side in the lane. The elderly woman behind the wheel waves her hand in invitation. I get in, grateful and amazed. Edith is bright-eyed, the same age as my mother, and a member of the Appleton Historical Society.

I tell her of my fruitless search for Ossemere, the house where Humphry lived. 'Maybe the name has changed,' says Edith. 'There is a house called Ossefield. Lovely Arts and Crafts. It's owned by a bookseller and he opens it up to the public once a year in the summer. It has a big garden with apple trees – I can see them from my house.'

It does not take us long to get to the station. I thank Edith again, and watch as the bright little car gets swallowed up in the traffic. I feel strangely energised, and not just because I have been rescued at the side of the road. My heart burns within me.

I recall a time, years earlier, cycling the Camino de Santiago pilgrim route in Northern Spain. A man is walking about a hundred metres ahead, weighed down by an enormous rucksack. Suddenly he disappears from view. When I come close, I see that he has fallen down a deep gulley and is lying, beetle-like, at the bottom. I feel sick with the certainty that he has done himself some serious injury. Then he springs up and clambers out with the agility of a free climber.

Acknowledging his good fortune, he says, smiling, '*Es un milagro del Camino.*' Miraculous things happen when you travel this route, when your steps have purpose.

On the Camino, you carry a pilgrim's passport which you get stamped in the cathedrals, churches, and villages on the way. Each stamp is different – some simple, some beautifully elaborate representations of Romanesque churches. Their variety is a reflection of the myriad experiences a pilgrim will have on the dusty road to Santiago de Compostela.

Leaving Appleton, my passport is unstamped. Then the heavens open and Edith comes along.

February 1933

Elizabeth sat on a bus as it wound its way out of Oxford. She loved a journey, though taxis were more her style.

The spark between herself and Humphry had been kindled quickly. Yet meeting one another in Oxford itself was rich in complication – there was Alan, their mutual friends, the question of where to go. From its inception, the relationship included a slice of intrigue. This was no hardship for Elizabeth – she was naturally secretive and a gifted schemer. And so she found herself on the bus, rattling towards the village of Appleton where a young man was waiting to meet her.

Humphry had recently moved from college accommodation to a house on the lip of this hamlet a few miles from Oxford. He was renting two large, semi-furnished rooms from the elderly owner, paying thirty shillings a week for board and lodging. The path to his new home ran up through an orchard. The large windows of his rooms commanded a fine view of the apple trees. He had managed to retire his landlady's knick-knacks and fill the space with his books before Elizabeth's arrival.

Humphry described her first visit in his journal:

> Tuesday 14th [February 1933]. Met Elizabeth from the 11-52 bus at Appleton Turn. Was not sure how we should find one another. She talked so much at first that I didn't know what to do. Conversation dashed on and on until I was floundering. The climax came when I wondered whether all Sicily could be seen at once from an aeroplane: this gave allowance to get an atlas, and we both breathed again. I do not know how far all this talking really belongs to her; and how far, eg: to-day, it all came out because she was a little nervous. She may not have needed breath and I attributed to her my awful need.

The day was a success – there was a walk along the Thames, a conversation about palm trees, and time spent with Virgil's *Aeneid* before Elizabeth returned home. In late-night pencil, Humphry started to compose a poem full of their day – Valentine's Day – and of the section of Virgil they had read together. When Aeneas's boat is carried up the Tiber by the gods to found Rome, the woods and the waters are wonderstruck by him – *mirantur et undae*. That would be the title of the poem. And Elizabeth would be Aeneas – her heroic qualities, her masculine intelligence, her sudden arrival (albeit by bus). The incomplete poem reads:

> *I wondered at your quick unweaving speeches,*
> *Which rolled together armies, maps and flying,*
> *Fall from the air upon a village landscape, […]*
> ……………………………………
> *At you then the waters wondered*
> *And the wood wonders.*

Months later, Humphry was to turn back to these pages of his journal. He would copy the entries and the fragment of poetry into a letter and send them to Elizabeth. His intention was to fill in the gaps in his poem, to reveal to her what he had been unable to articulate in Appleton: 'the first burst of you on me – strangeness, wonder, admiration; […] an extreme awareness of you as a woman for whom I felt a love, when we were standing together by the palm-tree.'

An unhurried morning greeted Humphry the day after Elizabeth's visit. He had no work to attend to in Oxford, and could spend the day reading, the flat February light falling into his room from the leafless orchard. There was time to reflect on this unexpected turn of events and where it might lead. A few months earlier, he had been expecting to marry; now he was beginning a relationship with a married woman.

Yet the other woman had not disappeared completely from his life. After a time of silent distance following the broken engagement, Madeline and Humphry were back in touch. In March 1933, a month after Elizabeth's first visit to Appleton, Humphry invited Madeline down from London to see him. However, not every day would be convenient as 'on Wednesday I think I shall be tied up with Elizabeth Bowen, novelist'. This single line reveals more than just Humphry's slightly awestruck feelings. It demonstrated that, from the very beginning of his relationship with Elizabeth, the two women were interwoven in the fabric of his life. This bond would find expression in letters Humphry wrote to each woman soon afterwards.

Humphry's research into the life of Gerard Manley Hopkins saw him exploring the countryside around Oxford for the context and cadence of the poet's life. By bicycle he retraced the poet's foot-steps – along the poplar-shorn banks of the Thames at Binsey, out to visit the church at Elsfield, and to Stanton Harcourt, famous for the Perpendicular tower which stands at the edge of its churchyard. Well known to Hopkins, the village had further poetic associations. It was here, in 1717–1718, that Alexander Pope translated part of *The Iliad.*

With matches and moonlight to guide him, Humphry climbed up the narrow stairs to the top of the church. He looked out across the roof of the nave, its lead gleaming blue, towards the Pope tower. Then with his literary musings over, he went to the Stanton Arms for a pint. Surrounded by darts players and old men, Humphry sat down to write a couple of letters, one to Elizabeth and one to Madeline.

There are phrases and observations common to both letters. Almost as though their proximity to one another on the pub table allowed words in one letter to soak straight into the other. A sentence about birdsong and bats is identical. As is one in Latin – '*mens curva in corpore curvo*' – a description of Pope's shrunken body and sharp mind. With neither woman could Humphry resist the urge to be conspicuously clever.

As soon as I embarked on my quest to uncover the affair between Humphry and Elizabeth, I realised it was far more than just an intellectual and emotional pursuit. Central to the whole endeavour, dictated inevitably by Elizabeth, was spirit of place. She writes at length about this idea in her autobiographical work *Pictures and Conversations* (published posthumously in 1975): 'Am I not manifestly a writer for whom places loom large? As a reader, it is to the place-element that I react most strongly: for me, what gives fiction verisimilitude is its topography.' My own ability to write their story depended on my evocation of their landscapes as much as their time, to be present where they once were.

Laying the letters out, many of which still have their original envelopes, I could see postal pathways that stretched not just round the British Isles, but halfway across the globe. A mental map presented itself to me – Oxford to Ireland, Calcutta to Cambridge – with important locations acting as 'dominants' in the story, just as they do in Elizabeth's fiction. Elizabeth herself was always seeking out places where something significant had happened: 'Such places are haunted – scenes of acute sensation for someone, vicariously me.' My journeys would not be a case of visiting a building, a ruin, a graveyard, rather they would mean laying myself open to the emotional archive contained in these places. It might be a case less of digging up facts, than of tapping into 'place-feeling', as Elizabeth refers to it.

And it wasn't only the locations themselves – just as important was the experience of getting there. For Elizabeth, travel went beyond mere movement: it had moral and psychological importance. When a character is in motion, he has the illusion that the landscape is moving too: 'He does not merely – as he would were he at a standstill – *see* scene, he *watches* its continuous changes, which act upon him compulsively like a non-stop narrative.'

Being in transit, following my map, would affect my perceptions of the characters, of the affair and its aftermath. My travels would even shape the way I wrote about them – I would be acted upon by the energy of the chase, become part of a 'non-stop narrative' myself. I decided that my trips would include something more – a photographic record of all the important places in the letters. I had worked earlier in my life as a documentary photographer and was keen to record my journey visually. The photographs would give me another way of responding to the correspondence: a different sort of picture and conversation.

Elizabeth writes: 'I may, too, impart to some of my characters, unconsciously, an enthusiastic naïvety with regard to transport which in my own case time has not dimmed. Zestfully they take ships or board planes: few of them even are *blasés* about railways.' I shared this love of travel with Elizabeth and her creations. I had grown up in West Africa, was lucky enough to have lived in several different countries. The necessity of visiting each cross on the map, even by public transport, was something I relished. I immediately started looking up ferry routes to Ireland and what injections I would need to visit India. Then I packed my bag – photocopies of the letters, map, passport, camera, a book of Elizabeth's ghost stories – and set off. Zestfully.

Beginning my quest, I was immediately conscious of the presence of my grandmother. On the one hand were my own memories of her from childhood – in the wardrobe of my imagination she wears a tweed suit; she is smoking, her eyes bright behind her glasses. She is a blend of quick humour and seriousness, and is, for this rather naughty child, occasionally fearsome. On the other hand is her role in the affair between Humphry and Elizabeth – in this she is, strangely, the other woman. Whether Madeline was to emerge as a dynamic individual or the pitiful, wronged wife remained to be seen.

The sinister power of the other woman is one that fascinated Elizabeth; it had already found creative expression in her short story 'The Shadowy Third', from the volume published in 1923. Claustrophobic and creepy, it describes a young marriage inhabited by the spirit of the husband's deceased first wife. The dead woman squeezes into conversations, is present in the bruised walls where her furniture once stood, lurks in the corners of the drawing room. She is invisible, but impossible to overlook.

A key problem about Madeline's representation is her destruction of many of her letters from this crucial period. The love triangle, in terms of correspondence, is far from equilateral. Through this incendiary act Madeline temporarily lost her voice, thereby echoing the fate of many women of the day whose histories are hidden. She also, inadvertently, gave to others – in this case Humphry and Elizabeth – the power to construct their own versions of her. However, though she may be a spectral scribe, she is not an emotional absence. She is Madeline to you. Linny to me. She is the only character in the story that I have touched.

Madeline's childhood had elements in common with Elizabeth's – hers also was one of journeys, maiden aunts, and time away from her parents. She was born in 1903 in Ceylon (Sri Lanka); her father worked in Colombo as an accountant in a tea shipping company. The family spent the hot season in the hills at Nuwara Eliya. Dubbed 'Little England', the town was a favourite of British expatriates. It sported colonial bungalows, rose gardens, and a Victorian-style post office. Polo was played in the cool evenings just before drinks were poured.

At the age of seven, Madeline returned to England alone to live with an aunt and begin formal schooling, benefitting from the surge in girls' education at the beginning of the twentieth century. A photograph of Madeline aged seventeen in her final year of school catches her standing in a garden, her parted hair drawn tightly onto the back of her head. Her cheeks are round, her lips full. She wears a scoop-neck dress of abstract design, and pert black shoes. With a confident gaze she greets the camera. Shoulders back, eyes forward, she sees life and opportunities opening up before her.

Whereas Elizabeth married young so that she would be free to get on with her life, Madeline chose instead to go to university. Women who wished to enter higher education in that time had to cope with the churlish exclusivity of the universities – many still saw women as a poorer class of student and withheld degree certification. The trailblazer in women's education was Royal Holloway College, part of the University of London, which first admitted students in 1887. It was here that Madeline began her degree in English in 1922, one of just under two hundred women to be enrolled that year.

When she graduated in 1925 (an education given her almost exclusively by female lecturers), Madeline returned home. Back to the comfortable affluence of the Church family home with its servants, library, and billiard room. A social circle of tennis parties, literary gatherings, and amateur dramatics. Madeline donned once more the narrow skirt of familial expectation. Her boyfriend at the time was eligible, attractive and successful: Guy Butler won four Olympic medals on the track between 1920–1924. Quite why or when he and Madeline broke up is unclear, but invitations to stay with Madeline's parents point towards him being considered a serious prospect as a son-in-law.

Yet within a year of her graduation, Madeline was making other plans – ones that did not include the dashing athlete. London was beckoning, just as it had for Elizabeth when she was in her early twenties. Madeline managed to get her father's consent to work for the Voluntary Aid Detachment in London, a job found for her by an uncle nicknamed 'Socialist Fred'. A branch of the Red Cross in both World Wars, the VAD had an interwar presence in deprived urban communities. Madeline worked in Deptford, one of the worst slums in the city, as a Schools Liaison Officer, visiting families to encourage them to follow advice given by school nurses and health workers. The job had a profound impact on her and shaped her political sympathies for the rest of her life.

Madeline Church (House)

In 1929, Madeline met Humphry at a book group in Sevenoaks. He was, at the time, still a student. There was no question of any hasty commitment, particularly as his family was less prosperous than hers. Humphry's earliest letters to her are full not only of youthful enthusiasm, but also book recommendations – titles by Ronald Firbank, Richard Hughes's *A High Wind in Jamaica*, and the little matter of John Donne's *Sermons*. No man is an island, and Humphry hailed many a passing vessel, often giving her suggestions for intellectual betterment.

When her parents moved to Eastbourne in 1931, Madeline headed for the capital. Here she rented a variety of rooms in boarding houses before finally finding a small flat of her own in Bloomsbury. By the early 1930s, the area was known not just for its bohemian life, but also as a desirable destination for that new breed of woman – the interwar 'bachelor girl'. Madeline, temporarily, joined their ranks.

Though only three and a half years separated Madeline and Elizabeth, they came from very different worlds. These collided in their shared love for the same young man – one who sat in the saloon bar at Stanton Harcourt drinking a pint, writing to them both. Having finished his beer, Humphry got back on his bike. He cycled home through the gathered gloom, leaving the village and its fine tower behind him. The letters sat snug in his pocket.

The view from the top of a church tower, particularly in moonlight, would have been a blur to Elizabeth. Extremely short-sighted, she was a woman of the first glance rather than the lengthy stare. She dealt in swift impressions, their soft edges subject to her imagination. Her eye must have fallen on many young men, but Humphry was the first on whom her gaze settled.

She could probably see that he was not a typical Oxford sort, despite his best efforts to find his place there. As well as his excellent brain, he had pleasingly rough edges. By her own admission, she liked people who had 'a slum quarter'. The dark streets of Humphry's personality were not only intriguing in themselves, but were a marked contrast to the well-lit avenue of husband Alan. Physically, Humphry was her type – a high forehead, sharp eyes. Several later lovers fell into this mould. And then there was his spirit – something Berlin touched on in his short description of his friend. People, both men and women, gravitated towards Humphry.

It was one thing for Elizabeth to admit that her companionate marriage to Alan did not fully satisfy her, quite another to act on this feeling. Taking rural buses in February to meet a penniless, attractive, twenty-four-year-old man must have given her a reckless thrill. Later in their relationship, Elizabeth would encourage Humphry to move about in space, to slip constraints. This was what her relationship with him allowed her to do – she could explore new identities and test the boundaries of her marriage. A game of hide-and-seek, perhaps, in the large house of her life.

In these early months as their relationship developed, so did a plan – for Humphry to stay with Elizabeth at her home in Ireland in April. For his Hopkins research, Humphry needed to visit Dublin as it was there that the poet had spent the last years of his life. Once the work in Dublin was complete, he would be free to travel to Bowen's Court. It would be the first proper opportunity for them to spend a sustained amount of time together, to shift the relationship on to a more intimate footing. Humphry, the scholarship boy from Sevenoaks, would also get the chance to experience a world far removed from his own – the damp grandeur of the Anglo-Irish gentry. There would be time to go on expeditions, talk of Flaubert, walk among the screens of grand trees that surrounded the house. Elizabeth could show him the huge walled garden full of spring colour, the little stone church on the edge of the demesne, her heartbeat of a home.

The trip to Ireland would mean that ideas, confidences, and feelings could be shared across a room rather than being committed to paper and envelope. Yet the letter itself was a crucial component in the affair between Humphry and Elizabeth and not simply because, for much of the relationship, they lived in different places. As for many people in the first half of the twentieth century, letter writing formed part of their daily lives. Theirs was an epistolary culture despite the advent of the telephone. They thought nothing of crafting a letter a few thousand words long, and then repeating the feat a day or two later.

But if the letter was a space of intimacy, the envelope that sealed it served to establish a very specific distance between them. Humphry addressed Elizabeth on the ones he sent as 'Mrs Cameron'. Anything else would have been vulgar and inappropriate. The tension between the contents of his letter and the mode of address was always in his mind. For her, there were no such issues. Married or unmarried, he remained 'Humphry House, Esq.'

The letter afforded, among other things, the opportunity for performance – something Elizabeth relished. There was also the question of posterity – one does get the feeling reading Elizabeth's correspondence, both to Humphry and others, that she had an eye on how she would appear to subsequent generations. Years later she would ask another lover, Charles Ritchie, to look after his diaries as she might want to cull them for publication. It seems that whatever was written to, by, or about her, in any medium, formed part of her story. One that she might wish to reinterpret at some point in the future.

Years later, Elizabeth lamented to a friend (in a letter, of course) the passing of the epistolary habit: 'The only sad thing is that, owing to the necessity to work so hard, I have altogether ceased to be able to write letters – as I used to do, if you remember, copiously in the 1930s.

Not that that's probably a great loss to anyone else, but it is a real loss to me, because writing to anybody is one great way of making oneself feel one is in their presence.'

For Elizabeth and Humphry, that epistolary tension – between the distance created by performance and the intimacy of being in someone's presence – was compounded by emotional wrangles that would emerge later in the relationship. This friction is evident even in their wildly different handwriting. Humphry's writing is tight, small, shapely. Elizabeth's is the flight of a drunken bird swooping across the page. She always finishes with a flourish and writes her name hugely. Elizabeth's letters to Humphry in the spring of 1933 do not survive. The few of his that remain are brief and focus largely on opportunities for seeing one another. This one, the last he sent her before his trip to Ireland, provides a glimpse of his anxious approach to the new woman in his life.

HH to EB

Ossemere, Appleton, Abingdon
Sunday [Undated, ?March 1933]

My dear Elizabeth,

Thank you for your card: I was just going to write to you when it arrived; and its effect has been to delay my writing for a day. Everything was all right on Monday – all buses caught. What with guest and work since then I have been very preoccupied. To-day I have decided that I should go to London to begin final references (among others the "lost" article) and plans for Ireland. I had hoped to see you here before going. But will you be in London during the week? You seem to go so often that I am banking on your being. May we meet then? My address will be 34 Fitzroy St, W. 1., where I shall have a completely furnitureless flat as office and dormitory. There is no phone, but letters will arrive. Will you let me know if you are going up during the week? I am sorry to go off with so little warning: but I had done all that could usefully be done here. What is your Chelsea address?

All questions. A packing hurry.

You must teach me how to exploit the spectacular possibilities of London as of the country. I will not write more as I am distracted and at the moment angry upon two distinct and justifiable pretexts; and since I am by no means angry with you it w[oul]d be absurd to let you suffer for it.

Humphry.

At first glance a simple letter of practical arrangements, an opportunity for Humphry and Elizabeth to escape Oxford's all-seeing eye. Elizabeth had a share of a flat in the capital and was a frequent visitor. Humphry on this trip was renouncing his favourite all-night drinking hotel, the Astoria in Soho, for an address slightly further north, in the heart of bohemian London. In his description of his sparse accommodation he hints at a chilly creative garret. He can only be reached by letter. But his flat was neither as spartan nor as empty as he made it sound. Indeed, it contained another person – Madeline.

Choosing his words carefully and withholding others allowed Humphry to negotiate this early intimacy with Elizabeth. If he was lying by omission, then so be it. As Elizabeth comments in a later novel: 'Never to lie is to have no lock to your door, you are never wholly alone.' Humphry may not have wished for solitude, but the attentions of two women would do nicely.

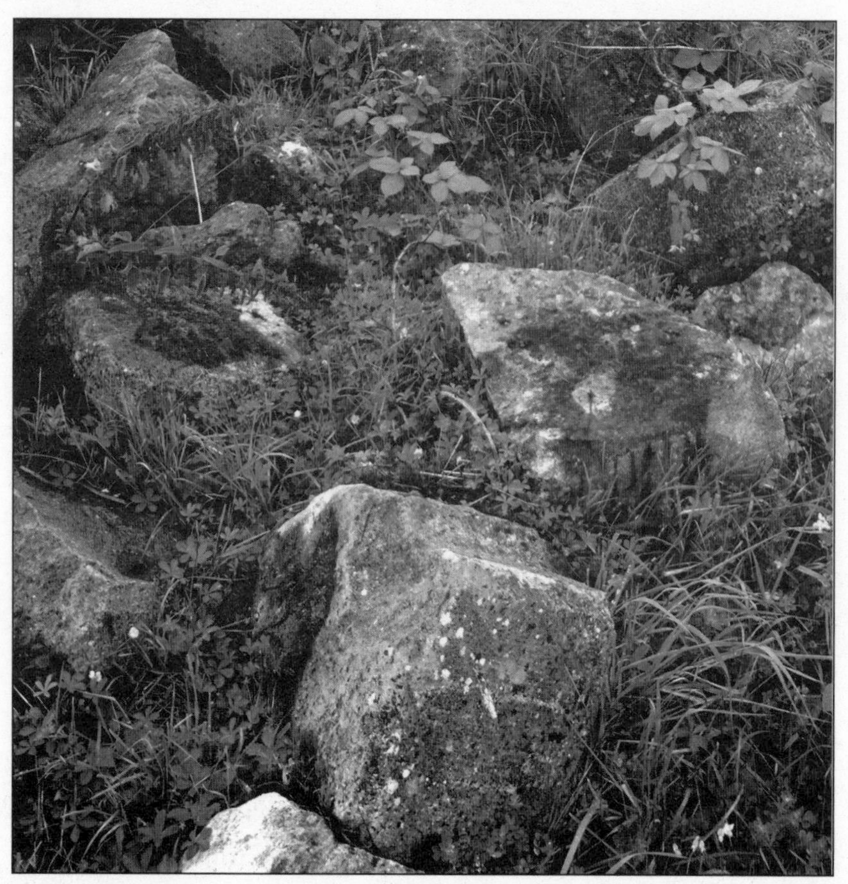

'Nothing beside remains.' The ruins of Elizabeth's ancestral home, Bowen's Court

Chapter 4

County Cork, Ireland: *Friends and Relations*

The damp barley brushes against my legs. My guide to Elizabeth's former home in Ireland wears a blue raincoat zipped up against the mizzle. She walks ahead with purpose. In the distance, a seam of low mountains struggles to be seen behind the dense cloud.

'This was the lower avenue,' Brigid says. 'The trees went all the way from Farahy Church up to Bowen's Court. Hundreds of years old, they were. The man who bought the estate from Elizabeth recouped the purchase price from the timber alone. And the house was demolished within a year…'

No trees swell into view. I just see yellow fields that fold softly down to the river, and more of the same in front of me. We walk up the slight slope, Brigid's light voice gliding through stories of the house, hamlet, and family.

She stops suddenly. 'We're here,' she announces.

A few blocks of limestone lie strewn about at my feet. Other lumps are shrouded in grass and bramble. I look down, conscious now of water seeping into my boots. The building's former outline is visible, but the core of the house is gone.

We squelch our way towards the only standing structure. The grey stone of the vast walled garden is greened by ivy. No flowers, no soft fruit, grow inside. The rain deepens as we turn to go. Walking back past the grave of the house, I avert my eyes as though there has been an accident.

Brigid sighs. 'If they'd burnt it down, at least we'd have a ruin.'

April 1933

Stepping into Elizabeth's life, as Humphry did in 1933, meant the crossing of a physical, as well as an emotional, threshold. This was at the top of the wide steps of Bowen's Court, something that you passed over before penetrating her ancestral home in Ireland.

Elizabeth's Welsh forebear, Colonel Bowen, arrived in Ireland during the brutal Cromwellian campaign of 1649. Swathes of land in County Cork fell to him. A later heir built Bowen's Court, the house which Elizabeth knew. Dating from 1776, it was a rather unlovely Italianate dwelling with a vast number of windows. It was boxlike, solid, and set among fine elm trees. Elizabeth describes the landscape's quiet, anonymous charm: 'The country conceals its pattern of life, which can only wholly be seen from an aeroplane. [...] From the air you discover unknown reaches of river, chapels, schools, bridges, forlorn graveyards, interknit by a complex of untravelled roads.'

Bowen's Court itself was a 'big house', both structurally and symbolically. These estates and their associated wealth were held by families of the Protestant Ascendancy (the roughly ten per cent of the population, an Anglican elite, that had dominated Ireland since the seventeenth century). This had long been a matter of considerable tension between them and their largely Catholic neighbours, and the early twentieth century saw such animosities intensify. Two wars of the 1920s, the Irish War of Independence and the Civil War, saw a huge increase in violence against the Anglo-Irish and their homes. The neo-Gothic castle at Mitchelstown, ten miles from Bowen's Court and well known to Elizabeth, was burnt to the ground in 1922.

Despite being occupied for a few days by Republican forces, Bowen's Court remained intact throughout these troubled times. Elizabeth's telling of the tale falls into the best tradition of family myth-making. Warned of the soldiers' arrival, the Bowens safely stowed away the family portraits and the silver. The young soldiers apparently spent most of their time in the house sleeping and reading Kipling. One day while the men were out, Aunt Sarah Bowen from Mitchelstown arrived at Bowen's Court and decided to stay the night. The absent soldiers never returned. The family force field was restored through the steely will of Aunt Sarah.

By the time Elizabeth met Humphry, Bowen's Court was hers. The power of this type of house, both over the occupants and over the imagination, was relentless. Young heirs were expected to deny their own feelings and perform expected rituals at the shrine of the family name. Elizabeth described herself as a 'matriarch' living in a manner that often outstripped her financial resources. But she was a childless matriarch who maintained the estate without providing it with an heir. In this, she embodied and anticipated the death of the particular group to which she belonged. The politics of her past, one that allowed her to play the role of Lady Bountiful of Bowen's Court, she did not struggle against. But painful shards of Irish history do appear in her writing.

Bowen's 1929 novel, *The Last September*, set in an Ireland dominated by big houses, explores this realm. It was published just before Elizabeth inherited Bowen's Court on the death of her father. Lois, the protagonist, feels that 'she and those home surroundings still further penetrated each other mutually in the discovery of a lack'. In the novel, the stasis of house and inhabitants is exploded by soldiers, fire, death. The narrative charts the big house's last gasp.

The dynamic personality of her house courses through Elizabeth's book, *Bowen's Court* (1942). It is, in part, an idiosyncratic history – of her own family, and of the tribe to which she belonged. She explores both the geographical and psychological space that enshrouds these 'house-islands' and their families, marooned in a time that is increasingly hostile to them. With successive Irish Land Acts, tenant farmers and farm workers were gaining a greater stake in land ownership. The fabric of the country was being necessarily, irrevocably, restitched. It is a change captured by Seamus Heaney in the poem 'A New Song', where he speaks of 'river tongues' flooding 'with vowelling embrace / Demesnes staked out in consonants'.

Bowen's Court is also a love letter. Elizabeth proudly conducts the reader, just as she would conduct Humphry, through the rooms of the house – we enter the hall with its apricot wallpaper, walk through the downstairs rooms with their friezes of Italian plasterwork, into the library smelling of dry calf binding and wood smoke. We hold on to heavy oak banisters going upstairs where all the rooms have mantelpieces of local marble. On this floor, there is a gallery and three large bedrooms with adjoining dressing rooms. Then it is up the back stairs to the top of the house where there are more bedrooms and the Long Room, a ballroom built with a hopelessly weak floor.

For Elizabeth, the restorative qualities of Bowen's Court were essential, and she sought it out as often as she could. She writes of her home: 'The sense of profusion, ease, courtesy, leisure, space drips like warm honey over one's nerves. Actually that only exists if one stays quietly in a country house.'

Bowen's Court was Elizabeth's fixed foot, from which her other selves adventured. On Alan's death many years later, she wrote to Isaiah Berlin: 'Really my next of kin is this house.'

Before leaving for Ireland in April 1933, Humphry spent some days in London. There is every chance he once again accepted double bed and board at Madeline's flat. Her reasons for breaking off their engagement at the end of 1932 seem to have been due to his poor behaviour, but his renewed presence in her life spoke both of her love for him and of the possibility that they might have a shared future after all. There must have been a twist of unease in Madeline's heart as Humphry left for Ireland and Elizabeth. Even so, her actions were measured – she sent him on his way with a guidebook.

For Humphry, it was first to Dublin for Gerard Manley Hopkins; then on to County Cork to see Elizabeth. He arrived at a time of considerable political upheaval in Ireland, still at this time a Dominion within the British Commonwealth. A general election in the Irish Free State in 1932 had seen a first victory for the fledgling Fianna Fáil party, under Éamon de Valera, with an ideology of Irishness at the top of their agenda.

This swift-moving current of Irish political life was in sharp contrast to Humphry's work retracing the measured, monastic tread of Hopkins, who was enjoying a surge in popularity following the publication of a new edition of his verse. The poet worked for the last five years of his life as Professor of Greek and Latin at University College, and died in Dublin in 1889. He then drifted into obscurity, and it wasn't until 1918 that a volume of his poetry was published for the first time. When he entered the Jesuit order, Hopkins burned his poems and it was only through copies he had sent earlier to a friend, the Poet Laureate Robert Bridges, that his remarkable verse was saved.

Humphry enjoyed Dublin, but his letters to Elizabeth were cloaked in Englishness – he was an outsider and felt it: 'I speak scarcely to anybody, always seeming the stranger. To-night a man shouted "Australian" at me! It is enough to put anyone in his shell.' This anxiety about where to fit in stretched to his feelings about the trip to Bowen's Court: 'I have a fear of blighting your whole stay.' He was a guest of Elizabeth, in a part of the world with which he was unfamiliar. The social world of Oxford where they had met granted a fairer distribution of power. County Cork was Elizabeth's milieu, exclusively.

Faced with the possibility of a railway strike disrupting his plans to travel to Bowen's Court, Humphry wrote to Elizabeth about arriving by aeroplane. In his imagination he donned the flying goggles of the romantic hero, telling Elizabeth he might be landing in her fields. At the time, Humphry did not even have a driver's licence for a car – one hopes someone else was to be at the controls. In the end, Humphry did not travel by plane, nor glimpse Bowen country for the first time over the wing's edge. Instead, he caught the train. On the journey, he was treated to a woman serenading the travellers on her fiddle as the train wound its way gently southwards through the hills.

In front of the main steps of Bowen's Court was a gravel road which crunched loudly under the tyres of arriving cars. Elizabeth probably heard Humphry before she saw him, before the imposing front door was opened to welcome him in. On entering he saw the family portraits on the walls, the fine grandfather clock, the vast windows that filled the rooms with crisp, spring light. And Elizabeth herself, dressed as she tended to in the country, in a skirt just below the knee, a blouse and cardigan, but still with her trademark chunky jewellery around her neck.

Elizabeth's invitation to stay did not mean a romantic getaway *à deux*. Humphry would have been expected to fit into Elizabeth's full and varied Irish life. Her family often came to the house: Noreen Colley, one of her cousins, was a semi-permanent fixture. Elizabeth socialised locally – both with immediate neighbours, such as Jim Gates, and at other big houses like Annesgrove and Byblox.

The doors of Bowen's Court were thrown wider still in the summer months when friends from England visited. Over came the Oxford crowd – Bowra, Berlin, and Lord David Cecil, the biographer and academic;

and later writers like Iris Murdoch and Eudora Welty. Some of the young men who visited in the 1930s, including Berlin and Stuart Hampshire, joked that Bowen's Court was straight out of Russian literature: a feudal backwater, an air of gloom, a way of life whose demise was as inevitable as the cutting down of the ancestral trees. Virginia Woolf, who was a guest of Elizabeth's in 1934, seemed to concur: in her diary she wrote that Bowen's Court was 'pompous & pretentious & imitative & ruined', filled with deathly furniture and carpets with holes. Her thank-you letter to Elizabeth was far more diplomatic – she declared that Ireland's seductive charms were so strong that she and Leonard had flirted with the idea of buying property there.

The novelist L. P. Hartley, another guest in 1934, describes Elizabeth's skills as hostess at Bowen's Court: 'You have a wonderful gift of interpreting your guests to each other – and to themselves as well. It is as though you furnished each with a passport to the others' personalities, and a unique sense of fusion comes from it.'

Sunny days at the house would result in a scattering of deck chairs, newspapers, cushions, and books on the wide front steps. For those rare bright moments, Elizabeth could imagine she was in Italy and bask in her home's '*villeggiatura* air'. From the house, guests would set out on expeditions which Elizabeth describes thus: 'the sort of expedition that survives only in this kind of Ireland, and, including rugs, picnic baskets, mackintoshes, is very much set out upon – I mean one doesn't simply frivolously start.'

Humphry's introduction to the house's rhythms happened immediately. Elizabeth's cousins, the Butlers, appeared at teatime on the first day. (One wonders how Elizabeth introduced Humphry, and whether any eyebrows were raised.) Bowen's Court would have been filled with cheerful conversation and familial shorthand. Here was a quite different Elizabeth from the one with whom Humphry had anxiously read Virgil in February. What Elizabeth asked of Humphry stretched beyond her desires and the requirement that he be a thoughtful guest. He needed to feel and respect the 'house's strong *own* life'. The italics are hers.

With tea concluded, it was time for a tour of the grounds – past the tennis court and croquet lawn, the other estate buildings that included stables and a disused dairy, round the higher lawn of pampas, conifers, and flowering cherry, and then down the wooded walk to the magnificent walled garden, all three acres of it. A sundial sat in the middle, a glasshouse on the sunniest wall, a pergola in one corner with vistas of the mountains. There were espalier fruit trees and vegetable plots sufficient to feed twenty people. The garden was full of colour. During Humphry's visit it was the turn of jonquils, polyanthus, lily of the valley, with vibrant parrot tulips preparing to flower.

Yet despite all the familiarity of place, light, people, Elizabeth had a delicate balance to strike. Her role as the chatelaine of the house, with its expectations and responsibilities, remained. Her skills as a hostess were instinctive, easy to extend to any guest. What was more difficult was finding the space within the knowing house, and among its various visitors, for her intimacy with Humphry to grow. In a letter to Humphry later in their relationship she explained this tension. She felt tired and constrained having other guests, 'with the superficial part of me that they stand for and bring into being, in the house at the same time with you and all you mean. It rattled me and divided me. I did not know where I was'.

This may be one reason why the most enjoyable day was one spent away from Bowen's Court at nearby Kilcolman Castle, a wreck sunk in marshland and garlanded with gulls. In the sixteenth century, the castle had been home to the poet Edmund Spenser. There he wrote part of *The Faerie Queene*, during his unhappy sojourn in Ireland as a royal official. Elizabeth loved the 'torn-open ruin', a broken building reeking of poetry and the past. (It is just the kind of structure she favours in her fiction.) But even on the trip to Kilcolman the pair would not have been alone

– neither Elizabeth nor Humphry had yet learned to drive in the spring of 1933. The presence of at least one other person, whoever they were, is not mentioned anywhere in Humphry's account of the visit.

On every subsequent trip to Bowen's Court, Humphry would be reminded of their day trip, thanks to a picture in the room he occupied at the top of the house. On the wall next to the mahogany wardrobe was a picturesque but wildly inaccurate print of Kilcolman. No matter that mountains had been added or cliffs chiselled for effect. What the picture held was the memory of their best day together – the mystery and magic of the ruin, Elizabeth's enthusiastic enjoyment of the melancholy tower, and the opportunity of spending time together in a different environment.

Humphry stayed with Elizabeth at Bowen's Court for a little over a week. Then it was back up north to take the boat home. Upon boarding the ferry to take him back to England, Humphry sat down to write to Elizabeth. Dublin was disappearing in the haze – a hot crossing lay ahead. He relaxed in a mock-mahogany chair in the bar. Priests of the Church of Ireland, dressed in tweed caps, sat bravely outside on the deck with their decorative daughters. There is a tentative note in his voice, as though he is conscious of his liminal position. What Humphry writes contains the gratitude of the guest, as well as the knowledge that he is something more: 'I shall not be able to write an adequate thank-you letter, because my stay at Bowen's Court was so good: not only because the place is so beautiful and the company, yourself in chief, delightful, but because movements and expeditions just happened unorganised and unexpected.' He signs off: 'I hope soon to see you under apple-trees.'

Once both were back in England, the relationship continued to evolve. There were further trips for Elizabeth up to Appleton. Their seeing of one another was more spontaneous – Humphry ringing up to invite her to see him the same day, warning her that he only had 'grim food' in the house. They went for dinner in Abingdon, which lay a safe ten miles from Oxford.

Despite the exciting novelty of the relationship, Elizabeth was inclined to tread cautiously. She was to say of Humphry, later in their intimacy, that he liked approaches – his difficulty arose in knowing what to do next. In an essay entitled 'The Art of Reserve; or the Art of Respecting Boundaries' she explores this ground further. Storming, or rushing, into the heart of someone was neither wise nor advisable – intimacy had to be wooed not ravished. She writes: 'The infinite possibilities of happiness within a single human relationship unfold slowly, with a deliberation of their own [...]. We grow to know one another: gleam by gleam, intimation by intimation the truth blossoms, the story comes to be told.'

Her behaviour towards him was also partly determined by a characteristic of the women in her family. Elizabeth describes her own grandmother thus: 'She must have been one of those women – in my experience more often *amoureuses* than mothers – who have the power to give an increased stature to anybody they like, love or are interested in.' Elizabeth could exalt Humphry, make him more than himself. A focus on these cerebral and psychological 'planes' (to use a favourite word of hers) gave her security, a supremacy over him. This majestic mentality would be evident throughout their relationship, and would later lead to tussles for power between them.

Though the sexual side of their relationship was not to begin for several months (correspondence reveals this happened sometime in the autumn of 1933), her physical attraction to him was real. As the year unfolded, her behaviour bore all the hallmarks of a woman who was in love – the thumping heart, the tears at departure, the jealous reactions. Responding to Humphry later in their relationship she confessed that one letter of his 'made me feel I was being hit in the breast when I should more justly have been hit in the head'. This was not simply a case of Elizabeth needing to inhabit the mind of a woman in an intimate relationship for the sake of her work. She had already written of complicated emotional and sexual tangles, of frustrated wives embarking on affairs. The involvement with Humphry may well have informed Elizabeth's work, but she did not require the relationship to make her writing of certain sorts of scene more authentic.

For his part, Humphry was dazzled by her status and stature as well as by her other qualities. He loved her Irish life, such a world away from his own. All his letters of 1933 are filled with a vicarious enjoyment of her community, her style of living. His feelings of inferiority, both in terms of wealth and class, seemed to shrink in the face of the warm welcome he received there. Unsurprisingly, he wasted no time in discussing a return to Ireland with Elizabeth. The last place he wanted to be was on the fringes of Oxford, now unemployed. Elizabeth's offer to let him stay most of the summer at Bowen's Court was a godsend. He could continue to work on Hopkins, reapply to All Souls, and hope that some kind of paid employment materialised. Meanwhile Elizabeth could go to Ireland at any point in the summer, knowing he would be waiting.

In early June, Humphry headed back to Bowen's Court on his own. But he was not alone – a crowd of Elizabeth's family having descended noisily on the house. With them he gossiped, and walked around the garden, inspecting the ripening peaches and gooseberries. He could, if he wished, lounge in bed in his yellow room at the top of the house, studying for his All Souls exam. Or sit around in the library reading Virginia Woolf all day, the smell of cut hay wafting through the windows, drinking his way through Elizabeth's store of sherry. Someone was teaching him to drive; a local 'boy' was engaged to type up material for his book; his razors were delivered by the postman. He was not just the guest of Elizabeth and her home. He could play at being lord of the manor.

His earliest surviving letter to Elizabeth that summer begins with a visit to her friends, the Annesleys. Their home, Annesgrove, was famed throughout Ireland for its beautiful, unusual gardens and was popular with Elizabeth's guests. The letter is written on the small, headed notepaper of Bowen's Court, the colour of Irish skies.

HH to EB

Bowen's Court, Kildorrery, Co. Cork
Sunday 18 June [1933]

Dear Elizabeth,

[…] To-day has been a comic delight. After a morning of vague reading I set out on what was meant to be a simple social afternoon, tea at Anne'sgrove and supper at Byblox. […] I was bowled over with admiration and curiosity by New Zealand flax plants so that Mrs. A. [Annesley] exhorted me to write a poem about them (for the other day they caught a guest solitarily composing beside the Awbeg). […]

We wandered and talked for apparently not long and finally got back to the house to find that it was nearly 7 o'clock, and that I was due by walking at Byblox at 7.30, and also I learnt that it was about 6 ½ miles instead of about 4 as I had guessed. I was given a pencil map on an envelope and sent off: it was a frightful walk, […] not even a donkey cart to get a lift in, and I sweated right through my coat, thinking hard about suicide or lying up despairing in a ditch. It just went on and on along minute roads. Finally arrived at 8.30, exactly an hour late, dripping with sweat, bursting with blood, lame, and having no breath only to find that the whole thing could have been carried off by saying that I was coming by old God's time. And then was shot breathless into a party of seven young women, myself only man. [...] They were funny: Noel Browne kept the whole party going with continuously able ridiculous conversation, using sort of Wodehouse phrases with natural speed – "rush of teeth to the mouth" etc – all about everything local, and it was delightful.

[...] I look forward to you on Saturday: you will add how much! We are asked to tea at Anne'sgrove on Sunday – or alternatively to play together in a tennis tournament!

How absurd of me to talk of you "adding" to your own house – it is the penalty of allowing vicarious enjoyment. But you know you will add, because the house will come to life.

I hope this reaches you not too late before you start: it ought to have been in 2 parts. Now more Irish history.

Humphry

Like Humphry, I arrived for the first time in County Cork by train. I did not, however, have someone from Bowen's Court to meet me at the station and whisk me back to the big house for tea. Instead I walked through the rain into the centre of Mallow, one of the three towns within shouting distance of Bowen's Court.

My sense of arriving in Elizabeth's orbit was very strong, but as important was a connection with Humphry. My reason for being in Ireland formed a part of his – we were both on the hunt for literary figures through their unpublished material. Elizabeth jokingly wrote to Humphry asking if he had found new Hopkins treasures hidden in the mattresses of Jesuit priests; I wondered what was contained in her land, her home, her bedding. I hoped, of course, for psychogeographical revelations. But I was also happy for something quieter, a metaphorical pilgrim's stone, something to be felt, pocketed, and carried home again.

Once the 'Bath of Ireland', Mallow's fame as a spa town is long gone. People now come mainly for the horse racing. The jumbled shop-fronts of Elizabeth's day remain, though not every business displays fresh wares to the passing pedestrian. Breeze block, not bread, fills the window of one bakery. It is a friendly place, however, with a burr of warmth in every greeting and a changing demographic. Mallow's Catholic church, with its echoing bells, faces a new Thai restaurant. The Church of Ireland has a female priest. In the church's graveyard are some of the very earliest Bowens. The rest are buried at Farahy, on the fringe of the Bowen estate.

A few days after my arrival, I arranged to go to Annesgrove Gardens, which form a central part of Humphry's first letter to Elizabeth from Bowen's Court. My reasons for visiting went far beyond a simple cross on my map. Of the big houses that stood in the cool hills of County Cork in Elizabeth's day, this was one of the last to be owned by its original Anglo-Irish family.

A party at Annesgrove, County Cork, in the 1930s

A cabbie with a cheeky grin picked me up in the main street of Mallow. We drove through the quiet lanes, past exuberant hedgerows towards Castletownroche. Arriving at the solemn gates, we were met with a sign: 'NO ADMISSION either by car or on foot.' Moving the traffic cones out of the way, the driver said, 'Always wanted to come up here.' Then he laughed. 'You saw my name, didn't you?' His tag was stuck to the dashboard – Michael Collins – perhaps the most important figure in Ireland's struggle for independence.

At the end of the drive, an elegantly proportioned house, mid-eighteenth century with seven bays, was waiting. A slightly decrepit wooden porch of later date drooped from the front. I rang the bell and was welcomed in warmly by a couple in their sixties. The porch was hung with hunting trophies; the drawing room was hung with nothing. Bright rectangles of salmon-coloured paint showed where the family portraits had once lived. Now just their sorry hooks were visible. The pictures themselves leant jumbled against the walls. There was a simple explanation: the Annesleys were hoping to sell up, preferably to An Taisce (The National Trust for Ireland). But since the financial crisis of 2008, the sale was looking increasingly precarious. One thing was certain – the next generation of this family would not be living in these high, fine rooms.

After lemon drizzle cake, Patrick Annesley and I headed out round the grounds. Everything vast, and green, and dank. A walled garden with well-tended borders; banks of rhododendrons shiny in the rain; an extraordinary exotic Japanese garden with a brutally grafted tree – half willow, half birch. A few years earlier, a great storm had plucked up and felled hundreds of trees, some of which still lay broken about. Parts of the garden had been devastated. Parts were now too unruly to reshape. Japanese knotweed gripped the steep banks that fell down to the river Awbeg. There was no one composing poetry at the water's edge now.

June 1933 at Bowen's Court. A clear watery light in the long evenings, flowers bursting into bloom, the trees around the house filled with rooks. The perfect setting for Elizabeth and Humphry to revel in each other's company after several weeks apart. What unfolded was quite the opposite – an explosive, fraught few days precipitated by the arrival at Bowen's Court of Isaiah Berlin and a carload of friends.

Berlin and his party were on a motoring holiday round Ireland. One of their number was a striking young woman, Maire (B. J.) Lynd. According to Berlin, Humphry found B. J. 'irresistibly attractive', and followed her around Bowen's Court 'like a huge, lovelorn dog'. When they left, Humphry tagged along with them, leaving Elizabeth without a second thought. The insult was not just to Elizabeth, but also to the house and the welcome it had given Humphry in her absence. At least she was not privy to the thoughts of one of the other young female guests who described Elizabeth as 'immensely hospitable, tho' worse made up than you can imagine, all shiney wet white & badly put on rouge'. Here Elizabeth is cast as the garish older woman, desperately using 'paint' to recapture past beauty. She is of an altogether different generation from her fresh-faced guests – their youth giving them naturally what was seen as most attractive in women of the day: clear skin and a good complexion.

Elizabeth must have felt a smart of rejection following Humphry's departure, but she was not someone inclined towards self-pity. One of her enjoyments at Bowen's Court was working outdoors, particularly when she was feeling low or irritated. This did not consist of surveying the flowers in the walled garden and selecting a choice few for the vases in the house. Instead it was clearing woods and slashing down nettles and undergrowth. These sorts of activities suited her, as she had, by her own admission, 'plenty of brute strength and aggressive instinct, but the reverse of green fingers'. It is not hard to imagine Elizabeth swinging a sickle through weeds, or hacking at a root or two to dispel some of her anger with Humphry.

Having left in Berlin's car, Humphry must have relied on public transport to get back to Bowen's Court. There is every chance that Elizabeth had to send someone to pick him up from the station just as she had on his first visit in the spring. One imagines less teatime jollity on arrival this time. Possibly as a way of avoiding the worst of Elizabeth's froideur in the following days, Humphry wrote a flurry of letters. He may well have written in his candlelit room at the top of the house, the bats beating at the window, a distant squawk of herons filling the night air.

One of the first letters was to Isaiah Berlin, in which he apologised for being 'tipsy and truculent' at the end of their road trip. The letter reveals how young men of the day viewed women, as well as the differences between Humphry and Isaiah. Characterising his friend as a fussy aunt, Humphry expressed resentment of Berlin's attitude of advisory patronage towards B. J. He made it clear that, despite finding B. J. exquisitely beautiful, he was not in love with her. Humphry's stated explanation for this was that he did not 'understand affection'. This wilful resistance to examining his feelings, whilst at the same time glorying in sharp bursts of attraction, was a trait of Humphry's as a young man. At the end of the letter, he offers a further justification of his behaviour, characterising both Isaiah and himself as 'incurably intellectual'. Humphry's thoughtless behaviour towards women was excusable, in his eyes, because he was pondering weightier matters.

Berlin was not the only person to receive a letter from Humphry in the distressed days after his return to Bowen's Court. Almost inevitably, Humphry wrote to Madeline acquainting her with the bones of the B. J. incident. Though Humphry did not mention the young woman by name, he told Madeline that his behaviour had resulted in being 'severely rated' by Elizabeth. Madeline did not have to use her imagination a great deal to construct a plausible reason for such a reaction – there was surely a woman involved. Humphry continues: 'It was all very difficult and complicated. As usual when I get in a complex social situation I acted in a way to hurt somebody; and I was very upset and unable to write. The final result has been to improve my relations with E. And everything is better than before.' A sentiment Madeline probably found difficult to share.

In the letters to both Madeline and Isaiah, Humphry identifies that the B. J. episode and its fallout has changed something between himself and Elizabeth. Her anger had, in all likelihood, given way to a mutual desire to heal the rift. After the storm their connection felt enriched. But what is evident from Humphry's letter to Isaiah Berlin is that this 'new contact and intimacy' was not sexual: 'no not what Maurice hoped: he is vulgar.' The Oxford men could imagine what they liked but the physical side of Humphry's relationship with Elizabeth was yet to begin.

For Elizabeth, there were several issues at stake. The first was geographical. Bowen's Court required a certain formality of her – its pinch-waisted dress was not easily cast aside. Her complicated relationship with her home was heightened by the portraits of her forebears on the walls. She knew she was being watched. There was also her position as a married woman, and a conservative one at that. Her love for Alan, the value she placed on their marriage, was very real. Furthermore, knowing Humphry's nature, her own sexual inexperience must have been a source of anxiety.

This more open-hearted, though chaste, understanding of one another was savoured for just a few days before Elizabeth left Bowen's Court once more. A short letter from Humphry on her departure begins: 'It was wretched seeing you off on Saturday: and worse to come back here and find it emptied of you while flowers you had done were freshest. Everything was subdued – the house, Sarah and everyone.' The letter then talks about soporific sunshine, chicken coops, and carburettors. Though he does say that he will write longer soon, his first inclination is to tell her of herself.

In his next letter he is allowed no such prevarication. Elizabeth had written requesting answers to tricky questions about his character and behaviour. Talking of poultry would not suffice. This sort of missive required thought and a drink – a large sherry from her cabinet. Uncut, his letter runs to fifteen hundred words and includes the extract from his journal about the first day in Appleton, and the poem 'Mirantur et Undae'.

HH to EB

Bowen's Court, Kildorrery, Co. Cork
Undated [July 1933]

My dear Elizabeth,

[...] I am glad indeed that my bad behaviour and worse account of it last week happened: it was bad – and as you showed you saw it gave you most of the worst and most inconsistent and blind traits in me in action all at once. I did not know when I went to bed on Wednesday night, eaten out and almost dead, eating my own bowels and deciding that you would above all not want me to try to find life again by knocking you up in your room, and wondering whether you had been as moved as I (and only in the morning did I realise how you had been moved, perhaps more than I) – I did not know then that your sense and care and understanding in the morning would make that really the beginning of an intimacy quite unlike what had been before. [...]

I am not grown up: still chase after too-complete intimacies in which touch and word coincide, the word is made flesh; still am unable to assess the power of word or touch, wondering and hurting; making and nursing illusions and ordering facts to fit them – and when they do not fit cynically repudiating both, and taking a cheap refuge in spiritual hostility and destruction. Still avid of experience without being able to co-ordinate or explain it; and avid for knowledge, with no idea how it is to be used. But in most of these ways many people older than I are not grown up, though many more have found some trick to hide this immaturity from themselves.

[…] Just because you are so much a woman and I so exclusively male, each in all ways, any emphasis of that had to be avoided if we were to be companionable: a balance could be best achieved by respecting one another's ground and remembering the nine years. And in the remembrance I said many quick unthinking hurting things – as over the dinner table at Abingdon. I was trying to make a mode of affection which was not that of a lover. In doing so inevitably I falsified my own character, not wilfully or malignly, but enough to make a surprised and horrid clash when it burst through.

[…] But now no more about characters: I am writing now after dinner and the full moon has just risen behind the circle of trees on the lawn, and is lighting up flecks of cloud above them which have been shredded out of rain-clouds by a rising wind. It has been sun-and-showers again to-day. The moon just swinging into a gap in the trees, bright silver coloured, not golden at all, and immense: trees like sea. […]

Am going to meet Miss Somerville of Somerville and Ross at Annesgrove to-morrow. How wildly odd. Mrs. Annesley's belief that all "literary" people jolt up well together produces most charming results.

How's your eye? It sounded horrid. I hope you are not still comic.

Love,

Humphry

Humphry's letter was waiting for Elizabeth when she arrived at her flat in Markham Square in London. She did not rush to read it; she was going out to dinner that night, and would read it at leisure afterwards. The letter exerted a perverse pressure on her throughout the evening – she dawdled at dinner, and stayed out talking on the steps with the person who had brought her home. She longed to read the letter, yet was shy of it. Finally alone in midnight's deep hush, she turned on the lamps, lit a cigarette, and began to read, her heart thumping. Then she put the letter down, wandered round the room, looked for an ashtray, lit another cigarette, and read it again. Her thoughts of him must have accompanied her to bed.

The following day, Elizabeth wrote an immediate reply, one that begins with a description of her nocturnal tryst with Humphry's letter. Uncut, the letter runs to ten pages. Her handwriting in the letter is almost illegible; the frantic mess of words a reflection of her emotional state.

EB to HH

46 Markham Square, SW3, Kensington 5732
Wednesday 12 July 1933

My dear Humphry

[…] About things you said – I wish you had knocked me up in my room that Wednesday night. I felt broken-off and felt we should not have parted, but thought ignorantly that you might be glad I had gone and would rather be without me. It was windy

that night, do you remember; I lay hearing sounds all through the house, step-sounds like people walking, then thought I heard your step on the landing outside, suddenly realized how much I hoped it was you and got up and went to the door. But it was all quite dark and you did not seem to be there.

The day before, when I wept in the library when I came back from Mitchelstown because you were not there, though I knew you would not be there and had under everything else profoundly dreaded that you would be there unwillingly, I felt the friendly solitude of the house, which had always been like a rock to me, outside and clear of everything that happened or that I felt, had gone bitter and unfriendly, or been invaded. I blamed myself thinking that some wrong feeling of mine about things had corrupted things. But I did still regard the great man in you. […]

I have been less hurt by what you do and may well do again in the exercise of a freedom that I respect than by a feeling of something factitious between us. A dread that I might be dealing with an unreal person. As a matter of fact, if I were all that grown-up myself, which I'm not, in spite of my years, I don't think factitiousness would exist or be called out in you. But I am still ignorant, nervous and dread touching the limits of feeling, if it has any limits. I still miss things and blunder and want perfection in intimacy so frightfully, and want the word to be made flesh.

I don't mind you hurting me inadvertently or deliberately, if it is not in the dark.

I remember standing with you beside the palm tree and I remember the moment, an extreme awareness of you and the man in you.

You know I love greatness, in the sense of Stephen Spender's "– I think continually –" My feeling for you has a touch of the subjection that is latent in any woman's feeling for any man: (unless she is first of all motherly, which I am not) the desire to be towered over spiritually, intellectually, morally. When I speak or think of your youth, I mean you have far to go.

[...] To be a so-called clever woman is to be moving blindly and dumbly under a crust of oneself all the time. I am partly a clever woman, but also very much more and very very much less. If when I do this nervous talk someone would put a hand on my arm and say: "That's enough: do shut up, do be calm, do let me breathe" I should be all right.

I talk most like this with anyone I most hope will be able to stop me.

[...] Alan has come up to go to a conference party and is wandering round the room, so I can't write any more.

[...] Someday I'll send you a blank page with '– love from Elizabeth.'

For the present –
Love from
Elizabeth
Thank you for telling me about the moon.

The speed of Elizabeth's reply, and the subtle shift in their relationship, sees phrases echoed, confessions shared. Her reference to the palm tree is prompted by the extracts from his journal that Humphry had included in his letter. They both cannot help rewinding to that early magical afternoon on the banks of the Thames. It is easier to mine memory than examine a past where the hurt is still fresh.

In the full text of Humphry's letter his poem is followed by this reflection: 'Then and often afterwards I was conscious of the "chaperone or drawn sword between us": indeed I thought I had put it there or asked her in – as also last week.' The allusion is to Richard Strauss's

Der Rosenkavalier, in which the lovers, Sophie and Octavian, have to face numerous obstacles. The sense of there being other people or situations to frustrate the relationship with Elizabeth suggested itself to Humphry strongly. He would take up the image again in another letter shortly afterwards, identifying Alan as one of the drawn swords of complication between them.

It is certain that Alan was with Elizabeth at Bowen's Court during part of the summer. Humphry writes: 'I was acutely conscious of Alan the whole time with you; figured a whole area of your life in which he was what you wanted – and above all did not want to intrude on that: in all of which I may have been hopelessly wrong.' Alan is imagined in one large room of Elizabeth's existence. He does not enter others, or invade the space Humphry wishes to inhabit. Humphry is able to state, quite openly, Elizabeth's impact on him: 'For you from the first I had more feeling as a person than I had ever had for anyone.'

Alan is not the only person pressing into Humphry's consciousness who makes an appearance in the letter. Madeline is also mentioned, painted as neither chaperone nor drawn sword, but as something else. Humphry writes: 'I have very strong and irritating lusts which emerge periodically and leave no peace, and bring with them the gloomiest thoughts about everything. They are in order: but this time they were particularly bad. For about a year Madeline Church has been my mistress and we have spent a night or a few nights together roughly once a month.' Humphry continues in this tactless vein by telling Elizabeth that he has recently suffered a degree of sexual frustration and melancholy as a result of his distance from Madeline.

Humphry often wandered through the rooms of his heart without shutting doors behind him. He thoughtlessly carried his relationship with one woman into the sphere of the second. He told each about his feelings for the other – unable, or unwilling, to imagine how this might distress them. (The B. J. episode was another occasion on which he failed to realise that his involvement with Elizabeth, let alone with Madeline, should preclude his pursuit of someone else.) Humphry's pattern of behaviour left both women in potentially vulnerable positions. Each was to devise strategies – very different ones – to deal with the man with the open-plan heart.

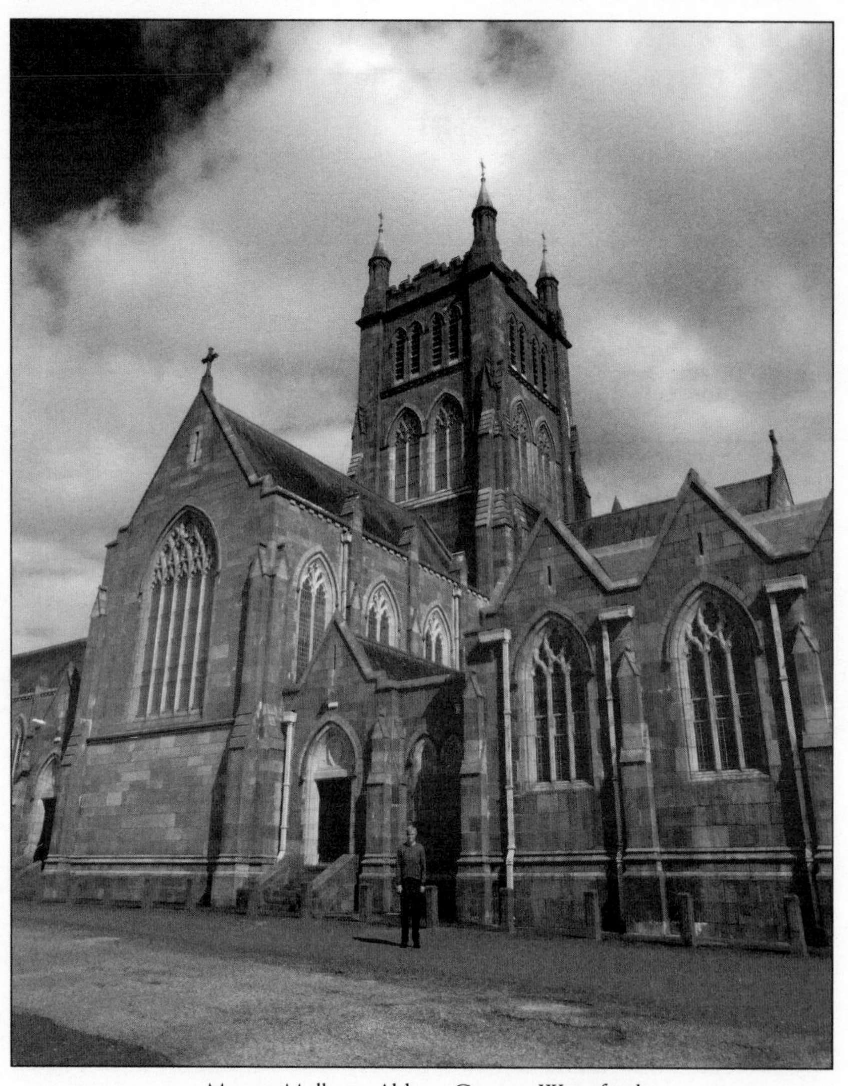

Mount Melleray Abbey, County Waterford

Chapter 5

County Waterford, Ireland: *The Happy Autumn Fields*

I wait on Mallow high street for another taxi. The journey is due east, into County Waterford. Retracing Humphry's songlines across Ireland, I am on my way to the Cistercian abbey at Mount Melleray.

There is a guest house, just as there was in the 1930s, open to anyone. On the phone to the abbey's guestmaster, I am reassured that my stay does not have to be silent. Nor is attendance at Mass obligatory. He encourages me to stay longer so that I can feel the full benefits of a retreat. There is a wisp of pleasure in his voice about the familial reason for my coming.

The journey from Mallow to Cappoquin is with a different driver, Paul. He knows all about 'feisty' Elizabeth, has a monied ship waiting to come in, and an effervescent intellect. 'A lot of history is based on the bitter word,' he says as we pull out of Mallow, passing both the Protestant and Catholic churches.

Approaching Mount Melleray, my heart starts to sink. The Knockmealdown mountains are visible in the distance. They are rolling out cloud, not a welcome mat. The cab moves through the vast gates and up the treeless drive of the abbey. I tell Paul about my anxiety.

'It's like that poem, the one about the nun,' he says. 'Who's it by again? You know the one I mean?'

I regard him quizzically. The cab slows to a halt in a vast expanse of grey gravel.

'It's only short, but I don't think I can do the whole thing by heart. Let me just find it, and I'll read it to you.' He looks at his phone, nods. 'Of course! I forgot it was Hopkins. It goes like this.' And then he reads, slowly, beautifully, the words humming on his tongue.

Heaven-Haven

A nun takes the veil

I have desired to go
Where springs not fail,
To fields where flies no sharp and sided hail
And a few lilies blow.

And I have asked to be
Where no storms come,
Where the green swell is in the havens dumb,
And out of the swing of the sea.

I sit for a moment, stilled. Give him a shake of the head, a smile, the fare, a thank you. Then I get out, and walk across the gravel to the bulk of monastery ahead of me.

July 1933

With summer at its height and Elizabeth back in England, Humphry decided to leave Bowen's Court for a few days. His destination was the Cistercian abbey at Mount Melleray which lay about an hour away from Bowen's Court. The abbey was originally built in the nineteenth century, and then reshaped with the stone from Mitchelstown Castle after its destruction by Republican forces in 1922.

Humphry wrote to Elizabeth that his reason for going on retreat was 'to see what silence does to men'. It had been a torturous year – one that included dashed hopes, emotional conflicts, and a loss of faith. Preparations for his stay at the monastery did not, however, include a return to Donne's *Sermons*. Instead he favoured a copy of Casanova's *Memoirs*, something he seems to have found on Elizabeth's bookshelves. He was driven to Mount Melleray by one of the men employed at Bowen's Court, and with the car horn broken, spent the journey furiously blowing a referee's whistle at children and donkeys straggling in the road.

His feelings on the retreat he kept to himself. The couple of lines he wrote to Elizabeth about the experience speak of practical considerations, not spiritual ones. He was reminded powerfully of the possibility of a religious life, but chilly vespers were not for him. His most ecstatic response came not at the monastery but on his journey away from it. He was stunned by the magnificent scenery of the Knockmealdown Pass – the one-time deacon seeing, like Hopkins, God's grandeur in the natural world. Within a year, Humphry was turning his critical attention to Samuel Taylor Coleridge, one of the high priests of Romanticism. It would not be God, but literature and ideas, that would keep Humphry's heart 'awake to Love and Beauty' for the rest of his life.

Even before his trip to Mount Melleray, Humphry was getting nostalgic about the summer drawing to its close, writing to Elizabeth: 'I feel terribly bound up with you and the house, and already by anticipation homesick. So much seems to have happened in these six weeks and I wonder.' These feelings were evident in the vast letters he sent her once he was back at Bowen's Court. The lime trees near the house filled the damp, warm nights with their sharp scent. The house itself was getting spruced up for her return – windows were being cleaned, rugs swept, the back stairs painted pink. The walled garden was rich with produce: 300 pounds of raspberries had just been sold in Fermoy, a local town. The gladioli were in full bloom, and the sweet peas being forcibly restrained so they could burst into flowery greeting for Elizabeth.

Humphry drank more whiskey, read Russian novels, and even ploughed through a book Elizabeth's father had written on the Irish Land Purchase Acts of the nineteenth century. But he did not hide away at Bowen's Court with Tolstoy. Instead he was very social in Elizabeth's absence, dropping in on neighbours, and helping with haymaking and weeding. One of the local women popped round to give him bars of chocolate cream as though he were a skinny boy in need of sustenance. All of this he described in detail to Elizabeth. And with no discernible embarrassment, he informed her of the possibility of Madeline coming to Ireland, though not to Bowen's Court, for a few days' holiday.

It was a glorious end to his stay – his vicarious enjoyment of her world as powerful as it had been at the start of the summer. This time though, the spell he was under went beyond the social and emotional and into the imaginative realm. In his last surviving letter to her from Bowen's Court, he speaks, for the first time, of Elizabeth's direct creative influence on him.

HH to EB

Bowen's Court, Kildorrery, Co. Cork
Friday [Undated, July 1933]

My dear this place is beautiful! This week there has been summer again, and a warm blush has come over everything. [...]

Two things have coincided and there has been conception. Man = your suggestion I should write a novel. Woman = my preoccupation with the Book of Ruth. Situation how and place where: fact of me being here and having fallen for Ireland, and reading Tolstoi. Novel is begun and already into some thousands of words: the plots fit perfectly and the vessel can hold nearly all my preoccupations. Naomi is the Irish Catholic wife of an Irish Catholic barrister who went to England to practise in London at end of last century – she was an only daughter and was left soon after her marriage (excuse the parallel) a house between Clogheen and Cahir. […] The Irish house had been burnt out in the bad times and sold. […] Chilion, as a Catholic, lapses – is a muddled excitable don who gives Ruth a hell of a time and finally after madly bathing in the river above Newbridge dies of pneumonia. Ruth goes to live for a bit with Naomi and Orpah in London. Naomi decides to go and end her days in Ireland. […] Ruth goes to Ireland with her, is caught up in it, becomes a Catholic of a sort and marries Boaz, a distant connection who by legal juggling has managed to buy back Naomi's Tipperary house for her. […]

How's that? The parallels are perfect. All my old emotional interest in the story and much else hangs to this. […]

Such elation and satisfaction have resulted from this that for the last few days I have quite neglected my history and am already wondering whether to go on with All Souls. […]

I owe this sudden burst into authorship entirely to you and here. So I tell you it is happening. Please don't tell anyone else, because I have so often talked to people about books which have come to nothing that now one is coming to something I want to keep quiet about it. […]

Love,

Humphry

Humphry's fondness for the Biblical story of Ruth, a story of migration and loyalty with three principal players, predated Elizabeth. In the lush summer of 1933, it blossomed inside him. But there was more than his increased receptiveness at play. There was also his suggestibility – Elizabeth had encouraged him to write a novel. In her critical essay 'The Roving Eye', Elizabeth writes about the connection between writers and their subjects: 'It might, it appears, be said that writers do not find their subjects: subjects find them. There is not so much a search as a state of open susceptibility.'

In his approach to the narrative, Humphry recasts the scene in Elizabeth's Ireland, using her life for his creative ends: 'excuse the parallel.' He is not merely writing because of her, he is sculpting her as fiction. There are many ways to compose love letters. Several thousand words about muddled dons in England and conflagrations in Ireland is surely one of them.

The novel was never finished. There remain about thirty pages of bark-coloured foolscap, all in Humphry's neat hand. *Sketch of Plot of Ruth as a Novel* is large on the title page. There follows a pencil drawing of the slice of County Cork he was introduced to by Elizabeth. A note on setting – 'Israel = Ireland. Moab = England' – is followed by a synopsis. Very few scenes are complete. Pages are numbered, but empty.

The majority of what did get written is set in Oxford. There is a character with 'affable teeth', and a young couple called David and Ruth who enjoy an evening glass of sherry. He is a young fellow, college unknown. She waits for him at home, in a village a few miles away. The narrative has elements of Humphry's life so far, as well as a projected autobiography which sparkles with more success than he had yet enjoyed. David has a job and a devoted spouse, with whom he sometimes discusses the Irish Free State. If Elizabeth's life and land gave structure to some scenes, it seems Madeline was making an appearance as the patient wife.

This letter, the fruit of his eventful summer in Ireland, affects me every time I read it. Here are snatches of Humphry at his most raw, real, vulnerable: 'Please don't tell anyone else.' With the cruel eye of retrospection, I see his keenly imagined story broken off, a rough first draft. Ruth and Boaz do not settle in Ireland. Nor does Naomi's old house in Tipperary rise from the ashes.

But there is something more in the tale of Humphry's unrealised novel – an intergenerational parallel impossible to overlook. For both Humphry and me, Elizabeth acted as some sort of creative catalyst, willing pens to be picked up and stories told. I feel drawn to my grandfather, connected to him in endeavour and inspiration.

Elizabeth would have received Humphry's spirited letter in Oxford. She was, at the time, writing short stories and planning her next novel, *The House in Paris*. A muddle of young people, a man and two women, would inhabit its pages. What name would she give to one of them? Naomi.

In Humphry's absence, Madeline was getting on with her London life. She continued her Voluntary Aid Detachment work, and made new friends, including a young male doctor. (Humphry judged her new acquaintance 'awful', though this may say as much about him as it does about the character of the doctor.) There is no suggestion that this was any more than a friendship, but it was evidence of Madeline's independence and attractiveness.

Her lodgings in Woburn Square faced fine plane trees, a patch of lawn, and a small summer house. A couple of streets to the east lay Tavistock Square, the home of Virginia and Leonard Woolf. During her years in the capital, Madeline had, unconsciously, followed the steps of the novelist around this precious pocket of the city. Woolf and the Bloomsbury set were described as living in squares and loving in triangles. Madeline, with her view of a Bloomsbury square, faced the same spatial and emotional tensions in the summer of 1933.

Madeline's contact with Humphry in Ireland was sporadic – there was his plea for sympathy following the B. J. debacle, and another letter in which he thanked her for lending him some money. The amount, £8, was not inconsiderable, amounting almost to a month's pay. While Elizabeth was giving him free accommodation for half the summer, Madeline was helping to subsidise the rest of his stay in Ireland.

While Humphry was away, Madeline continued to support his work. From its inception, she was a part of his research into Hopkins, helping him organise and collate the material he uncovered. She contributed to the notes, corrected transcripts, and drew the maps. What he requested of her from Ireland was less creative, more prosaic: 'I will be sending you some things for typing soon.' Clearly the local boy enlisted to act as secretary at Bowen's Court was not of a high enough standard.

Humphry also gave her advice about various job opportunities and work experience that she was considering. He encouraged her, if she was to do unpaid work, to continue with a socio-economic survey she had started, either alone or at the London School of Economics. That was much better, he felt, than another possibility she had mentioned, as 'secretary – hostess' to Alexander Farquharson, the head of the Institute of Sociology: 'An ineffectual rarified ascetic is exactly the sort of man one would expect to want most ardently to get hold of an uncertain attractive woman to do his dull work for him for no salary.' It seems the irony of this sentence was completely lost on him.

As Elizabeth prepared to leave Bowen's Court at the end of her stay, Humphry wrote at more length to Madeline. What he suggested was that she come to Ireland for a holiday and 'live with me completely as my wife somewhere in the country'. Here was a renewal of their sexual relationship (one that dated back to the months following his loss of faith) as well as a vision of marital commitment between them.

For Madeline, this plan would mean foregoing a trip to Russia she was hoping to take. And there were clouds over Ireland – both meteorological and emotional. There seems to have been an understanding that a summer apart would be good for them, for her in particular. Nevertheless, she went to Ireland for three days at the end of July, spending the time with Humphry in County Waterford. Now the proud bearer of a driver's licence, Humphry managed to borrow an old car – from Bowen's Court.

Humphry noticed immediately that Madeline seemed changed, more sure of herself. The holiday itself was a great success, he felt their love was fuller and more certain than before. In his first letter to Madeline after her return to England he wrote: 'I love you now without panting into the future and wondering about it. I must keep from that: it is what wrecked our love before. We have a daily present.'

The wedding was back on. The only hurdles were the usual – family, money, employment, and other people.

The summer of 1933 was a time of considerable political turmoil in Ireland, something Humphry witnessed first-hand on his return to Dublin. On 13 August a parade in the city was planned by the Blueshirts, the Fascist-leaning National Guard. The gathering was banned by de Valera, who feared it might lead to a coup d'état. Hearing shouting from his room in a nearby hotel, Humphry resolved to go to Stephen's Green, in the city centre, to see whether there was any sort of disturbance. He wrote to Madeline that he found the developments in Irish politics of the time 'very exciting', before concluding: 'It is suddenly pouring with rain. That always stops revolutions!'

For Humphry and Madeline more pressing problems lay closer to home; both families needed to be fully won round to the idea of the marriage. In a fit of fantasy, Humphry imagined an elopement – with both sets of parents being presented with the marriage as a fait accompli: 'I think even your father would melt a little if he saw you were happy.' Clearly the Church family, particularly Madeline's father, had not yet warmed to the idea of Humphry as a suitable son-in-law. He had, after all, let her down before.

Then there was how best to placate his own father. Harold House had given Humphry a fair amount of money on the understanding that he would again enter for the All Souls exam. This financial obligation weighed heavily, as did his father's opinion of the marriage: 'He would be utterly unsympathetic to the idea of my marrying you without a "job" – and not a job merely, but a fat bank balance.' Humphry proposed a meeting so that his father could see them happily reunited: 'He must be got up to London, where the obvious place to discomfort him most is your room. Will you allow this? Also, should it be a three-power conference? Should you be there?'

Madeline's participation in the proposed marriage conference is not written as a speaking part. Her presence in the room – her room, no less – will chiefly act as a balm on the acid tongues of father and son. Her own wish to marry Humphry is not imagined as carrying any weight with his father. Though Madeline might be able to express her will and independence in her choice of husband, it was harder for her to disturb their patriarchal presumptions of her secondary importance. Humphry was taking a wife; she was being received.

In his last letter to Madeline from Ireland, Humphry talks about a subject close to his heart, head and body – women, and more specifically, Elizabeth.

HH to MC (Madeline Church)

Maris Hotel, Lr. Fitzwilliam St, Dublin
Tuesday evening [Undated, August 1933]

Madeline darling, I am on the way towards two things (a) being drunk for the first time for months (b) being angry with you for not writing to me. [...]

A thing I meant to talk about in one or other of my earlier letters, but did not mention because I was shy (and now the shyness is gone because I am towards being drunk) – is – are you consciously jealous *when I talk of my attractions to other women? You have never said anything, and I know nothing. Chiefly, at present, are you jealous of my feeling for Elizabeth? This is a solid and extremely valuable thing for me, and I think a permanent one; the history of it you know, but you have not commented on it, so that I do not know what your attitude is. Inevitably you will meet her. I have already told her that we are going to be married, and she says that it makes her extremely happy. I want to know how you feel.*

Secondly, I cannot cure myself, even now our marriage is settled of violent and casual physical attraction to all kinds of women whom I meet or see. I think *this will be different when we live together, but am not sure. [...] A purely sensual attraction is of no importance, and will lead nowhere because of the feeling that I have all over my body that it is yours. I may even do sensual acts which are technically "unfaithful" but would you be jealous of those? To me they will not be betrayals or falsifications, but trivial and regrettable incidents – but there even may be none – I do not know. Last summer at the gate of the Oast House I said that you would be Alpha and*

> *Omega in my affections, but there might be intermediate letters – you said nothing to that.*
>
> *[…] I suppose in the end it is only trial and practice that can determine how we stand: but your everlasting silence has made me want to press you about this: it is in our independent relationships to other people that our marriage will stand or fall: you know that as I do; and we saw last year how it can fall.*
>
> *[…] Good night darling. I wish we were together to-night.*
>
> *My love,*
>
> *Humphry*

I have the unsettling feeling of reading over my grandmother's shoulder. I find this letter both gripping and awful. Beyond Humphry's selfishness and insensitivity lay assumptions about sexuality and its expression. He was of the school that believed nature had endowed men with a strong, natural sex drive which required regular release. Implicit in what he writes is the paired belief that women's (in this case Madeline's) sexual instincts were quieter, less urgent. He was aware, however, that his narrative of independent, erotic satisfaction was at odds with societal values that placed sex at the heart of a procreative marriage. Though Humphry's attitude was not unusual for the time, his frankness and his demands probably were.

Madeline, for her part, was expected not just to tolerate these encounters but to understand why Humphry needed them. And even that was not enough – he wanted her to express, immediately and in writing, what she felt about these extramarital liaisons. But the power of a letter does not lie simply in the words that are committed to a page. As significant is the reaction of the recipient. Madeline decided, at that moment, not to enter into a discussion about Humphry's infidelities – technical or otherwise. Her unlifted pen tells its own story.

My four days at the abbey were drawing to a close. I like to imagine that I spent my time there much as Humphry had done – going for walks in the rain, reading poetry in the bare bedroom with only a crucifix hanging on the wall, going to Mass when the feeling took me, relishing the silence. My last morning was a Sunday. The thin ranks at early morning prayers were swelled with visitors, most of whom stayed on for porridge and toast afterwards. A lively, chatty woman in her fifties who seemed to know everyone sat on the bench opposite me. Niamh was an ex-teacher and wore a large, capable denim skirt.

I mentioned my grandfather's visit to Mount Melleray and his description of the stunning road that ran up from the abbey to Clogheen and beyond. Without a second's thought, Niamh generously offered to show me both the route and her home in the mountains.

Half an hour later, we were off. The hills had a bleak, sheep-sheared beauty to them. They shone velvet green after rain. It was as spectacular as Humphry had described.

We stopped at the isolated farmhouse where she lived, a dwelling that even in high summer seemed starved of light. The place felt empty – no people, no dog. Niamh explained that her mother had recently died and that she now lived alone in the house. She showed me into a big room opposite the parlour. Hundreds of oil paintings hung from hooks, leant on every wall, sat in piles on the furniture.

'My mother's paintings,' she said haltingly.

There were seascapes and still lifes, paintings of the hills and valleys that had surrounded her mother's home and heart. The life's work of an accomplished painter.

'I don't know what to do with them. Do I sell them or give them away? I can't keep them all. And at this point, I don't even have the energy to sort them.' There was a hint of tears in her voice.

We left the farmhouse and got back in the car for the trip down the mountain, and then to Dungarvan, from where I could catch a bus to the ferry port. As we drove, I reflected on our different circumstances. Treasured but overwhelming, Niamh's inheritance still filled the space in the farmhouse where her mother had sat. Her painful dilemma – what to do with all the hues of her mother's life – was paralysing. I felt fortunate about the heirlooms I had received. Admittedly the letters did not take up half my house; they had merely taken up residence in my head. But more importantly they had generated energy, and opened up a new path for me across the mountains of family history and memory.

I hope Niamh has kept several of her mother's oils. Ones she loves, ones through which her mother speaks. There they should hang, on the walls of the lonely farmhouse in the rainy hills above the abbey.

The soft fruit season in Ireland was well over. September approached, and the first chills of autumn thinned the air. Humphry, unemployed and poor, headed reluctantly for the ferry back to England.

It was a journey common to Elizabeth's characters – both her visitors to Bowen's Court, and those who move through the pages of her stories. The heaving decks and skylines suspend normal existence. Caught between A and B, travellers 'seem bound for nowhere'. Time is fluid, yet a consciousness of it is sharpened by the voyage. Chance encounters colour every crossing. In *The House in Paris*, Karen, one of the young women in the love triangle, takes the ferry. She gets caught by 'Yellow Hat', a brilliant Bowen grotesque, with a 'highly respectable kind of flashiness' and a mole on her back. Karen leaves Ireland, watching from the deck as its 'hills, houses, trees slip behind to become the past'.

On my own trip back from Ireland, I took refuge in the only cabin not filled with piped music and faded photos of Hollywood greats.

The couple on my left were Slovakian and offered me some Toblerone. The man on my right, with hair as red as his indignation, discussed the migrant crisis with his knitting wife. The grimy windows looked backwards, over the ferry's wake. I shared Karen's thoughts: 'You look at places you are leaving, thinking: What did I hope to find?'

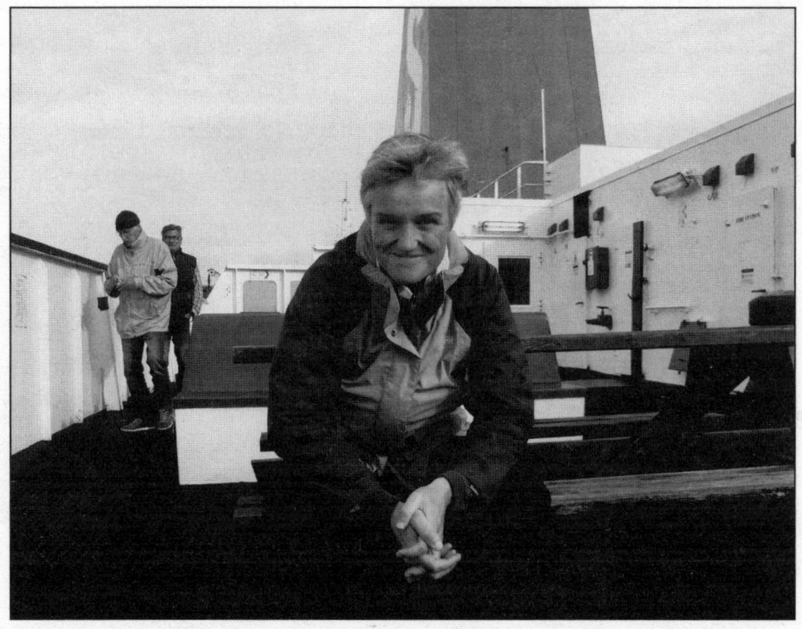

'Bound for nowhere.' The author on the ferry back from Ireland

The wreck of the Royal Clarence Hotel, Exeter

Chapter 6

Exeter, The Royal Clarence Hotel: *Recent Photograph*

I am telling my aunt Rachel about a fire. We are in her aquamarine sitting room, digesting a home-made curry. Against one wall is a wooden chest, on another a portrait in oil of a young man. It seems familiar, but I can't place it. There are books, Indian fabrics, and a few family photographs visible. Winter light dances through the large French windows. Outside is a dormant garden and a couple of recumbent stone lions.

'Didn't you see it in the news?' I ask. 'The fire at the Royal Clarence Hotel in Exeter? It was sometime just before Christmas. Totally de3few things about the Clarence – its laying claim to being the first hotel in England, one where Franz Liszt played a concert, and a dead royal was embalmed. That it was a hotel favoured by Admiral Nelson, Clark Gable, and Elizabeth Bowen. And that it was an important staging post in Elizabeth's relationship with Humphry.

I show Rachel pictures of the blaze on the internet, the smoke rising up across the cathedral and the city. The unique character of Cathedral Close, with its curve of sixteenth century buildings overseen by the grand hotel, is lost.

'Next door was the house where your parents lived. In fact, they think that's where the fire started.'

My aunt seems unmoved by the story of the fire. 'I did have a photograph once of Madeline in front of the Clarence,' she says, without a trace of nostalgia. 'I don't know where it is. Like so many things, it seems to have vanished.'

September 1933

Returning to the quiet cottage in Appleton was, for Humphry, a sharp slap back to the real world. The All Souls exam awaited, menacingly. He wrote to Madeline of his three reasons for wanting a fellowship: 'pride, money and opportunity.' There was possibly a fourth reason – remaining close to Elizabeth – though he was wise enough, on this occasion, not to mention it to Madeline. His account of the All Souls exam points towards preparation that was neither thorough nor wholehearted: 'I used some Keats I had learnt while shaving; but not very appositely.' Berlin's judgement was slightly harsher: 'Humphry House wrote poor papers & a tremendous struggle will take place over his body which I dread.' One of these papers was the essay with a single word as its title – that year, 'Patriotism'. It was an idea that would occupy Humphry in the years to come, even if he wrote about the theme badly in 1933.

In a letter that Humphry wrote to Elizabeth in the thick of his exams, he attempted to arrive at an understanding of his attraction to her. To do so he compared his feelings for her – 'based on complementary qualities of mind and sympathetic admiration' – with his emotions for not one, but two other women. One was Madeline, whose qualities he characterised as diminutive and domestic. The other was a woman he referred to as his first mistress, impressive and far above him in personal power – a woman more like Elizabeth. Her name, uncannily, was Madeleine, spelt with an extra 'e'.

There was a further crucial piece of information – Humphry mentioned that he might, with his first lover, have fathered a child. Elizabeth was made aware of Humphry's sexual experience (if not irresponsibility) just as their own sexual relationship was to begin. The psychological elements of the revelation – the questions of lost children, unknown paternity, barren or fecund women – would have found fertile soil in Elizabeth's creative, as well as emotional, consciousness. In a little over a year, all these issues would rise to the surface in the relationships between Elizabeth, Humphry and Madeline.

Possibly fearing rejection from All Souls, Humphry had applied for other jobs, away from Oxford, even before the results of his unsuccessful attempt were published. One of these was in Exeter, as an English lecturer at the University College of the South West of England. Though not appointed to this role, he was offered a post there in Classics. Humphry was amazed to receive the offer as he felt unqualified for the role. But doors open for Oxford men, even ones they do not knock upon.

He returned to Oxford one weekend in October 1933 soon after taking up his post in Exeter. Possibly it was an opportunity to see Elizabeth one final time. She would have had time to decide that, despite the distance that was opening up between them, she was unwilling for the relationship to come to an end. Humphry too did not wish it to be goodbye, either to her or to his Oxford life. He was invited to dine at All Souls by John Sparrow, a fellow of the college who would later become its warden. In a letter to Isaiah Berlin, who was now a fellow there himself, Humphry confessed a sense of failure: 'It will be like coming into the dock as an already condemned criminal to dine there; support me.' Then it was a last goodbye to the city that meant so much, before turning his eyes westwards.

When Humphry arrived in Exeter, there was a grand total of two hundred and thirty-one students reading for degrees, of whom about three quarters came from the West Country. A majority of the students were receiving a grant with a view to entering the teaching profession. The university's proportion of female to male students was more nearly equal than any other British institution of higher learning of the time. Humphry ungenerously characterised some of his students as the daughters of plumbers – his condescension springing from very definite ideas about women not of the middle or upper classes.

Humphry initially felt that Exeter was 'rough and crude', and found few like-minded colleagues. He was a long way from Oxford, with its air of gilded, erudite masculinity. Nevertheless, he was conscious of the financial benefits of full-time employment. He settled down in his new accommodation, a men's hostel on the edge of the university. Able to catch his breath, he cast an eye back over the last month – the sudden change in his fortunes, the new terrain, and his abrupt departure from Oxford and Elizabeth.

In his first letter to Elizabeth from Devon he wrote: 'I had begun to see that in some ways at least you were right; that in future our relationship will be thinner and more distant; and I was empty because that meant a great lot was being drained away from me, for which there was no substitute.' There were fewer chances to meet – the relationship ran the risk of drifting into the shallows. Though Humphry would also see less of Madeline, this was not a source of such anxiety for him. She was ringed into his life and future in a way that Elizabeth was not.

With his two female leads offstage, Humphry could concentrate on the chorus of young women in front of him – his students. Within a week of arrival, he wrote to Madeline: 'More than half of my pupils are women! So far not one that I have seen is fit to look at beyond a blowsy vulgarian with eyes who is bad at Latin. She, I am sure, is the sort of girl dons have to beware of, who tries to carry off a bad mind with a pitch and a toss.'

Humphry felt that his female students did, or should, care more for hairdos than Horace; that attracting a man was more important than declining a verb. Yet the same women were writing impassioned articles in the student magazine, *The Ram*. As well as raging about that perennial problem – lazy male students borrowing their lecture notes just before exams – the young women wrote about their societal position and rights: 'In every branch of College life, the triumphant feminine voice rises shrilly above the tempest of masculine inanity, with words of counsel and calm. […] Raise the war-cry, my unhappy, oppressed, and desperate sister. "Vive la Femme!"' These young women were looking forward to greater professional opportunities and relational freedom in a system not so much tilted towards men, as tailored for them.

The catch-22, for ambitious women of the 1930s, was marriage. On the one hand was the expectation that women were meant to marry. On the other was the fact that many employers denied women the right to continue working once married. Even nursing and teaching, professions dominated by women, operated this 'marriage bar'. Marriage would mean a loss of one's professional life as well as the sliver of security and independence it afforded. In the 1930s, eighty-five per cent of female teachers were unmarried, so much so that the word 'teacher' became synonymous with the word 'spinster'. A job as a teacher was the chosen path of many of Madeline's peers from Royal Holloway College, as well as the young women receiving educational grants in Exeter.

The contemporary author Winifred Holtby, best known for her novel *South Riding* (1936), described how such single women were viewed: 'Today there is a far worse crime than promiscuity: it is chastity. On all sides the unmarried woman today is surrounded by doubts cast not only on her attractiveness or her common sense, but upon her decency, her normality, even her sanity.' This judgement was exacerbated by considerations of age. In 1931, the average age for a woman to marry was twenty-five. Madeline was a week short of her thirtieth birthday when she married. Perhaps like Elizabeth Elliot in Jane Austen's *Persuasion*, she 'had the consciousness of being nine-and-twenty [...] she felt her approach to the years of danger'.

Married at twenty-four, Elizabeth Bowen had avoided the marital pressures faced by some women. But the peculiar world of marriage, its disappointments and dilemmas, she exploits to the full in her fiction. Women anxious to settle into matrimony (as well as a number of frigid teachers) crowd her pages. They aim for the comfort of marriage, its 'upholstered happiness', at the same time as they chafe against its constrictions. In her 1927 novel, *The Hotel*, a spirited young woman, with more than a sprinkle of sapphism in her make-up, finally accepts the proposal of a whiskery dullard. She is 'appalled at the misapprehension', on his part, that she could be in love with him. When she finally comes to her senses and turns him down, she cites the 'funny law of convenience' that propels people, unthinkingly and often without love, towards marriage.

For Madeline, marriage to Humphry hinged less on convenience than on commitment – both to a person and to a social expectation. However, the pattern of both their lives had changed considerably since she met him at the age of twenty-five. Then it had looked as if he would have the security and income of a life in the Church. She probably did not imagine herself as a stereotypical vicar's wife – presiding over teas, herbaceous borders, and knitting circles – but she would have seen a future laid out for her that was pleasingly ordered and comfortable. The years following Humphry's loss of faith saw estrangements and infidelity and Madeline moving up to London independently. Though she did not take up full-time employment, she dipped a toe in the life of the urban, working woman. Despite this glimpse of a different life, her desire to be married remained undimmed. She, like so many women of her generation, had no wish to be left on Pa's hands.

In the autumn of 1933, Madeline was in London, some distance from her fiancé. Also in the city, on regular occasions, was Elizabeth, who was growing out and away from Oxford and was enjoying new friends in the capital. Humphry's opportunities of seeing either woman were limited, but with both swirling in his mind, he actively, and perhaps paradoxically, promoted their acquaintance of each other.

In August he had written to Madeline that 'inevitably you will meet her [Elizabeth]'. And in one of his first letters to Madeline from Exeter, whilst having a drink in the Royal Clarence Hotel, he wrote: 'This hotel was recommended by Elizabeth. About her I am rather worried, and do not know what to think and feel. She is going to look you up this week in London. I hope that happens. I wonder about it. I want to hear; I am anxious.'

The meeting between Madeline and Elizabeth happened soon afterwards, over a glass or two of sherry. This most civilised of drinks (one drunk with vigour in Elizabeth's fiction and enjoyed by Madeline throughout her life) was the ideal choice for the two women, who shared polite conversation and the same man. The women made each other's acquaintance on a Friday. Humphry did not have long to wait to find out how the meeting had gone.

By Tuesday, he had received a letter from Elizabeth and dashed off a note to Madeline the same day: 'Since your letter the only news I have had of you was from Elizabeth: the fact that you met: and her quick opinion "I think she is a <u>great</u> girl". I thought about you two having sherry together on Friday evening: [...] and I wondered how you would get on and what you would say to one another.' Humphry seems unaware of Elizabeth's slightly patronising tone in describing Madeline as a 'great girl'. Madeline herself was probably more alert to what the use of the phrase implied.

Within a fortnight of their first sherry, the two women met again. A further intriguing element to these meetings is their possible location, and where Madeline was staying at the time. With the marriage delayed and provisional plans for a trip to the continent being made, she needed a room for just the month of October. Her postal footprint arrived at Red Lion Passage in Holborn – an address well known to Elizabeth.

The room Madeline rented belonged to Elizabeth's cousins, the Butlers – the same couple that Humphry had met his first day at Bowen's Court. Hubert was a well-respected historian and writer. His wife Susan (more often called Peggy) was an arts promoter and sister of the theatre director Tyrone Guthrie. The month of Madeline's occupancy saw Butler's translation of *The Cherry Orchard*, starring Charles Laughton, receive excellent reviews at the Old Vic Theatre. Of the rental arrangement Humphry wrote to Madeline: 'I'm glad you're having the Butlers' room. It is rather expensive: but very pleasant, and you really have quite a lot of money behind you.' His niggling discomfort at the slight difference in class and wealth is again evident, even though he was a beneficiary of the Church family's affluence.

Madeline's stay with a member of Elizabeth's family evinces characteristics of each woman. Self-assurance on the part of Madeline. Civility and the exercise of subtle power on Elizabeth's. And for Humphry a comforting thought – the triangle, as far as he could see, had no sharp edges.

Humphry's letters to Madeline, in the weeks immediately afterwards, do not mention Elizabeth. By contrast, his letters to Elizabeth are full of his bride-to-be. This letter, like many of this period, is on Royal Clarence Hotel notepaper. Humphry most likely wrote in the Drake Lounge of the hotel – it had writing desks complete with paper, blotters and inkwells; there were hunting trophies on the walls and an open fire. It was warm, stylish, and redolent of Elizabeth.

HH to EB

Mardon Hall
25 October 1933

Elizabeth my dear I am going to write you a hurried note in your hotel – which amuses me – over some beer after reading a pile of bad translations.

First about Madeline: you have got to the core of her. She always goes straight to essentials: essentials and ultimates are in her head all the time and inconclusive circular worrying about them is a part cause of what you call her emotional tiredness. The loneliness and the apparent lack of "personality" at first meeting are both closely joined up with this. […]

The question is what are the ways in which she is at present unsatisfied, and I don't satisfy her? I don't think she knows herself, and I don't know. I think from her side that they are all things which would become clearer in the having, ie: after marriage. […] I think always now of marriage as the only possible condition of working our relationship out. If we didn't marry there would be for both of us a lifelong feeling that we hadn't let our mutual affection have its chance. Quite apart from the gap that would be left in me there would be the anxious and biting sorrow that I hadn't let her have the chance of working out the thing on which she had banked and spent so much. You are right in finding her 'moral' qualities – courage, simplicity, honesty etc – her strongest. It is these things that make her (apart from the charm, which is very real) so much a worthwhile woman; but hitherto she has lacked the best sphere for them and squandered them on second-raters. Instinctively she has always gone with people inferior to herself: it is difficult to understand.

The lack of 'social personality' is difficult: she rarely contributes anything to a general conversation which is of real value. I think it is marriage she needs.

[...] I have written more and more seriously about M. than I thought I should: but she is in a sense "on" my mind always as well as "in" it; and so there flows a stream of what have been my thoughts.

[Ends]

Another letter from Humphry to Elizabeth, written after the women's second meeting, is in much the same vein. While in the first letter Humphry discusses Madeline's personality and their relationship, he focuses on her intellectual qualities in the second: 'I think the capacity for interest and intelligent work is there and might develope [sic] itself or develope her into something quite big.' Though aware of Madeline's gifts, he is quite clear that there was a hierarchy of cleverness in their relationship: 'She has a strong feeling of inferiority about the fact she is less well read than I, and quickly despairs because I do not manage to hide the difference.'

Humphry's obsessive discussion of Madeline points both to his insecurity and his position in relation to both women. There is a deferential tone throughout the letters to Elizabeth. He subjects his years of knowledge of Madeline to Elizabeth's first impressions of her. Elizabeth's view of Madeline is right, good and wise. After two letters full of Madeline, Humphry apologises to Elizabeth for making her a 'confidante'. His tendency to blur emotional boundaries was one reason for these outpourings, but there were a number of others. One was the fact that he had received from Elizabeth detailed appraisals of Madeline's character.

Elizabeth could be brutal about the women on the arms of her young male friends. Of Stephen Spender's fiancée, Inez Pearn, she wrote to Isaiah Berlin in 1936:

> Miss Pearn I do regard with deep disfavour – but what is the good of saying so now? To begin with, being a snob, I found her common. This need not have mattered if she had not had the manners of one of the lower animals. [...] She was impartially rude to us all, including Stephen – who, I felt, did not enjoy the lunch a bit. Which made me furious with her. And she looks like a girl hiker, or one of those young women who ride tandem bicycles in the home counties. I am unhappy at not liking her, as Stephen so clearly wishes his friends should. But really she is hopelessly unpalatable. If only she would be run over by a bus.

Madeline escaped lightly. Admittedly there was criticism, but Elizabeth did not wish death by public transport on the poor woman. There was, however, one other crucial event that coloured relations between the three of them in the autumn of 1933. It might have been a further reason for Humphry's confessional tone, and for Elizabeth dealing with Madeline in the way she did. It might also explain why Madeline seemed, in Elizabeth's eyes, emotionally tired and lacking in personality.

Sometime between Humphry's summer visit to Bowen's Court and Elizabeth's trip to America in November, the couple slept together for the first time (judging by Humphry's letters to Isaiah Berlin in June and to Madeline in December). This might have happened when Humphry came up to London, or even on a visit to the West Country. Humphry's letter to Madeline in August about the strength of his attraction to Elizabeth explained what was on the cards. Madeline had been warned. It must have been an extremely difficult, lonely time for her – the convivial sherry evenings with Elizabeth a trial of the worst kind. Small wonder she was quiet.

For Madeline it must have been a relief to know that Elizabeth would shortly be leaving for America – Humphry was not to see Elizabeth again before his marriage. Elizabeth set sail from Southampton in November for several weeks away. Before she left, she received a last letter from Humphry. In it he said that, despite his impending marriage, he felt 'remarkably unchanged' towards her. That he was glad the love he gave her was what she wanted, and was now more solid than before. He imagined her reading his letter on board the next day, as she sailed out on the tide. And echoing Othello (a man better known for his jealousy than an understanding of love) he asked her to 'think kindly but not too well of me'.

On her return to England in the middle of December, Elizabeth wrote to Isaiah Berlin about her trip to New York and about Humphry's impending marriage. The letter is an appreciation of the city's benevolent spirit, manifest both in its people and its architecture. She writes appreciatively of the houses 'salmon-coloured in the sunshine', of the city's 'extreme speed' and glittering beauty.

Elizabeth's gush of well-being about New York is in marked contrast to her thoughts about the House marriage. If she had been even-handed in her assessment of Madeline's character earlier, she had sharpened her nails, and her pen, since:

> We must just make the best of this. There is still a strain – to me at least – of the priest in him: one cannot combat the exultation of someone doing what they think right. Perhaps

> it is right. So long as he is happy I don't mind anything. There is a chance he may be. He is, I know, embracing mediocrity with his eyes open. I think he is really fond of the woman which would be enough to make things all right if I were really certain that she's really fond of him. I know she once was. But she grumbled to me when we last met about their relationship in a masochistic sort of way that appalled me. I think she is really a nice girl (as you do, too, I think?) if she would only cheer up. Perhaps marriage will cheer her up. – Anyway, there it is.

Elizabeth's letter indicates that she imagined Berlin might share her ambivalent feelings, if not her jealousy, towards Madeline. Berlin was himself unconvinced about Humphry's decision to marry. In an undated letter written some time just before the wedding, Humphry explained why he had not told his friend of his plans. He knew Berlin would be 'unsympathetic' to the idea. He goes on: 'I am not choosing a wife as I would a housekeeper – and as for the other it depends what you want a mistress for. Madeline is a much better woman than you know; and if it happens that I marry her without you discovering this I hope you won't leave me in the position of being bound to think of you always as an enemy to my wife. I should dislike to give you an explicit justification of her: and only ask you to pray it may be revealed to you that you are mistaken.'

Though Humphry felt he needed to explain his actions, he left Berlin the task of discovering Madeline's worth. Yet that autumn her actions spoke volumes about her character and proved she was not the dreary woman of their imagination. Rather than sitting at home waiting for the great day, Madeline travelled to Europe alone, enjoying for the last time the particular freedoms of being an unmarried woman. As she boarded the train that would take her East, then to the ferry at

Harwich, and on to the continent, Madeline knew she would not see Humphry again until hours before their wedding.

Madeline was bound for Frankfurt, where she spent a month learning German. It was a time of rapid change across the country, following the rise to power of the Nazis in January 1933. Frankfurt was second only to Berlin in its number of Jewish citizens. By the time Madeline arrived, the anti-Jewish boycott was in place, and an infamous Nazi book burning had taken place in the Römerberg, the city's historic market square. In a letter to her mother she describes her impressions of the political climate: 'Everybody here seems to be a staunch Hitlerite. They just say "ah he's a great man" and nod their heads. But there are no signs of political excitement: Swastikas on flags, boys drilling: but all very comfortable about it.' As yet, the non-Jewish life of the city seemed unruffled.

Madeline stayed as the paying guest of the pleasant Frau Hagen in a flat which took up one floor of a large whitewashed house with shutters and balconies. She and the two other female guests, a chubby Dutchwoman and a German, were fed plates of butter-heavy food. At least Frau Hagen knew how to make a decent English cup of tea. Madeline started exploring and socialising immediately. While she walked through streets hung with invasive flags and cycled along the banks of the Main, she had time to reflect on her situation, her future, her choices.

She must have been conscious of what she was giving up – there would be no more solo trips to the continent, no more taking herself off to the opera alone in a foreign city. She would lose those freedoms, as well as her independent working life. Her name she would give up to a man who had been a feature, if not a fixed point, in her life in the last four years. Marrying Humphry, she was embracing inconstancy with her eyes wide open. Madeline's feelings about the marriage are expressed in a letter sent to her mother. On the envelope, added years later are the words: 'In this, my letter to my mother from Germany, written on the Sunday before we were married.'

MC to her mother, Margaret Church

Sunday [17 December 1933]

Darling Mother,

Thank you for your very dear letters. They made me very happy. Thank you and Daddy for being so awfully sweet and kind. I do so awfully not want to hurt you by my manner of getting married. I loved your letters. Yes, I know one never can speak openly where feelings are concerned: it is very difficult. You have not been "fearfully unsympathetic". You have always been very true to what you thought best: and this sort of clash is bound to arise, – I mean the clash of loyalty to one's parents and to the man one wants to marry. But I am very happy now. I think things in future will be much better between all of us.

[...] I will stay Wednesday night with you: go down to Exeter on Thursday morning and get the legal marriage done: return to London at once, and come back to the hotel to stay Thursday night also with you, and with Daddy too if he can come. I hope Humphry will come round to the hotel to see you both during that evening. Then on Friday we can be married in S. George's, and then go straight off to Cornwall. This I think will be a good arrangement, don't you?

Forgive my not writing about my recent doings here, today. I must write so many other letters. I will write to Aunts Edith, Agnes, Vi and Florence. They are the most important, because they live in London (except Aunt Flo.), so would most expect to be at the wedding. Perhaps sometime you could tell Aunt Bea, and explain to her? And I will write from Cornwall to Aunt Nellie. […]

Well, this I expect to be my last letter from here. I hope to see you at 11 o'clock at Victoria on Wednesday, under the clock: and I hope to see Daddy on Thursday evening.

Much love darling Mum to you both. […]

Your loving daughter

Madeline

Such poignant calmness. (As a loving aunt, this letter cuts me to the quick.) Madeline's clarity of purpose was a marked contrast to Humphry's state of mind in the week before their marriage. He had managed to get his times mixed up at the church in London, and was desperately scrabbling around to find a slot that would enable a close friend to attend. He was still struggling with the fact of having two women in his life. In the forty-eight hours before his marriage, he wrote to both of them.

HH to MC

Tuesday [19 December 1933]

Madeline darling,

Things seem to be settling themselves fairly well; except that there are still two large doubts. 1. What Hotel are you staying in to-morrow night? […] 2. There's still a fearful muddle about times at S. George's.[…]

The quite definite things are these:-

1. *I have arranged the wedding here at the Registry Office for 2.0 o'clock on Thursday.*

2. *You must catch the 9.0 o'clock train from Paddington on Thursday morning, arriving Exeter 12.35. I will meet you at S. David's Sta.*
3. *Between then and lunch you will have time finally to decide what wedding-ring you are to wear for life, as I shall have made a provisional selection. I am choosing very thin gold ones: no platinum or thickness.*
4. *About 1.0 or 1.15 we have lunch at the Clarence: 2.0 wedding.*
5. *Short gap for love-making.*
6. *We catch 3.25 for London, arriving 6.50 Paddington.*
7. *Arrangements separate dinners, later call by me as already suggested.*

[...] I love you a very great deal: I look on all this as the confirmation of your everlasting mistresshood: you may be a mother as often as you care to arrange: but do not ever be a wife! – But it may be I sometimes want a wifely mistress! Darling I love you. To-day Elizabeth wrote to bless us: as, I suppose, a sort of Apollonian rather than Aphrodisian priestess. Anyway she blessed. I was glad, because in some odd way I seem to have come into her life rather. I do not love her in bed. It is you I love.

On Friday, I think it would be good to come back here and spend our first real night together at the Clarence, looking out at Hooker and our Cathedral. On Saturday on to Cornwall.

[...] I expect you here 12 Thursday leaving Paddington 9.0 o'clock.

Dear,
Humphry

The buzz of New York was over. The hush of Headington wrapped itself around Elizabeth once more. She was not in the best frame of mind, commenting to Berlin: 'England is never a good place, I think, to come back to, and at present I feel rather Anglophobic.' Her low spirits may have been partly due to Humphry's impending marriage. Anxious to stay visible, she wrote to him immediately on her return. In the envelope she seems to have enclosed something else – an eight by ten inch, black-and-white studio portrait of herself.

The photograph is a stylised head-and-shoulders shot. The head is turned slightly to the right. Elizabeth gazes out of the bottom corner of the frame. Rear-lit, her jaw is pronounced, her thick hair aflame. There is something sharp about the line of her mouth. A line of decorative buttons runs over each shoulder, enlivening the plain, round-necked woollen top she wears. One eye appears slightly lazy, but its intensity is undimmed. Her identity is fixed, her moment is the present.

Solicited or unsolicited, the timing of the gift seems extraordinary. If Humphry had asked for the photograph, he was choosing to bring Elizabeth's potent presence into the nuptial home. The photograph was unlikely to have been displayed on the mantelpiece, but she would haunt the third chair at their table. Had Elizabeth sent the photograph of her own volition it was a reminder, in gleaming silver albumen, that she still had her eye on him.

The photograph Elizabeth sent Humphry shortly before his marriage

The following letter Humphry wrote to Elizabeth the day before his wedding.

HH to EB

Wednesday 20 December 1933

Elizabeth my dear, your excellent letter reached me yesterday morning on the steps of my "Mardon Hall" when I was gladly leaving it for the last time. [...] And the photograph fell out first into my hand.

Thank you very much. You are generous to us.

Yes; I am sure I am doing a good thing. We shall be happy. All the strains and changes of our relationship have left few gaps: we both know what this marriage will be like. I know what I hope to build on it. In a few months I shall be very changed. But I shall not be changed in my feeling for you. All along you have known that would not really change from its first quality and direction: we are complementary in many things. I admire you, love you admiringly, deeply. We shall go on meeting I think now for always as specially belonging; "one another's truth", as you once said, on a most exacting plane. You have come to a new knowledge of style lately. I am going here through humiliations and searchings which I know I needed.

This is to wish you a good stay at Bowen's Court. Give my love to Barrys. I hope to write to Sarah to-morrow; and my love to Noel.

I am sleeping here to-night; my last one unmarried; am very tired with letters and arrangings. Good night, my dear; Good-night.

Humphry

Will you wish Alan a good Christmas from me please?

Humphry's perpetual struggle to find his place in relationships often led to him defining the roles of others. In his letter to Madeline, he betrays his anxiety about shifting identities: he uses the word 'mistress' for his fiancée, and 'priestess' for his mistress. He looks forward to marriage whilst recoiling from the word 'wife'. To Elizabeth, he writes of a married self evolving, without this development straining their relationship. His aim is to stay visible in her world, and so he mentions her Irish friends, and even her husband.

The position of Alan Cameron throughout the affair between Elizabeth and Humphry is a curious one. The Cameron marriage was housed in one wing of Elizabeth's life. That space had clear boundaries – Humphry was not invited to stay at their marital home in Oxford but was a guest at Bowen's Court, Elizabeth's home, when Alan was also there. Beyond Elizabeth's feelings about her marriage and its parameters was the character of Alan himself. Like Elizabeth, he was completely committed to their shared life. Nevertheless, there are suggestions that he, too, enjoyed extramarital liaisons with young men. In later life, he was also increasingly wedded to alcohol, which might have made him see, or care, less about Elizabeth's emotional involvements with other people. If he is a further shadowy presence in the story, it is for very different reasons from Madeline's.

What Humphry wished to emphasise just before his own marriage was his constancy – not to his wife, but to Elizabeth. He was conscious of one of Elizabeth's complaints about him visible in the letters from Ireland – that he was inauthentic, that he falsified his character. This incoherence of character was distinct from having contradictory elements within it. Elizabeth was a hybrid, a woman rich in internal oppositions. Sean O'Faolain, a later lover, described her as 'heart-cloven and split-minded'. She thrived on duality – it was in her blood. But she also valued continuity of self, in those she knew and in her fictional creations. Characters who lacked it might be enigmatic, appealing, but they were less to be trusted. One such is Harrison in her novel, *The Heat of the Day*, who is described thus: 'By the rules of fiction, with which life to be credible must comply, he was as a character "impossible" – each time they met, for instance, he showed no shred or trace of having been continuous since they last met.'

Changeable Humphry may well have been frustrating for Elizabeth. But that did not make him unattractive.

On Thursday 21 December 1933, Humphry House and Madeline Church were married in a civil ceremony in Exeter. No photographs were taken, and there was only the required witness in attendance. The next day, with sandwiches, closest family, and Madeline wearing a green suit, they reprised the event at a church in Bloomsbury. As soon as was feasible, they dashed away from the small party.

At the end of 1932, before their first engagement had disintegrated, Humphry had imagined a European destination for the honeymoon: 'Mussolini offers a 70% fare reduction to those who honeymoon in Rome. Viva il duce.' In the end, there was no bargain break in Fascist Italy for the Houses. Instead they partook of the sea-salted pleasures of the Wellington Hotel in Boscastle, in Cornwall. According to handwritten hotel records, they were the only guests.

Twenty years earlier, Thomas Hardy had stayed there following the death of his first wife Emma. As a young man, he had come to Northern Cornwall during their courtship. Then, in his seventies, he retrod the haunted hillsides of his youth and grieved for the woman – lightly-loved in life, but much-missed in death. Like the great novelist, Humphry was marrying a woman whom he considered inferior to him. Hardy only counted Emma's worth when it was too late; Humphry's appreciation of Madeline grew throughout their marriage, but he, like Hardy, never was able to appreciate his wife's full potential.

A couple of miles to the north of the hotel is Beeny Cliff, the dramatic headland which gives its name to one of Hardy's most celebrated poems about Emma. One chilly afternoon, Humphry and Madeline hiked up to appreciate the 'chasmal beauty' of old Beeny and the 'opal and the sapphire of that wandering western sea' beyond.

From Beeny Cliff, the waters of the Celtic Sea flow up towards Ireland. Sailing across that body of water at the same time went Elizabeth – on her way to Bowen's Court with Alan. Christmas was one of the times of the year that the Camerons, husband and wife, loved and shared most. Elizabeth revelled in the role when tradition demanded it. The house rang with their convivial welcome, with the merry footfall of guests. A huge Christmas lunch, served promptly at midday, was thrown for all the relations in the seldom-used dining room. Light splashed from a coloured candle, enclasped by a wreath of holly, that stayed lit night and day until Twelfth Night. The library shutters, the thick, deep curtains, kept in the warmth and cheer.

Elizabeth writes of Bowen's Court at Christmas: 'All winds dropped then: a miraculous quiet rose from the land.' There were no storms. Any tempest she experienced in December 1933 was not meteorological. At the year's deep midnight, Bowen's Court was the best place for her – as an individual, as part of a couple, and as a woman whose young beau was getting married to someone else.

16 Cathedral Close, the first home of the Houses,
to the left of the Royal Clarence Hotel, Exeter

Chapter 7

Exeter, Cathedral Close: *Her Table Spread*

I clamber down the steep cellar steps of the Well House Tavern in the heart of medieval Exeter. The air is hung with the scent of stale beer and humidity. Reaching the bottom, I see a room in two halves separated by a couple of rounded brick arches. To the right is the well, thought to be Norman, that gives the building its name. In a flat a couple of floors up, immediately after their marriage, lived Humphry and Madeline.

I peer into the well. Local legend has it that John the monk and Martha the nun, unable to find an earthly space for their love, flung themselves down it to their deaths. A metal grid prevents any copycat foolishness and catches tossed sweet papers.

At the other end of the cellar, embedded in the wall, is a glass-fronted case. Inside a skeleton turns slightly towards me, its ribcage raised, its legs foreshortened. The bones are the colour of tobacco. Though I am normally squeamish, I don't find it disturbing. It seems murky, distant. It is the sign above the broken figure that I find far more affecting than the remains. Written in suitably gothic hand-writing, white paint on black wood, are the words: 'Birth is the first step unto death.'

To the right of the skeleton box, up against the wall, is a beautiful wooden settle – an incongruous feature in any pub cellar. I sit down facing the kegs. There are ghosts here certainly, but they aren't familial. Maybe they are of the shattered Anglo-Saxon youth in the case, or John, or Martha.

I ascend the steep stairs, and sit down at one of the tables facing the cathedral. Humphry, I know, would appreciate the fact that his first married home is now a pub. I drink my half pint of ale, looking across the green at the statue of Richard Hooker, with the warm-stoned cathedral beyond. My line of vision is that of my grandparents – their front window is just above my head. A large hen party sits down at the next table, dressed in pink sashes and rabbit ears. Shots are drunk, laughter and lewdness splash across their table. I smile at the women as I leave, walk past the Royal Clarence Hotel, out of the medieval close, and down to the station.

January 1934

In her 1932 novel *To the North*, Elizabeth explores the idea of a relationship squeezed in time and geography's tight grip. The encounters of Emmeline and Markie, the ill-matched couple at the centre of the story, are described thus: 'Their brief and irregular meetings – so little fair weather between the last frost of arrival, the earliest shadow of saying good-bye – were unsatisfactory to both of them, wretched for her. Their free time was too short for travel; the risks and banalities of an English hotel she refused to contemplate.' Many of the same complications and frustrations applied to Humphry and Elizabeth at the beginning of 1934. The dreariness of a hotel was compounded by a new distance from one another – the fact of Humphry's marriage.

Whatever Elizabeth's feelings as she came back from Ireland after Christmas, she had her work to fill her imagination. The year would see the publication of another collection of short stories, *The Cat Jumps*. It was an instant success, the first edition of 1,500 copies selling out almost immediately. Some of the stories had been written on demand for magazines, and she was not particularly enamoured of them. She told her publisher, Victor Gollancz, that they had an 'escape from life' theme. One of them describes an unwise affair with a crooked chauffeur; another, a suicide in an apple tree. It is an uneven collection – violent, strange. There are two outstanding stories, 'The Disinherited' and 'The Cat Jumps'. Both have agitated houses which press their spirits on the people within. This idea would find fuller, richer expression in the novel *The House in Paris*.

Humphry was similarly busy professionally; the new term allowed him to teach English, his chosen subject, as well as Classics. He was engaged in finishing the first draft of Hopkins's letters and notebooks, as well as beginning to write reviews for periodicals. For Madeline, the marriage wrought many changes, not all of them pleasurable. She had left her job and circle of friends in London; there would be no more singing of Gilbert and Sullivan operettas. Her family was far away and the city seemed friendless. As a result, Madeline paid an early visit to both their families in south-east England. Humphry wrote to her while she was staying with his parents encouraging her to 'exact a cheque from papa, and do remember to spy round for things we want'.

Madeline Church (second left) before her marriage in a production of Gilbert and Sullivan's *Trial by Jury*, performed by the Sevenoaks Players in 1931

The newly-weds' physical space was, at least, beginning to take shape. They began to accumulate essential furniture. Family pieces were given and new purchases made, such as a black glass table that reflected the magnificent cathedral into their living room. There were wedding presents from friends; Isaiah Berlin planned to give them a dumb waiter.

Elizabeth, too, prepared to send them a gift. Her sense of propriety remained unscathed. Something for the house seemed a good idea. She would give them a fitting for the flat, a silent reminder that she was a fixture in their lives.

With Madeline off visiting the relatives, Humphry sat down to write to Elizabeth. This first letter is warm, chatty. He tells her of setting up home – of leaking pipes, painting the furniture, deliveries from shops, 'disasters to things on our narrow stairs'. He opines about Yeats's new poems, speaks of an article he is writing about T. S. Eliot, and of his new study looking out over the back of the Royal Clarence. Writing to his lover, the newly married man seems untroubled by any emotional conflict of interest: 'I think this is a good thing I have done getting married.' And of Elizabeth's proposed wedding present he writes: 'How sweet of you to offer something! I feel really that you are bound up in this marriage so much that you are yourself enough: but it would be good to have something as symbol of this.'

Soon after this first letter, something passed between them that made Elizabeth's blood boil. Quite possibly, Humphry had misjudged how much Elizabeth wanted to hear about his marriage.

Humphry's next letter, towards the end of the month, is of a quite different colour.

HH to EB

16 Cathedral Close, Exeter
29 January 1934

My dear Elizabeth,

The rug has come. It is quite lovely, and has put a terrific liveliness into a floor which was rather dull. Thank you very much indeed for it. I agree I must cancel my earlier letter; your answer to it was entirely just. It was so just that I have not looked at it again since a first quick reading. It stung for days. At first I thought of defending myself and all the language; but now I shall not even bother to excuse. I do falsify landmarks. The rug puts them back again. It is good to have it.

No; I can't go on without recurring to your letter. I can't look at it again; I may be falsifying again. But it hurt so much at the time that I simply cannot forget it. I do not know that the pain is more because it showed how wrong I had been before, or because you had come into my utter solitude as an adversary. I have read into my memory of it as much too much as you read out of mine. I still feel alienated, and while this is so I can't write easily about anything. Will you let me have a note (not perhaps built upon the details) which will take away this alienation, or feeling of it that I have? I have a lot to say, but there is a stop to saying it at present, and I don't know how to move it.

In a few weeks I mean to get up to London, when there will be an ease in work here. I am very hard put to it at present. Then we must meet. But before then I want to be able to write to you.

My love,
Humphry

Elizabeth's rug might have covered the gaps in the floorboards, but it did not seal the cracks in the relationship between her and Humphry. In a letter to Madeline, written to her while she was visiting their respective families, he suggests she might like the rug for her room. If that is where the gift ended up living in their home, it is hard not to see Madeline standing in the centre, pressing what little heel she wore into its heart.

Few stories have been handed down through my family about Madeline's life in Exeter. One of them is a conversation she had with Humphry sometime early in their marriage. Madeline asked him whether he would like a divorce so he could marry Elizabeth. Humphry apparently roared with laughter and exclaimed, 'Good heavens, no!' Such a reaction is in keeping with Humphry's desire to have the best of both worlds. Though Madeline could not have known of Elizabeth's commitment to her life with Alan, her question to Humphry is revealing both of her state of mind and of the degree to which she considered Elizabeth a threat.

A divorce in 1934 was no easy matter. Laws which had not been revised for eighty years stated that adultery was the only ground for divorce and that there had to be an innocent and a guilty party. Divorce by consent was not a possibility. The absurdities and cruelties of these laws were highlighted in a novel by A. P. Herbert entitled *Holy Deadlock* published that very year. (Later, Herbert became a Member of Parliament and played an instrumental role in the Matrimonial Causes Act of 1938. This allowed a petition for divorce to be filed after three years and broadened the terms of divorce to include desertion, cruelty, and drunkenness.) The social stigma attached to divorce was almost impossible to escape. This was proved vividly soon afterwards in the trials of Wallis Simpson, the divorcée for whom Edward VIII abdicated. If being unmarried at twenty-nine was dangerous, being a divorcée in your thirties was disastrous.

Having been given Humphry's confirmation that he wished to remain in their marriage, Madeline assumed her role as a wife. Raised in an affluent family, she was ill-prepared for a life of electric stoves, linoleum floors, and housekeeping. Her family had a cook; she had not expected to become one herself. Her skills in the kitchen at marriage extended to the successful boiling of an egg. She needed to learn, fast.

One of her cookery books was *Simple French Cooking* by X. Marcel Boulestin, originally published in 1923. A classic of its day, its recipes ranged in difficulty from omelettes to preserved goose: 'Put the meat for twenty-four hours in a jar with coarse salt, thyme and bay leaves.' The book expresses incredulity at the English inability to make salads, pours scorn on our gravy with its 'deplorable taste of soup', and recommends that women take the recipe book to bed with them much as if it were a Bible. On page one, entitled 'Remarks, General' he writes: 'I can imagine no more charming picture than the wife seeing to the perfection of the evening meal, and the husband on his way home from the office looking forward to it. Happiness sits smiling at their table.'

Madeline was conscious both of the economic necessity and social pressure to be wife, homemaker, and cook. It was not a role she found easy. A kitchen disaster with burnt sausages (she was not even attempting an exotic French dish that evening) prompted a humiliating confrontation with Humphry. Anguished, she rushed out of the flat on her own into the chilly winter night. When she got to the bridge over the river, she stopped and looked into its murky depths. She was approached by a policeman who, fearing some desperate action on her part, implored her not to jump into the rushing waters.

Though my mother tells this tale with a laugh, its comic element cannot mask a more disturbing side. Madeline knew the dark colours of Humphry's character, but that night soon after their marriage she needed to leave their flat, going out into the cold to recover from the heat of his censure. The situation with Elizabeth must have contributed to her insecurity; the distance from her family exacerbated her loneliness. There was one further thing that had a significant emotional impact on her in the early days of the marriage – Madeline decided to join Humphry in his new-found agnosticism. Though never an evangelical believer, she left behind the comfort of organised religion. She was in every way leaving Church to become a House.

When my letter-map brought me to Exeter, I was more conscious than ever of disappearances – of people, buildings, and elements of my story. This was, principally, due to the merciless malevolence of fire. I was haunted, in a way that I hadn't been before, by the knowledge of Madeline's lost archive, of the correspondence that she chose to burn in old age. As though shot on Super 8 film, the scene judders and flickers before me.

Madeline stands in a garden; it is a cool evening and the scent of roses is strong in the dusky air. A small bonfire has been prepared close to the back wall. She bends and strikes a match. The fire catches quickly: it has been a dry summer. Madeline picks up the first bundle of letters, yellowed envelopes with George V in green profile on the stamps. The papers crackle, become threads of matter that rise into the smoky air. It is a quick death. On goes the next bundle – some of the letters she had written when she was young; a few racy letters Stephen Spender had written Humphry in the 1930s; perhaps some correspondence between Elizabeth and her husband in the early days of their affair. It does not take long. The fire dies down, the smoke drifts over the back wall. Madeline walks across the lawn, up the steps flanked by stone lions and into the house. She locks the door firmly behind her. Her incendiary edit is complete.

This paradox, that in the destruction of evidence a person may strive to make the narrative of a life clearer and cleaner, lies at the heart of one of Elizabeth's radio plays, *New Judgement: Elizabeth Bowen on Jane Austen* (1942). The narrator confronts Cassandra, Jane's sister, about the burning of letters pertaining to Jane's one major love affair, and accuses her of destroying the clues to Jane's life and art. The narrator argues that as Austen 'belongs to the world', so the letters should have become public property. Cassandra's riposte gets to the heart of the conflict between family loyalty and literary posterity: 'My first solicitude was that the secret her heart guarded should not pass, after my death, into vulgar hands. Yes, I burned *those* letters – one packet. The others, Sir, I have left – to you and your world.' Perhaps these were feelings Madeline shared; she, like Cassandra, preserved some but not all of a famous writer's correspondence. Perhaps, too, the vulgar revelatory hands she feared are mine.

It was a bitterly cold day as I stood next to the statue of Richard Hooker in the shadow of Exeter Cathedral. Part of the physical archive of my story was gone; missives from the past had disappeared (albeit accidentally) in one flame-bright night and I needed in some way to acknowledge this.

In front of me was a cold white security barrier, eight feet high. Embedded in it, a door outlined in do-not-enter red. The gap of sky where the buildings had once been was criss-crossed by scaffolding, skinny-limbed and chaotic.

Suddenly a man was at my shoulder. 'I saw the fire. The hotel façade was just one brick thick, rippling in the wind like a curtain.'

I told him that my grandparents' house was number 16, the Tudor house next to the Royal Clarence that also got swallowed up by the flames. And how glad I was that I had visited before the blaze.

We stood quiet for a moment. Then he said, 'You know what today is? It's the anniversary of the fire. We are both here to lay flowers on a grave.'

Though Humphry might write and imagine otherwise, the marriage had inevitably shifted the co-ordinates of all their lives. Elizabeth's young lover – her first – was now a married man. He was tiresomely far away. Emmeline in *To The North* reflects that if she and her lover 'were to be little together they must be calmly apart'. Yet neither Humphry nor Elizabeth had tranquil spirits.

In one of his letters, Humphry extended an invitation to Elizabeth to stay with the Houses in Exeter. An impractical suggestion borne of unsatisfied desire perhaps, but also an indication that he feared losing his Oxford life. One person from that world who did visit in the early months of 1934 was Isaiah Berlin. Always fond of a good gossip, he writes to his mother about the visit: 'I found the Houses rather melancholy and had to act as a sort of ice-breaker: you know how difficult that is even when your husband or your son are melancholy & require restoration: but if one *is* going to enjoy oneself one must try & cheer one's hosts up.' He picked up the gloomy mood between Humphry and Madeline even if he did not go as far as guessing its cause.

Leaving the awkward atmosphere in the little flat behind him, Humphry often walked across Exeter in search of a decent pub from which to write to Elizabeth. Easier for him, and no doubt for Madeline. (Elizabeth, similarly, did not like writing to Humphry when Alan was around. In her letter of July 1933, she comments on how Alan's sudden appearance in the room has affected her ability to write.) These Exeter letters are written on the printed notepaper of the marital home – a reminder to Elizabeth, before she had even read a word, of where he was coming from.

The letters are a jumble of feelings, ideas, and observations. He describes the nuns who dash across the cathedral yard like black lightning, dodgy paintings on pub walls, a woman as she shakes a duster from a guest-house window. Local birds, churches, and accents. He sends her thick Devon cream. Consciously echoing Hopkins he writes of her 'inseeing letters', of barriers between them, of recent excoriation. He speaks of being smoothed and exalted by Elizabeth one minute, and of his unhappiness about the state of their relationship the next: 'By far the most painful thing in this long distance is not seeing you more.' There is a frankness in his voice: 'Because you can hurt me more utterly and deeply than anybody you are more valuable than anybody. You are vigilant; you read me.'

Invisible in these letters is the exterior world, of politics and social change. There is no mention of the travails of Ramsay MacDonald's National Government in a time of continued recession. Absent too is the rearmament debate in which many prominent writers such as Storm Jameson and Vera Brittain were engaged. With Elizabeth, there is the sense that external events always came a poor second to her internal life, and Humphry probably understood this. Humphry might also have realised that there was not much common ground politically between them; he was firmly to the left of centre, while Elizabeth sat more to the right. She preferred monarchs to ministers. Through their conscious construction of epistolary personae, Elizabeth and Humphry removed themselves from the world around them. This allowed them to engage on a plane that was exclusively theirs, one seemingly untroubled by discussion of the issues of the age.

One topic of considerable interest to them both, however, was the whole question of writing – as form, content, and bearer of one's identity. Elizabeth not only requested words unsaid, but required a high level of emotional and intellectual discourse when he did write: 'You demand me at my best; and that I rarely reach here.' He was conscious of her cramping his style, literally and metaphorically. At the same time he was searching for a new self, wondering whether he should aim to be a scholar or an artist. His uncertainty was a contrast to his clear understanding of her inked-in persona, as 'Elizabeth Bowen, novelist'. This was how Humphry had referred to her the first time she appeared in a letter to Madeline, in February 1933. Now, a year later, he writes: 'I am glad your book is going well.' She was on her fifth novel; he was publishing his first review.

There were, however, some opportunities for Humphry and Elizabeth to see one another. The two of them met several times in London between March and May 1934. In the middle of March, Humphry went up to London for a few days for his Hopkins work, staying in Hampstead with Arthur Calder-Marshall and his new wife, Ara. An April visit to the capital was tacked onto the end of a few days visiting both his and Madeline's family in south-east England. During this visit, he saw Elizabeth and was introduced to T. S. Eliot by her, something he was keen to happen despite being 'shy about trying to see known men'.

It is not clear whether the sexual relationship between Humphry and Elizabeth continued during these months. However, there were opportunities for this to happen as Humphry travelled up to London alone. Humphry's feelings about marriage – that in some respects his wings were clipped – may have made him more determined to indulge his footloose, sexual self. As for Elizabeth, a continuation of a physical relationship with Humphry would have provided her with pleasing proof that Humphry's marriage remained irrelevant to the progress of the affair. Whatever the state of their intimacy, their letters reveal that both felt frustrated in these months by the fresh distances between them.

Their months of dislocation and dissonance reached a climax in late May and early June 1934. Elizabeth, after visiting friends in Devon, paid a trip to Exeter, seeing the Houses together. Shortly afterwards she saw Humphry on his own in London. It is unclear where he was staying on this visit. After a fiery scene with Elizabeth, he spent a night on the streets. The next day, the rapprochement – Elizabeth and Humphry paid a visit to the Botanical Gardens at Kew. They might have hoped that a healing balm would descend in the quiet leafiness of the Palm House. Instead, they found themselves in the Rock Garden of recrimination – all alpines and boulders, cold to the touch.

When Elizabeth next sat down at her writing desk it was with a different heart – one that still held Humphry in her affections, but saw the first shadow of their parting. Gone was the chain-smoking woman of nervous talk, conscious of her vulnerabilities and how she appeared to men. Instead Elizabeth reflects on her 'exacting' behaviour, her high-handedness, and her inability to get Humphry to behave as she wished:

> Remember that you had Elizabeth Bowen to contend with – I mean, a confirmed writer. Someone accustomed to getting herself, or himself, across without outside

> opposition. […] One spends one's time objectifying one's inner life, and projecting one's thought and emotion into a form – a book. Which, once one's inside difficulties are overcome, is the exercise of an unchecked power. […] Because it is hard for me (being a writer before I am a woman) to realize that anything – friendship or love especially – in which I participate imaginatively isn't a book too. Isn't, I mean, something I make what it is by my will that it shall be like that.

Identifying herself in this letter as a writer before she is a woman is not simply about Elizabeth's vocation being paramount. The 'unchecked power' afforded by writing, the inking a person into existence and controlling them, was central to Elizabeth's sense of self. With Humphry, the aspiring writer, it was her trump card.

She goes on to describe what she found challenging about his personality – a 'lack of wholeness', a Janus-like propensity to speak alternate truths, his antagonism. Pulling away from him she writes that this is 'the last "serious" letter I shall write you'. She signs off: 'Goodbye for now.' If she was going away from the affair it did not seem to be far, or for long.

Humphry began his reply immediately but, unusually, took three days to complete it. He needed time to organise his thoughts, to state very clearly what he meant. In the letter he does not focus on Elizabeth as an artist, but as a woman – and not a sufficiently quiet, compliant one at that. He takes issue with her powerful personality – the word 'demonstrative' appears repeatedly in his letter. The social enthusiast, the woman of 'diplomatic' manners seems to him insincere. At the end of his letter, he hopes they will be able to write the relationship afresh, despite the ink of understanding running dry between them.

Conspicuous by her absence, in both letters, is Madeline. Though Elizabeth mentions her right at the end it is when she is acting as social secretary, hoping to introduce the Houses to friends of hers. Humphry mentions his wife only in the shortest of sentences, when he tells Elizabeth that they have been house-hunting. And yet there is one phrase that reveals far more about their marriage than Humphry was probably aware. He says: 'Have hardly spoken to anybody for weeks.' His underestimation of Madeline's intelligence, discussed in an earlier letter to Elizabeth, is again in evidence.

This is the first surviving letter of Elizabeth's since July 1933, eleven months earlier. The question arises about why these two did not join Madeline's bonfire, if that was indeed the fate of the others. On the one hand there are the literary qualities – both letters show Elizabeth in top gear as a writer. On the other is their emotional content. The first letter may have been spared as it highlighted Elizabeth's vulnerability, and contains an appreciation of the 'great man' in Humphry. This 1934 letter was Elizabeth's first attempt at goodbye – something less likely to have distressed Madeline.

Central to both these earliest extant letters is a discussion of creativity. One letter addresses the idea of being a 'clever woman'. In the other, Elizabeth is the 'confirmed writer', bending plots and people to her will. Yet true 'unchecked power' resides not in the one who sculpts a sentence, but in the one who decides which words endure. This role, as far as Elizabeth's letters are concerned, falls to Madeline. She is wife, editor, guardian. She is both the burner of the letters, and the keeper of the flame.

The fire that consumed the Royal Clarence Hotel, and the disappeared photograph of Madeline in Cathedral Close, are potent metaphors for my grandmother's life in Exeter. The trail that leads back into the forest of family history has never been so empty of pebbles to gather and guide. I find it hard to conjure her. Difficult, too, not to pity her. But a conversation after breaking my ankle, whilst dancing at a village fiesta in Northern Spain, altered my vision of Madeline and her early married life.

I was lying face down, in considerable pain, speaking in halting Spanish about my grandparents and Elizabeth. Isabel, the chiropractor, kneaded and probed. I found myself talking openly, the way you do when you are in the hands of a healer. Words come easier, too, when there is no eye contact. I was telling her about the marriage ceremony, about the first months in Exeter.

'Your grandmother must have been so angry,' said Isabel. 'You know what happens when anger like that is buried? It has to find a way out, and the trauma often skips a generation.'

Slightly sceptical about the whole idea, I remained silent. But I felt a jolt of surprise, a realisation that I had accepted the family version of Madeline at that time – a picture of devotion and long-suffering stoicism.

Isabel continued, 'It is no accident that you are writing this book, that you have felt compelled to return to the past. Even your injury – it is linked to your mother's side of your family. *Estás comiendo la vida de tu abuela*.' (You are eating your grandmother's life.)

The phrase was so vivid, dreadful. But its effect on me was immediate. I felt an electric charge running through the meridians of my body from my head right down to my wounded ankle. The session at an end, I lay in the dim room for a few minutes to recover. Then I trembled my way back to my flat and went straight to bed.

That Madeline was not visible – a fate suffered by many women of her generation – did not mean she was weak or passive. Instead she was like an underground river that would eventually have to burst above ground once more. In Exeter she was just biding her time.

A few weeks later, my mother gave me a present – Madeline's tiny travel clock. It is housed in a buff leather case with hard sides. Two doors, held together by a clip, swing back to reveal the clock. The face is simple, the decoration around it floral, of jade enamel. It is beautiful, quiet. The hands, inevitably, do not move. The inherited clock speaks of her time, without telling mine.

Greenslinch, Silverton, Devon

Chapter 8

Greenslinch: *The Man of the Family*

A deserted lane deep in the Devon countryside. Birdsong the only sound. A huge hedge of yew encircles a coral-coloured house. In the hedge is a gate – its latch clicks loudly under my hand. I walk across the rising grass towards an open postern door. Tentatively I knock. The two women standing at a kitchen table look up, surprised. I produce, rather like a calling card, the correspondence between Humphry and Elizabeth that mentions Greenslinch.

'You're lucky to catch us,' says the taller woman. 'We're packing up the last of the house. We'll be gone in an hour.' On the kitchen table lies family flotsam of three generations. A decorative Turkish tray; three bone-handled knives; several plugs; a biscuit tin.

Conversation about the house fills the kitchen like steam. I tell them of Humphry and Madeline's years living there without electricity in the early thirties. Wistfully they recount tales of their lives in the house, bought by their parents in the 1950s. One sister was born in the house. Another sibling still lives in the remote hamlet of their childhood.

'Feel free to have a look around,' says the more talkative sister, as she turns back to a pile of coffee cups on the cluttered table.

Stripped of its furniture, the house reveals its fine, weathered face – tiled floors, cob walls, wooden beams. I follow a dim passage to the foot of an extraordinary winder staircase built inside a crumbling wall. The house moves under my hand as I climb. I come out into a vast, sun-splashed room with a vaulted beam ceiling. It is more like the ballroom of a country house than the upper floor of a Devonshire farmhouse. This is Humphry's study. There is a spinning wheel, a sewing machine, a few pictures propped against the wall. Several children's books – E. Nesbit, the Moomins. Boxes and suitcases into which the family has packed its past. I follow the right angle of the house into the bedrooms, where Madeline and soon a child and nursemaid would live. Despite the loud wallpaper of past decades, a deep quiet hangs over the house.

Back in the kitchen, I thank the sisters for their kindness.

'You came at just the right time. Next month the builders move in. It's a young couple with children. There's going to be a football pitch in the garden. The place will be gutted, totally gutted.'

June 1934

Elizabeth had stated, at the beginning of June 1934, that she had written her last 'serious' letter to Humphry. To her mind the 'snags of joint ownership' inherent in every relationship were insurmountable. She could not compose him, or the affair, in a way that was still pleasing to her. The relationship with Humphry was not, however, sealed up neatly with her envelope. It would continue throughout that year and into the next, despite the increasing pressures – both logistical and emotional – that were being felt by both of them.

As summer shone, Humphry sought to leave the tumultuous falling-out in London behind. His letters to Elizabeth discuss their relationship alongside other more quotidian concerns – work, friends, reading matter. The most important news he had to impart was about living arrangements. Despite the flat in Exeter having several months left to run on its lease, it was proving too small for the couple. Its convenient location meant that Humphry continued to use it during term time throughout the year. But he and Madeline now had a different marital home – a farmhouse called Greenslinch, which lay in the quiet hills north of Exeter. Here was green space for books, creative thought, and a family.

The hamlet of Greenslinch is mentioned in the Domesday Book. In 1086 there were four villagers, three smallholders, and a 'slave'. By the 1930s the number of inhabitants had not swelled, though one presumes the slave had gone. Local legend tells of doomed Lady Jane Grey stopping here for a night when the house served as an inn during its heyday in the sixteenth century. The story seems unlikely given how inaccessible the house is, approached up steep gulleys and sudden dips in the road. Not to mention that it is on a road to nowhere, or Tiverton.

In early July, Humphry returned to the island of Ireland, but not this time to Bowen's Court. Madeline's younger brother, Geoffrey Church, was marrying an Irishwoman, Kathleen O'Neill, in Belfast. Geoffrey was a vicar, Kathleen the daughter of one. For both Madeline and Humphry the trip to Ireland must have felt strange. There were echoes of Elizabeth – in the air, as well as in Kathleen's Protestant family. Geoffrey's career in the Church was a reminder of Humphry's failed foray into the priesthood. This wedding rang with family; theirs had been a quiet affair.

Just before leaving for Northern Ireland, Humphry contacted Isaiah Berlin, who was planning to be in the country at the same time. He and several female friends, including B. J. Lynd (the woman who had caught Humphry's eye at Bowen's Court in the summer of 1933), were reprising the fateful motoring tour of the previous summer. Humphry wrote: 'Elizabeth says you are crossing "To the North"; and I have to be in Belfast the week after next for a wedding. Will you be in or near Belfast the week after next? If so we must meet, [...] and you can have all the pleasure of seeing my sexual dangerousness minimised by an attendant wife, and I can have all the pleasure of seeing you.'

A rendezvous duly ensued, after which Berlin wrote to Elizabeth:

> Humphry – the word fruitful always recalls him to me – we saw with Madeline in Belfast; she livelier, securer, more of a person, almost a mother already: he, reduced, I thought rather gloomy, altogether deflated, unnaturally flexible, fangless, and gentle, it rather frightened me. He was plainly expecting to be taken joyriding by us, but my companions thought it inconceivable that he be asked without her, so nothing was suggested, to his obvious chagrin. However he is married and why should he be allowed to forget it? this sounds unkind but he mustn't be tempted deliberately to desert her. That he is not happy I now have no doubt of.

Berlin's image of Humphry, frustrated and lacking bite due to his marriage, was unlikely to have distressed Elizabeth. What she found much harder to digest was the news of Madeline – the wife was lively, blooming, and pregnant. On hearing the news, she immediately wrote to Humphry, who shot back a reply.

HH to EB

16 Cathedral Close, Exeter
23 July 1934

My dear Elizabeth,

Your letter came to-day, and must have an immediate answer: I do not like, and do not wholly understand, the charges against me for lacking 'simplicity' because I did not tell you that Madeline was having a child. To begin with, you are right in thinking that one of the reasons I did not mention it was that I thought you would be hurt. You will have seen in my letters since we last met that I hardly ever mentioned her, and only rarely spoke of "we", when it could hardly be avoided. You did not like to be reminded of my marriage.

But there is much more in it than that. I do not think I told Shaya [Isaiah] about it. I may possibly have done so in an unguarded moment which I have forgotten in Belfast: but I now honestly think that the only person I have actually told is my father, who had a certain right to know. Madeline, I know, has told a number of her friends: and if friends over-lap and exchange gossip I can't help it. The channel is probably Jacquetta Hawkes, a nice girl, and a friend of the Lynds. But the important thing is the charge of lacking "simplicity". […] When I married Madeline we agreed that we should have no children for two years: we took a flat (on an agreement until next March) which could not be lived in by more than two people. All contraceptive arrangements were in Madeline's hands, and she said they were good enough: yet a child was begotten – a child I had not intended to exist, nor provided to house. […]

I do not resent the child. I look forward to it. I have a full share of fatherly instincts: but I do feel some bitterness – aliquid amari – that the child should be coming when I did not intend it: almost against my will: should be forcing me out of this flat before I intended, settling and domesticating my whole life before I wanted.

But if I had told you 'simply' unprovoked it would have seemed a wanton (whereas this is a conscious) antagonism to Madeline.

I cannot believe that I told Shaya in Belfast, when we talked philosophy and Frankfurters, that I was to have another child. His source must have been indirect.

But for 'simplicity' – directness, why, Elizabeth, did you not tell me when we first slept together that you were a virgin? I thought you had some malformation: for you said only: 'I am as difficult as a virgin'. I could not know you were one: and had I known, with what more tender slowness I would have come to you, and how much less gloom would have sat across that breakfast tray!

I do not want to seem to give a childish tu quoque*: but I want you to see that in urging 'simplicity' upon me as a criterion of letters and our whole relationship you are urging something which I cannot say I have wholly found in you. […]*

Oh dear! I feel this is too argued and thrust home: but no more now than ever do I know where I am. […]

You say you are coming down to Dorset for the week-end of this week. May I drive over there and meet you on the day your stay finishes, and bring you away? And can you spare a few days more? I should like to bring you back here; for many reasons. Anyway I must see you *when you are so near. […]*

My dear,

Humphry

When Elizabeth received this letter, she was hard at work on *The House in Paris*. In the novel, the tangled, illicit affair between Karen and Max culminates in a night in Hythe on the Kent coast. A child is conceived but unwanted. The baby, Leopold, is shuffled into the adoptive hands of the Grant Moodys, 'proper parents' with the requisite qualities. The scandal safely behind her, Karen marries Ray Forrestier. They become a couple who are 'delightful to meet', but have no children: 'It was understood that their childlessness, though an infinite pity, kept their companionship uninterrupted and close.'

For more than ten years, Elizabeth had shared a similar companionate union with Alan. Humphry's letter exposes the Cameron marriage as a sexless union – something Elizabeth, unsurprisingly, was loath to discuss with her young lover. He details their first night together, laced with awkwardness and despondency rather than passion and laughter. Any distress Elizabeth might have felt about Madeline's pregnancy was surely heightened by how Humphry spliced the news – with a reference to her recently virginal self.

Beyond the contrasting fecundity and frigidity of the two women lies the question of power. Not simply over Humphry, but over their own bodies. For Humphry the timing of a child was inconvenient. For thirty-year-old Madeline the time was ripe. Humphry writes: 'All contraceptive arrangements were in Madeline's hands.' Judging by her actions before their marriage, Madeline was dexterous in the use of birth control. The question is whether she let the precautions slip through her fingers, secretly hoping to get pregnant. If so, she was doing more than putting her own desires first – it was she who was determining the rhythms of the marriage.

But Madeline's pregnancy is not the only one to obtrude in this letter. Humphry mentions, just as he had in a communication to

Elizabeth before leaving Oxford in October 1933, the existence of 'another child'. Faced with this sensitive revelation, I am again conscious of the sensibilities of my aunt and my mother. But the treatment of this information is not so much determined by me as dictated by my grandfather. In 1948, Humphry wrote and broadcast an essay entitled 'The Present Art of Biography'. In it are the following lines: 'I believe strongly that whatever can be known about a man, however trivial it may have been, however smelly, or however grand, is proper material for the biographer, and that to conceal is as great a crime as to come forward as an uncritical eulogist.' Humphry, of all people, would not wish me to falsify his character through omission.

This is what I know, told to me by my mother in a coffee shop at Clapham Common Station several months after I received the box of letters. Following Madeline's death, my aunt, uncle, and mother took the decision not to look for their half-brother. They had little to go on beyond the first name of the mother – Madeleine with that extra 'e'. The illegitimate child by then would be grown-up, and might always have been ignorant of his birth father. In fifty years, there had been no contact made with any member of the House family. They decided to let the matter rest. The mystery of Humphry's child echoes that of the unplanned Leopold in *The House in Paris*: 'No one knew about Leopold. The husk of silence round him was complete. Even outside England, not a soul whose discretion was not absolute knew the facts of his birth.'

At the end of July, Elizabeth went to stay with friends in the West Country. The trip presented her with one of the few opportunities of seeing Humphry that summer. She took him up on his offer in the letter of 23 July to spend a couple of days in Exeter. Her visit coincided with the opening of an exhibition that Humphry had helped to organise at the university about Samuel Taylor Coleridge, a hundred years after his death.

Born in Ottery St Mary about ten miles from Exeter, Coleridge remained, throughout his life, a West Country man at heart. Some of his greatest poems, 'The Rime of the Ancient Mariner' and 'Kubla Khan', were written in Nether Stowey, Somerset, during 1797–1798. Humphry's Exeter exhibition brought together pictures, manuscripts, and first editions of his work. Miscellaneous items included a rhyme song of the Greek alphabet written by Coleridge for his son Hartley to learn, and a sword said to have been used by Coleridge during an undistinguished spell in the Dragoon Guards. The exhibition was something Humphry had brought into being, something he was proud of, something to show Elizabeth. She, for her part, loved Coleridge – later in life she would learn 'The Rime of the Ancient Mariner' by heart. The shared pleasure of the exhibition was one of the moments of 'sureness and delight' that Humphry would refer to in a short note he wrote Elizabeth after her departure.

Far less enjoyable was an evening that Humphry orchestrated to bring Elizabeth and Madeline together again. The women had, of course, met before. That had been before the marriage, before the pregnancy, and in a neutral space. Crucially, Humphry had not been there. This time the three of them were present, dining at the Royal Clarence. The hotel's Wellington Room had an ornate plasterwork ceiling and a distinctive oculus window. There were large landscape paintings on the walls. Its stylish air – silver service, starched tablecloths, balloon-backed chairs – was at odds with the mood at the table. The game soup, roast chicken, and chateau potatoes were accompanied by forced civility rather than good cheer.

Months later, Elizabeth described in a letter to Humphry the 'spiritual dumbness and numbness' of the occasion, and remonstrated with him for trying to force these necessarily conflicting elements into the same sphere. Elizabeth felt that she and Humphry could be different people when they were alone. Now with Madeline, they were compromised; normal communication was impossible. Elizabeth, who was engaging and entertaining when the occasion demanded, struggled to find something to say.

If the dinner was difficult for Elizabeth, it must have been excruciating for Madeline. She was with her husband and the other woman, one who traded on her big personality and saw Madeline as mediocre. Elizabeth might be well known for her sparkling wit, but for Madeline there was little to smile about. Even Elizabeth's nasal voice, with its pinched vowels and unnatural rhythm, was grating. There is every chance that, at the end of the awkward evening, the Houses decided to spend the night in their centrally located flat in the shadow of the cathedral. That would have left Elizabeth just the other side of a thin wall in the Royal Clarence Hotel.

Despite seeing one another in the West Country, where Elizabeth most desired to be with Humphry was in Ireland – on her land. She understood how emotional co-ordinates lined up with topographical ones. Her house was more accommodating; her relationship with a married man would breathe better there than in an airless hotel. Inviting Humphry to Bowen's Court in September was more than him simply returning to her home and emotional space. This time she required of him a temporary rejection of his new marital home, where the scattered seeds were bearing fruit and his wife was five months pregnant.

When Humphry left for Ireland, Madeline travelled to south-east England to visit family. Better for her to have the support of her parents in Humphry's absence. The cottage was no place to be alone, particularly when pregnant. The buzz of her family home would also have gone some way to lessen any discomfort about Humphry's stay at Bowen's Court.

As in the previous summer, Humphry overlapped in Ireland with other guests and family members. Elizabeth told Isaiah Berlin of Humphry's visit: 'he flowered out into his old self and was in fact more mellow, nicer than I have ever seen him before. The "fanglessness" which I had noticed during a rather difficult visit to Exeter at the end of July entirely disappeared, and he flung his weight about heavily, hilariously and I must say charmingly.' As well as describing her transformative influence, she gave an opinion about the major changes in Humphry's life: 'I don't know if you gathered how terribly depressed he has been about being a father – or being a father so soon. His marriage we didn't discuss, of course. But rather anguish hangs over the whole affair.'

The marriage was not discussed. Naturally. But its influence had spread into every corner of Elizabeth's mind. She could not help seeing Humphry's new married self, shadowed by a pregnant Madeline. The feeling was evident in letters to friends, and in particular in a letter to Berlin about an unexpected guest at Bowen's Court: 'a Miss Ursula Branston, from the Empire broadcasting dept. of the B.B.C.'. The woman, who had cycled over for tea to meet Elizabeth, had got lost on the way. She arrived late, saddle-sore, and in a temper. Elizabeth was obliged to offer her a bed for the night.

Humphry's immediate reaction to Miss Branston was extreme: he announced that he couldn't possibly tolerate her and would have to get drunk. Elizabeth commented to Berlin that she had seldom seen Humphry, or indeed anyone, as drunk. And Elizabeth had seen plenty of intoxication in her time. She noted: 'I do not know why Humphry took on so. Except that she was in some ways unhappily like Madeline – I mean, she had the same talent for earnest and inauspicious remarks.'

Sitting by her own fireside, Elizabeth listened to the unfortunate Ursula Branston and heard Madeline's voice. She projected her feelings of discomfort onto Humphry, so that they appeared to be further proof of his unhappiness rather than of her jealousy. His behaviour towards the female guest might simply have been bad manners. As is evident from his opinions of his female students, Humphry found bright women a challenge. Having one clever woman in the room was fine – particularly if that person was also your host and lover. The arrival of another intelligent female, possibly from a very similar class background to his own, upset his equilibrium.

Unimpressed with Humphry's behaviour, Elizabeth duly made him pay for it. The next morning, she and the rest of the guests went off to Limerick for the day. Humphry, presumably irritable and hung-over, was obliged to take charge of Miss Branston and return her to the station. Instead he decided to drive her to Kilcolman to look at Spenser's ruined castle. The hood blew off the car immediately and the rain lashed down on the pair. Eventually, a bedraggled Miss Branston and her bicycle were deposited in Mallow to catch the train. The next day she wrote to thank Elizabeth for her hospitality and to tell her that she was in bed with a severe chill.

The rest of Humphry's visit – card games in the evenings, walking, picking mushrooms – was a pleasure for them both. There was even a ride in an aeroplane down the Blackwater valley under the curve of a rainbow, with Humphry peering dizzily over the wing as Elizabeth's land sped past below. Elizabeth commented to Berlin: 'I have enjoyed the summer and wish it weren't nearly gone.' Leaving her at Bowen's Court, Humphry sailed back from Ireland on a night full of fireworks. High on the hillside above the port was a bonfire which threw jagged shadows onto a row of cottages. A group of hollering boys were on the water letting off Roman candles, setting ablaze a boat which splashed its light across the wake of the *Innisfallen*. Then the fires of Ireland, the pleasures of the big house were behind him, and he was back to his real life in the hamlet from the Domesday Book.

A new academic year brought no settling of Humphry's spirits – his university job he increasingly saw as 'drivelling schoolmastering'. Other professional work, such as reviewing for the *Morning Post*, was far more rewarding, especially as it allowed him to sit around all day at home in pyjamas. He sent Elizabeth a gift of John Donne's poetry, repaid her some money he owed, and informed her of his choice of name for the unborn baby: 'If a son turns up in December I am thinking of calling him Gerard Humphry.' It does not seem from the letter that he got as far as imagining a daughter.

A relaxing day at home he describes to Elizabeth thus: 'I was reading a life of Heine, and a translation of some of his prose, and then in the evening I read most of Eugénie Grandet, and finally went to bed with Balzac's letters.' Though not always swift to acknowledge Madeline's intellectual gifts, Humphry relied on her help with any text in German – she translated the original Heine texts for him. It was just one of the many times she played an almost invisible role as amanuensis, contributing her talents and intelligence to his academic ventures. Humphry's interest in Heine was sharpened by parallels he saw between Heine's experiences as a Jew in Germany in the mid-nineteenth century, and the rise of Nazism in the 1930s. Madeline had fresh tales from Hitler's Germany after her month in Frankfurt before the wedding.

As ill winds strengthened across Europe, it was Elizabeth's turn to experience these first-hand. On her return from Ireland, she spent only a few weeks at home before setting off, with Alan, for Rome. The city would exert a lifelong grip over her imagination, resulting in her distinctive travel book *A Time in Rome* (1960). For her, the city had everything – melon-coloured ruins that asked to be entered, art in its veins, local restaurants with proper napkins and large plates of veal. It was a city that breathed the interpenetration of past and present, an idea at the heart of Elizabeth's world view: 'whatever went on, goes on, in one form or another.' The city that autumn was beautiful – dazzling with zinnias, roses, dahlias. But for all her enjoyment of its history and spirit, Elizabeth could not ignore the smell of fascism. She went to one of Mussolini's rallies and saw him, absurd on his white horse, reviewing his tanks and dogs of war. The experience was chilling.

Of Rome, Humphry received not one but five postcards. In the only one posted in Italy, Elizabeth complained that Roman cafés made letter writing difficult – being either too noisy or full of wobbly tables. The others, sent in a bundle on Elizabeth's return to England, were the surplus postcards, keenly bought but unsent, that characterise many a foreign holiday. The black and white images echo her tread across the city – temples, churches, statues. Like a tour guide, Elizabeth gives single sentence explanations on the reverse of the cards. 'This is Venus' one says. Another: 'This is the green bronze door.'

Finally back at a sturdy desk, Elizabeth sat down to write Humphry the promised letter. The flood of preoccupations that had nagged at her consciousness all year – the shape of their affair, the meaning of home, the nature of marriage – burst their psychic banks. Uncut, this letter runs to almost three thousand words. And even that is not enough. Extra thoughts are added up the sides of pages, signposted with insistent asterisks in the main text. She launches in without even a salutation.

<u>*EB to HH*</u>

Waldencote
8 November [1934]

Your letter to Rome has just come, sent on by the p.o. – Facist [sic] efficiency. […]

Do you know one odd – more than odd – effect our relationship has had on me? Late in life – at an age, I mean, when most people are past strong upheaving intellectual and moral feelings, it has made a Communist of me – I expect modern Italy completed this – Facism [sic], a militant bourgeoisie, that armed defense [sic] of the 'Mine', a sense of the ego feeding on material owned things – national or domestic. Their terrific propaganda for the home and the family. […]

Do you remember much of your Rome letter? It was written some time ago. But it is in a way the text of this. Because you said in it what I had always felt you felt – though more strongly since your marriage. I mean, what you said about "settings". Speaking of the fortnight at Bowen's Court you say: "You see, I walk into your life and fit there, in your setting and everything." If I had known you thought of Bowen's Court as my 'setting', I should not have asked you – not you, of all people – to come there ever, and if that is how you will always think of it you must not come there again. To me it is a good and great place in the same sense that Rome is a good and great place. It is not my work to keep Rome going, it is my work to keep Bowen's Court going. […]

I feel you want me to be in your home because it is something that belongs to you, an expression of you, something that you have made. I want you to be at Bowen's Court because it is something that does not belong to me, that does not express me, that I have not made.

[…] I do not want to stay with you and Madeline because your daily life with her is something which it would be most insincere of me to pretend to have any part in. If you cannot emerge imaginatively from your daily life enough to meet me imaginatively and to keep up this imaginative communication between us, then you and I have no future. But the idea of you letting me go fills me with despair on your behalf as much as on

my own. If you did let me go, if later your home life and your marriage ever ceased to satisfy the whole of your nature, then you would have nothing to fall back on but petty muddles and lusts – unless you had found meanwhile, as I should like you to find, another and better Elizabeth.

If I can love, as I do love, deeply and steadily, my home life and my life with Alan, and love you, and not only be content to keep the two loves apart but wish to keep them apart for the good of both, why cannot you do the same?

This house not being Bowen's Court but being my married home, I never ask you to come here and stay with Alan and me. Why should you wish me to stay with you and Madeline?

If we want to see each other, we must see each other outside the ordinary course of things. [...]

If you cut away our sensuous feeling for one another there would be nothing left. While this sensuous feeling exists I cannot be your and Madeline's family friend. [...]

Write soon

Elizabeth

The dust of Rome and a return home combine to produce one of the most extraordinary letters in the correspondence. For Elizabeth the political is personal – it hinges on families and homes, on emotional boundaries rather than physical borders. At the same time as eschewing possessiveness, she maps out her domain. The framework she rejects, manifest in the Italian family, is the very one that gives her certainty: 'my home life and my life with Alan.' Conversely, even Bowen's Court, a building that bears her family name, she resists calling hers.

Her position in relation to Humphry is similarly complex. Truly rejecting possessiveness, and embracing emotional homelessness, would mean giving up Humphry altogether. She shows little sign of that here. Not for her the idea that 'if you love someone, set them free'. Yet Elizabeth's awareness of Humphry as part of a couple is evident throughout. In her earlier letters, she had described Madeline's character in isolation, as though she were an anthropological specimen. Now, Madeline not only shares Humphry's life, but also many of Elizabeth's sentences about him.

The pregnancy is studiously avoided, despite Elizabeth having three thousand words in which to mention it. Within a month there was a baby – not a boy, but my aunt Rachel, born on 9 December in Exeter Royal Infirmary. Now there was no escaping the fact of Humphry's parenthood or of Madeline's fertility.

Madeline is not merely a potent presence in this letter of Elizabeth's – her fingerprints are actually all over its pages. Sometime late in life she not only reread the letter, but added jottings in pencil on the back of the envelope. They read as follows:

> Why can't we keep loves apart?
> Without E, marriage failing, fall back on "muddles and lusts"
> The Exeter evening a "spiritual dumbness and numbness"
> If sensuous feeling cut away, nothing left
> Good that love outside marriage is homeless
> Greatness in both of us
> an artist
> Life to be suffered, exposed to senses
> The gates of the spirit

Madeline's notes are written in a spidery hand, quite unlike the swirling script in her letter to her mother from Frankfurt. It is similar to the wobbly handwriting on the back of the postcards she sent me as a child. These scribbles were those of my grandmother in later life. The scratchy pencil marks testament to a rereading undertaken for a specific purpose.

I imagine Madeline reading the letters, sharp-eyed despite her failing vision. She is a confident editor – one sufficiently detached to set down another woman's passionate connection with her own husband. As well as picking out some of Elizabeth's more rhetorical flourishes, Madeline highlights Elizabeth's frustration about how to manage the affair with Humphry. But perhaps the most striking feature of these jottings is her recording of Elizabeth's claim that she was an essential component in the House marriage. Dispassionately, Madeline writes down Elizabeth's version whilst carrying in her heart a different one.

Madeline's active engagement with the letters – her scribbles on envelopes, her accretions up the sides of pages – radically shifts her position. Both Humphry and Elizabeth tried to exile Madeline to the marginalia of their narrative. Yet she claimed this space for her own, keeping herself visible, commenting on the action. She was in dialogue with the letters long before I was. Like a medieval scribe, Madeline decorated the edges of the manuscript, leaving me to do the colouring in.

Norfolk Square, the site of cheap lodgings close
to Paddington Station in the 1930s

Chapter 9

Norfolk Square: *Careless Talk*

I am in a hotel room behind Paddington Station with a young Greek man. The beds lie unmade.

The room is a bit shabby but much of its beauty remains, anachronistic, impractical. The Edwardian fireplace with its hand-dipped aquamarine tiles. The decorative frieze above the dado rail. An acanthus rosette around the light fitting. The floor to ceiling double windows are flanked on one side by the most exquisite feature of the room – a vast, flamboyant mirror twelve feet high with gold floral twirls in its border.

My companion, the receptionist of the Shakespeare Hotel, tells me some of the history of the building. It was built as an elegant residence in the 1850s. There was a mews at the back where carriages rested. The wrought-iron balconies still look over the mature trees of the square, but war damage took out most of the decorative glass. Much of Norfolk Square was transformed into hotels or boarding houses in the early twentieth century, its proximity to Paddington Station being essential to its reshaping.

I think of the convenience of the address for Humphry and Elizabeth in the 1930s – both used Paddington Station regularly. They likely met in this building, possibly in this very room.

Suddenly I feel a shift in the air as surely as if someone has opened a window. The room's spirit expands into the dormant space between the tousled beds. It is strong, fierce, bitter. No other place has made my skin tingle like this, robbed me of breath. I feel overwhelmed, almost stifled.

'OK?' asks the young man.

I do not know whether it is a question about my health or my readiness to leave. I nod swiftly. We head towards the door. The room has her hand at my back, ushering me out. Whatever secrets she has, she hoards them haughtily.

Was this the place they met? I may wonder, but the room knows.

January 1935

The world of temporary accommodation – full of glancing encounters, quick intimacies, and lost souls – is much favoured by Elizabeth in her fiction. One of her earliest short stories, 'Breakfast', brilliantly evokes the world of the paying guest – irritation, mottled bacon, and train times swirl amongst the boarders and their odd hosts. The hotel is an even more popular setting, used to particularly telling effect in the novel *The Death of the Heart* (1938).

Portia, the dispossessed teenage heroine, not only grows up in hotels but flees to one, broken-hearted, at the end of the narrative. Here she tracks down the dreary, older, family friend Major Brutt, who has made the Karachi Hotel his home. Leaving behind the eyes of the bar, the couple go up to his 'temporary little stale room'. Behind closed doors, Portia offers to marry him. Recognising the wild neediness of the proposal, Major Brutt turns her down. The hotel's atmosphere, built on transience and anonymity, allows passions to be expressed quickly, frankly. Sometimes erroneously. There is relief that the walls are not yours. Though they will hear your conversation, they will not remind you of it later.

In the second week of January, Humphry was back in London still working on the notes for the Hopkins book. He was not, this time, staying with friends but renting a room short-term in a boarding house. These establishments, along with a couple of cheap hotels, were to be a feature of his life in the next few months. Letters to Madeline come from a range of London addresses – Westbourne Grove, Paultons Square, Norfolk Square. In one he is pleasantly surprised by the boarding house being 'a real grown-up place with a grandfather clock in the hall, and all the furniture quite impersonal, quite flawless in leg and texture'. Another time he rents a slightly cluttered room from a Mr Jeeves, paying five shillings for B & B. In January 1935, Humphry was in rented rooms in Norfolk Square.

It was little over a month since the birth of Humphry and Madeline's first child. Domestic responsibility and his new identity were both left behind in Devon. Now back in the capital, he was free to see whom he liked. To go out late. To ascend unseen to his room with Elizabeth, who was a visitor to Norfolk Square. The couple had seen little of one another in the last few months, failing to meet on Humphry's trip up to London in early November 1934, after Elizabeth's return from Rome. (This Elizabeth blamed on his poor organisation.) There is no evidence they saw one another before the year's end and, with Rachel born on 9 December, it is likely that Humphry remained in Exeter with Madeline throughout that month. Elizabeth and Alan would, in all probability, have been in Ireland at Christmas as usual.

Now reunited in London, they could make up for lost time. The boarding house itself would have given Humphry and Elizabeth every opportunity to refresh their sexual relationship. The freedom afforded them by the place – its beige atmosphere, the unrecorded footfalls – may have been a reason for Humphry delaying his trip back to Exeter.

He wrote to the Principal of Exeter University saying he had been kept up in London unexpectedly on family business. This 'necessary lie', as he referred to it in a letter to Madeline, enabled him to miss the beginning of term. To her he wrote that a 'great internal change' had happened, and he now found himself 'twice as strong, fertile and happy, and more serious'. A couple of days later, he apologised to Madeline for being away for so long, and explained that he had 'forced up gargles of old and bad breath'. Though Elizabeth is not mentioned directly in these letters to Madeline, Humphry's new-found vigour seems to be as a result of some emotional shift. It is unlikely to be an excitement caused by discoveries about Hopkins's sprung rhythm.

For Elizabeth too, the events of those days in January were significant. Just as she had in the wake of his marriage, she wanted to restake her claim in Humphry's heart. A year earlier, this had been comparatively straightforward – she had asserted her belief that their affair stayed outside their marriages. This time the complication between them was one that she had not earlier rationalised – Humphry's fatherhood. Months later, in a letter to Humphry, she harked back to conversations they had in the deaf room in Norfolk Square, to the valuable time they shared. There was catharsis on both sides. Lines were redrawn, breath freshened.

Madeline, meanwhile, was no longer alone with baby Rachel in the isolated, ill-lit cottage. There was a recently acquired car, and the arrival of a nursemaid to help look after both the baby and the house. Though for her it seemed an inauspicious start to the year, Madeline's position in the complicated triangle would become more pronounced, more powerful, as the year progressed. Her alignments, in relation to both Humphry and Elizabeth, changed. With a baby on her lap, Madeline became the fixed foot of the compass to whom thoughts and people travelled.

Elizabeth was reminded of choices not made, children unbegot, as she drifted into her mid-thirties. Humphry had mixed feelings – he accepted his fatherhood, but work always came first. His

Madeline with her daughter

recent work on Coleridge would have reminded him of the poet's celebration of his firstborn son in the poem 'Frost at Midnight': 'My babe so beautiful! it thrills my heart / With tender gladness, thus to look at thee.' There is no evidence in Humphry's writing of such an outpouring on the birth of his daughter.

In her letter of 8 November 1934, Elizabeth had discussed the idea of visiting the Houses. In the postscript to that letter, she had written of her desire to stand beside Humphry at a 'fire in the abstract', rather than at one that burned in either of their homes. Yet a result of the renewed urgency between them at the start of 1935 saw a change of heart on Elizabeth's part. She travelled down to Devon to stay with the Houses in February. A visit at such an inhospitable time of year speaks of Elizabeth struggling to adhere to her own rules of engagement where Humphry was concerned. Now she was both in his setting and warming herself at his hearth. Her indignant rejection of his marital realm, so visible in the letter from Rome, has dropped from view. Standards are only double, it seems, when they belong to people other than her.

Two events during the visit attest to the swift-shifting dynamic between Humphry and Elizabeth. The first was work related. She had been asked to write an essay about Jane Austen for a book entitled *The English Novelists: A Survey of the Novel by Twenty Contemporary Novelists*, which was eventually published in 1936. While at Greenslinch, Elizabeth received assistance from Humphry on the essay. The two of them would have worked in the high-beamed study, the low-slanting February light coming in through the expanse of window. Once satisfied with the longhand version, there remained one dreary task – typing it up. Happy always to let his wife do his typing, Humphry sat down willingly in his own home to do that of his lover. One can see Elizabeth smoking and relaxing in an armchair nearby, while Humphry clanked out the words with two-fingered diligence.

If Elizabeth was in the ascendancy as they worked in the study, a snatched moment elsewhere shone a different light on the relationship. In later life, Madeline recalled looking in through the window of the cottage one day and seeing Humphry and Elizabeth together. Unaware they were being observed, Elizabeth was on her knees in front of Humphry, kissing his hands. Her position was vulnerable, submissive; his more solid, authoritative. What was said between Humphry and Elizabeth drifted unheard into the chill air of the cottage.

The emotional visit at an end, Elizabeth returned to Oxford. Ever conscious of propriety, she chose to send Madeline a tea service by way of thank you. To Madeline, the cups and saucers seemed a mocking reminder of her role as the little wife – Elizabeth was a woman scornful of certain domestic virtues. Madeline stayed silent for a fortnight before eventually thanking Elizabeth by telegram.

Elizabeth was soon back in the swing of her colourful social life; the queen surrounded by her clever courtiers. Berlin and Bowra were joined by Goronwy Rees, another of Humphry's university friends. Rees had, gallingly for Humphry, been made a fellow of All Souls. It is this dazzling world of the Oxford college that fills one of her few surviving letters of early 1935.

EB to HH

Waldencote
Saturday 23 February [1935]

Today is a very good morning, like spring. At this moment, 11.5, you will just be beginning your Saturday morning lecture. Is it three weeks since I stayed with you? [...]

I thought of you very often this day – or night, rather – last week, dining with Shaya. The food was superb, so I smiled.

I can't remember it all, it began with oysters, then lobster Newburg, then there were a great many other things, finally cherry-pink ices with chopped up cherries inside. Tragically, my stomach was not its best, as I had been kept awake by the wind the night before and got up in the small hours and eaten aspirin which always makes me feel sick the next day. […] I felt odder and odder but trusted it didn't show. A gigantic whisky sour after dinner, mixed by Goronwy, put everything right.

It was a very good evening. Before I started, (owing to the bad stomach and tiredness owing to having been caught in the fields round here, that afternoon, in the 70 m.p.h. gale, head on) I had a bad attack of pre-party low morale, but from the moment I got there I enjoyed myself very much. The people there were Maurice, John Sparrow, Goronwy (who joined the party at 10 o'clock), and two nameless (I mean names inaudible) undergraduates, decorative, decorous and much impressed by being there, who seemed if anything, to be called Peter and John. We dined in a room miles away, to which we walked through a string of other rooms, mostly full of iron bedsteads, ricketty wooden washstands and photographs of what Maurice said looked like people's dead wives. On the way back, Mr Austin, a Latin (isn't he?) young and outstandingly unattractive Fellow, was crouched angrily over his fire like a caged rabbit and didn't seem to like being used as a passage at all. Everyone was in black ties, which looked very grand. […]

After dinner I got upstairs first and turned off several of Shaya's lights, which had been too loud before dinner, and monopolized on the strength of being the only woman Shaya's nice high-backed white armchair in the shade of the gramophone horn. I read Shaya's invitation cards, examined the photo of Stephen [Spender] and read a picture postcard I had written him while in Rome. His scout looked in while I was doing this and asked whether I was lonely; I said no, thank you: then the others came up. The evening then became very mellow. Goronwy shot in, not in a black tie but looking very pleasant, sober and well-brushed. Written down, the talk might sound rather silly: it was argumentative and rather emotional and great fun at the time. Goronwy started an argument with John S. by saying he never liked anybody who was "nice": he didn't and he didn't see how one could. I said I certainly never liked anybody with no slum quarter. We talked for about an hour about what each of us there meant by nice. […] The undergraduates, who had listened, left at ten to twelve, and the last hour without them was the best, really. They were very nice, but undergraduates at a party like that are always rather like young girls, aren't they, there rather on their physical qualities, and, so far, definitely adding something: impressed, agreeable, just intellectual enough. I can't remember much what we talked about the last hour: I must have been rather drunk.

Ends

This letter must have set off a rapid pulse of emotions in Humphry. There was probably jealousy, resentment, even self-pity in what he felt. He recalled himself being the decorative object of Elizabeth's interest a couple of years earlier. He did not like to be reminded of Oxford's glamorous intellectual world – not being a part of it he felt strongly. The conversation, though at the end slightly inebriated, ranged across topics that he longed to discuss in such company. They were eating lobster; he was eating cottage pie. Then there was Elizabeth herself, demonstrative and dynamic, acting no doubt, in just the way he found both attractive and unseemly. While she and his friends slept off their hangovers, he heard the cry of his baby in the lonely farmhouse.

When the end of term came, Humphry gladly went up to London, this time for a month. There was plenty of opportunity to see Elizabeth when she was in the capital, though any meeting the two of them enjoyed does not get a mention in his letters to Madeline. As for Elizabeth, she travelled to Bowen's Court for Easter before making her way back to Oxford. Nagging still at the edge of her consciousness was Madeline who, with baby Rachel, was coming to stay with her at Waldencote in early May. The plan was for mother and child to stop off in Oxford on their way back from visiting family in the south-east. For Elizabeth, propriety was uppermost. She had visited the Houses in the West Country. It was right that such an invitation was reciprocated. Elizabeth had already made it clear to Humphry that he would not be welcome in her marital home, but it was different for his wife.

That the prospect of Madeline's presence discomfited Elizabeth is evident in a letter she wrote to Berlin from Bowen's Court: 'Madeline House is coming to stay with me on the 8th. Can you help me set up her morale by coming to a meal any time while she's there, also do help me think of some nice husband for her in case T. Brass falls through?' A spare man is invited to Elizabeth's dinner party to play Humphry's role as the 'nice husband'. For both women, the presence of a stand-in must have sharpened their sense of the man who was absent. Despite this, the visit (according to Elizabeth) was a success – there was spring in Oxford and shopping to keep them entertained. Madeline and Alan got on well with one another, talking of Ernest Renan's *Vie de Jésus* as they all went for a walk.

Left out, Humphry was the person who found Madeline's stay in Oxford most galling. He was stuck in Devon on his own. The garden was full of lush wallflowers, bluebells, bees. He doused some of the paths in weedkiller, and then took a break in a new deckchair, bought on special offer for the Silver Jubilee of George V. He could survey the overgrown garden and reflect. His twenty-seventh birthday was imminent. His gnawing dissatisfactions seemed larger than ever. Back inside the house, his fine high room was filled with heat and the peep of hatching starlings.

A swarm of letters, some indignant, was despatched to Oxford. One of Elizabeth's replies is the following.

EB to HH

Waldencote
Saturday [Postmark: 18 May 1935]

My dear, you must be calmer. I am truly sorry that I wrote as I did when you were overwrought about work and other things. No, your letter neither shocked nor troubled me, but did make me sorry – how am I [to] show it? – that the trouble of mind in which you wrote should be my fault, or at least aggravated by me.

Goodness knows your life is difficult just now, and I don't want to make it harder. Until the torturing uneasiness of your relation with Madeline resolves itself, one way or the other, your relations with anyone else, either friend or lover, are bound to be poisoned, distorted and uncertain. Without this (that uneasiness) your either loving me or not loving me would be comparatively straight forward, either way. Simply because I am incapable of loving anyone who does not love me. Most people are.

What you say about my overwhelming love for you makes me feel dishonest. It seems to be about some other woman. My dear, I am too selfish idle and 'literary' to be capable of a love like that. I have been, I'm afraid, often selfish and hedonistic where you are concerned. You must not mistake an artist's impatience and wish for everybody to live at the full height for an ordinary (and better) woman's craving love. Saying I love you too much you in a sense honour me. Hence my feeling dishonest. I am not capable, and perhaps never may be, of a feeling like that. I am dishonest, too, and play act more than you know, and I know myself.

[…] The part of your letter that seemed to me most nearly nightmarish was your saying you didn't like Madeline staying with me. You had always wanted her and me to 'get on'. Now we do. Isn't that one pleasant thing? I asked her because I liked her; I think she liked being here and I liked having her. The sun shone, Rachel liked the garden (apparently) and I enjoyed the tulips from having someone to share them with. In fact, 2 women and one small baby were happy. Aren't you being a little ungenerous?

I am working very hard as I am trying to rewrite the novel in 3 weeks, and these are crucial weeks as they make it either bad or good. I think it is good. I hope you will. I wish it (the weather) wouldn't be cold, as that distracts one and lowers one's vitality, which wastes time.

I must go on with it now. I know times are bad, but let us enjoy May. I hope the 'obstacle' will clear away soon, it seems bad luck it should be there. Write when you can – Have you got time to look at those Flaubert translations some time? I'd like to send them.

My love,
Elizabeth

Elizabeth's interest in both the nature of attachment and its expression is central to this letter. This idea she revisited in an essay entitled 'Disappointment', written for the *Reader's Digest* in the 1950s: 'Have we insisted on being blind to the true nature of the man or woman on whom we set our hearts? If so, a false situation has arisen: the loved one sooner or later must give us pain by no more than being himself, or herself. By trying to force another person to conform with our notion of him or her, we virtually force them to disappoint us.'

These ideas were central to the relationship between Humphry and Elizabeth. Each was, partially, in love with the idea of the other. For Humphry, she was still the glamorous, successful writer. For Elizabeth, the model was of a young, clever lover free of relational constraints. When each exposed their fuller selves, irritation and frustration were often felt by the other. In these moments each of them retreated – to territories where they felt most comfortable, and the other at a disadvantage.

In one of his letters that spring, Humphry identified the central problem of the relationship as sexual. In doing so, he played his best cards – the royal flush of his virility. This is where Elizabeth felt awkward and embarrassed, as the account of their first sexual encounter, in Humphry's letter of 23 July 1934 laid bare. As well as this position of sexual supremacy, Humphry imagined her to have an 'overwhelming love' for him. Elizabeth's response to this plays to her unassailable strength – that of the artist. Her skilful sidestep (and my dear, you need to take note here, she lectures him) into the cerebral and creative leaves him tongue-tied. She is adept at having the last word.

Gleam by gleam, the inhabitants of the box of letters were beginning to reveal themselves to me. Their hopes, anxieties, insecurities. And also their shared passion for literature – Hopkins, Austen, Donne, Coleridge. All writers whose words form a crucial part of my inheritance.

And yet, as is so often the case, these new relationships of mine were born from the loss of a previous one – the bright presence of my uncle John. Any odyssey loops simultaneously away from and towards family. I kept coming back to one moment shortly after his death. I was with my mother practising the poems we were each to read at his funeral. Mine was 'Binsey Poplars' by Hopkins; loved first by Humphry, then by John. (An art historian, he used the poem alongside Monet's poplar paintings in his inaugural lecture as professor at the Courtauld Institute. It was a thrilling lecture, as were all of his I was lucky enough to attend.)

I read the poem aloud to my mother, much as if I had been reading it in front of a class. Her back was turned; there was something to stir on the stove. Unimpressed, Mum turned round. My reading was monotonous, the rhythm not sufficiently wired. 'Oh, and you rushed the end.'

We went through the poem together carefully. I marked all the syllables to stress and drew horizontal lines where I needed to pause. Our conversation about enunciation was, perhaps, a way of refining a grief that was harder to articulate. We talked of the importance of stressing the word 'felled' rather than dwell on the person who, like the trees, had been cruelly cut down. I tried my reading again. This time Mum was satisfied and rewarded me with a wide smile.

Then it was her turn. She burst into a dynamic recitation of John Donne's sonnet 'Death Be Not Proud'. In the words, in the timbre of her voice, in the spirit of her delivery, was a gleeful rejection of death's final power. Though 'soonest our best men with thee do go', death will die too. Donne's confounding of expectations allows the poem, paradoxically, to be a celebration of life.

And so it was when Mum read the poem a few days later at John's funeral, her rich voice filling the small chapel, falling on the family members gathered. A joyful acknowledgement of John's life. A valediction forbidding mourning.

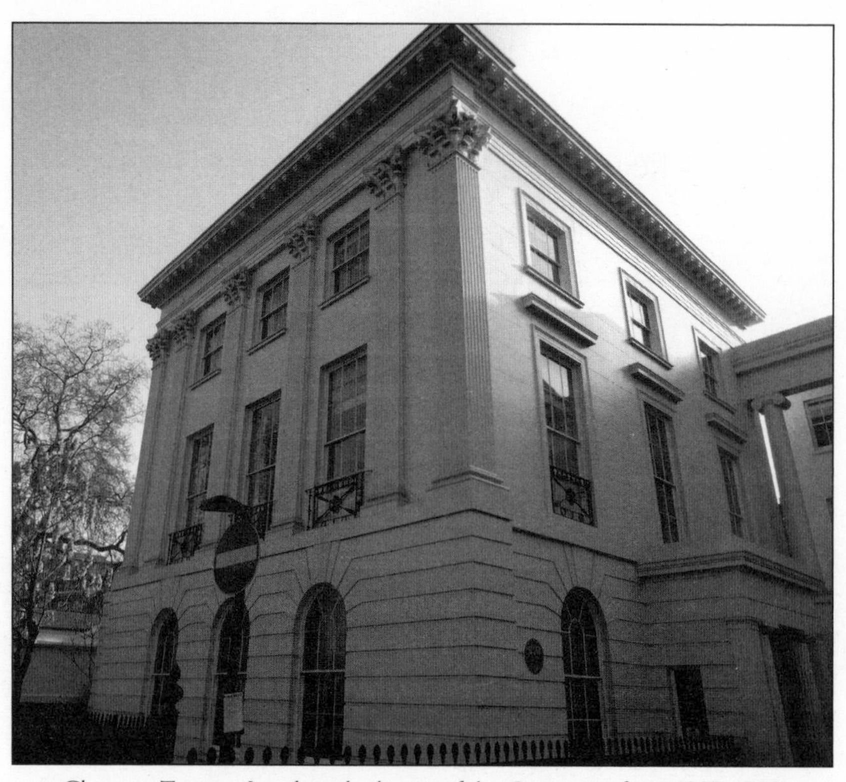

Clarence Terrace, London, the home of the Camerons from 1935-1952

Chapter 10

Regent's Park: *The Death of the Heart*

There are ten different bells at Elizabeth's front door in Clarence Terrace, her London home. A notice on the left warns me that CCTV is in operation. Another sign below directs the visitor to the porter's office in the centre of the terrace, under the grand Corinthian pillars. I make my way across the deserted street and go in.

In front of me, the inner doors are firmly closed. Light falls on the green carpet from a small doorway on the right. I approach and greet the man seated at his small desk. Thin, fierce-eyed, dressed in black, he sits in his windowless cell, no wider than a single bed. On the wall is a clock announcing 'London showtime'. To my left lie a red visitors' book and a can of air freshener.

I mention Elizabeth, her house at the corner, the blue plaque. And Humphry, visiting in the thirties. The porter listens, but is not very interested in people of the past. It is talk of the building, not any former inhabitants, that brings him to life.

'It's the Germans' fault,' he says bitterly. 'The whole terrace had to be rebuilt after the war. There was a hotel just the other side of the park… the White House Hotel… then it was a gleaming new block of apartments. Beautiful Art Deco. It had a ruddy great star on the roof. The Luftwaffe…'

He breaks off to swill the word slowly round his mouth. 'The Luftwaffe used it for orientation.' As he speaks, he draws a wide circle in the air to show the imagined circumference of the bombing. 'A huge area round here was flattened as a result. I bet you didn't know that.' He concludes, his hands returning to his sides. Finally, he smiles. I reply in kind.

I do not find out who now lives on the ground floor of Elizabeth's house, its velvet curtains shredded with decay.

I head out again into the spring air, filled with vivid green and cherry blossom. The terrace is deserted except for a grey car parked just at the corner under Elizabeth's plaque. A single woman, glamorous, bejewelled, hair pulled back off her face, emerges from the house. There is a touch of Elizabeth in her look, her style of dress. She closes the front door behind her. A click of heels on the pavement, a glance in my direction, a car door opening. Then she slips behind the wheel, pulls out into the traffic, and is gone.

July 1935

After ten enjoyable years in Oxford, the Camerons moved up to London: Alan had secured a new job as Secretary to the Central Council of School Broadcasting at the BBC. Elizabeth was ready for the change and for a new abode. The one they found was in Clarence Terrace, facing Regent's Park. Elizabeth fell in love with it immediately – the Nash pillars, cream stucco, parquet floors, and trees reflected into the rooms from the park outside. There was a long Regency mirror on one wall. A large vase of flowers always brightened the room. The windows were at the perfect height for her to lie on the sofa and look through the railings into the greenery beyond.

Before properly being welcomed by her new home, Elizabeth was off to Ireland for her usual summer stay. The Houses, meanwhile, entertained both Isaiah Berlin and Madeline's parents at Greenslinch. And as summer slipped into autumn, Humphry once again travelled to Bowen's Court on his own. The house was winding down. Alan was not there, and the only other guests were Noreen, Elizabeth's cousin, and the literary editor William Plomer.

Elizabeth gives an account of the holiday in a letter to Isaiah Berlin: 'He [Plomer] was here with Humphry and they blended beautifully; in fact we had a very excellent week. Then poor Madeline got indisposed, got nervous and started sending telegrams. So Humphry had to go home. He arrived here looking overwrought and rather ill, but brightened up immediately and was his most healthy and charming. I think whiskey agrees with him better than beer.'

Her story was similar to that of the previous year – about how Humphry had blossomed at Bowen's Court in her presence, and about the inconvenience of his clingy wife. A very similar version of events was sent to Plomer who had returned to England a few days earlier: 'Humphry left the Saturday night after, because his wife's state of health and mind crystallized into telegrams which made him have to go, and made us send him off. A bit of a barren muddle, and deteriorating in the long run, I feel.'

In both letters, Elizabeth makes Madeline's nervousness seem either pathological or motiveless. Yet she chooses to omit a couple of crucial details as to why Humphry had to leave Bowen's Court so abruptly. The roof had blown off the ill-starred cottage in Devon. And Madeline's ability to deal with this was compromised by a single fact – she was pregnant again. Elizabeth, apparently, sent a note back with him for Madeline. It expressed her disappointment that Humphry had been obliged to leave Ireland earlier than planned. Small wonder, perhaps, that this communication does not survive.

That Humphry was called away by telegram was not only an irritation to Elizabeth. It was also highly symbolic. In *To the North*, one lover rages to another about this wired disruption of plans: 'But you and I – wherever we go there is something to keep us separate. Someone is out to break us.' So Elizabeth might have felt as the curtain came down on Humphry's visit.

The last of the guests, Noreen, followed Humphry away from Bowen's Court a few days later. Returning to the now empty house with Jim Gates, her neighbour, Elizabeth was hit by a sudden burst of depression. Large whiskeys were poured and the wireless put on. Quite by chance, what she and Jim heard was a woman called Helen Simpson reviewing Elizabeth's recently published novel, *The House in Paris*. What a pleasing coincidence. How apposite. Her home was filled by a discussion of characters who had brought themselves into being during her relationship with Humphry. His footfall was no longer heard in Bowen's Court, but his presence was abiding – on the air waves, in her memory, and in her novel. Even his name – 'House' – ran down its spine.

The House in Paris sits at the heart of my family's myth surrounding Elizabeth. I was told by my mother years ago that there were elements of my grandparents in the shaping of two of the protagonists, Max and Naomi. I have allowed the association to sit with me, to become part of my constructed versions of relations I barely knew. Rationally, I know these characters are not my grandparents. Emotionally, I want that bond to exist.

The story itself interleaves past and present, adults and children, the lost and found. It opens with two children who are, for different reasons, parked for the day at the leering house near the Jardin du Luxembourg. An old crone, Madame Fisher, is upstairs in bed. Her pitiful daughter Naomi fusses and frets about below. The central section of the novel is a flashback which brings to life the lost affair between Naomi's friend, Karen Michaelis, and Max Ebhart who at the time is half-heartedly engaged to Naomi. There are further emotional twists including a hint of lesbian longing and an inter-generational crush. Karen manages to sweep the affair with Max into memory and marries well. Max effects the most unlikely suicide. The conclusion of the novel is a taxi journey across Paris with Leopold, the illegitimate child of the affair, heading for a reunion with his unknown mother.

The passionate collision between Max and Karen was highlighted by Gerry Hopkins, the nephew of the poet, and a friend of both Elizabeth and Humphry. In a letter to her soon after the novel's publication, Hopkins wrote: 'There is no comfortable illusion in the book that love is either a happy or a satisfying event: it appears rather almost as a form of Greek nemesis, a devastation falling on people for no reason and with no solution. [...] What, perhaps, centrally emerges for me, is the overpowering feeling that what your two people did was not what they wanted, but what they were forced to do. It took hold of them and exhausted them.'

Here, then, is the emotional climate of Elizabeth's relationship with Humphry in the early 1930s. There remains, however, the important issue of the characterisation in the novel. Of the connection between fictional and real people, Elizabeth writes '*Physically*, characters are almost always copies, or composite copies. [...] Though much may be lifted from a specific person in "real life," no person in "real life" could supply everything (physical) necessary for the character in the novel.'

Biographers of Elizabeth are divided about the interplay between the figures in the novel, Elizabeth, and the Houses. Patricia Craig comments that 'we needn't assume there is anything of Humphry House in him [Max], any more than Karen resembles *her* (however tempting it is to see a parallel between the nerve-racked threesome of the novel, and the events surrounding Elizabeth while she wrote it).' Yet certain traits and gestures are common to Max and Humphry, ones that were apparent to Madeline when she read the novel – his fidgeting with objects on a tea table, his tendency to think quickly and act more slowly. Written inside one of the copies of *The House in Paris* that has come through the family (a 1967 Sphere paperback with the children rendered in scratchy purple on the cover) is the following: 'Max is supposed to be based on Humphry House.' The handwriting belongs to my aunt, with whom my grandmother lived in old age.

Elizabeth's first biographer, Victoria Glendinning, makes a direct link between Madeline and Naomi Fisher: 'Elizabeth did seem to model Naomi on the wife [Madeline], or on her own version of her.' It is not a flattering portrait. Naomi seems to have her own microclimate – of ordinariness and shivery virginity. Yet Elizabeth found herself affected, almost haunted, by her own creation. She wrote to a friend: 'Naomi Fisher I see the whole time, even her clothes.'

While Elizabeth seems to have used certain physical characteristics of Madeline, the more complex, psychological slant of the young woman is harder to fix. Madeline was later to refer to herself as a 'pillow' for Humphry, consciously echoing the passive description of Naomi given by Max in the novel. He says: 'A fatigue I had not admitted made her my pillow. Desire of what she gave seemed to be desire of her.' Here the woman is seen as both comforting and malleable.

My mother, on a recent reading of the novel, exclaimed hotly that there were 'absolutely no similarities whatsoever' between Madeline and Naomi. She went on: 'You feel Naomi is almost frigid, quite the opposite of Linny. But then maybe Elizabeth chose to see her like that, because she was a rival.' My mother's comments are about Naomi's personality; my grandmother's about the role she plays in a man's life. It is a crucial distinction.

Wishing to remove the make-up from the characters in *The House in Paris*, I decided to go to Austin, Texas, to visit the archive where the majority of Elizabeth's papers lie. On a budget and travelling alone (an activity undertaken by the dispossessed in Bowen's world), I rented a room in a stranger's home. Owned by a wide-smiling woman in khaki shorts, it was a brightly painted bungalow with a hammock on the porch and an open-air shower.

My host's ebullient personality was matched by the strong spirit of her house. Elizabeth, throughout her life, was keenly conscious of a building's peculiar power. She writes: 'Each house seems to live under its own spell, and that is the spell that falls on the visitor from the moment he passes in at the gates.' Whether in a big house in Ireland or a clapboard bungalow in Texas, the effect is the same: guests are bewitched. My host's sphere of influence spread not to the gates of a demesne, but to the fairy-lighted porch of her fuchsia home. I felt the house's energy on entering; over the next few days it lapped at my ill-shutting door, it metamorphosed into the fat cat that colonised my space. I was staying in a Bowenesque house; strange, watchful, lopsided. It seemed the ideal place to be during my exploration of the uneasy rooms in *The House in Paris*.

My days in the chilly archive fell at the end of October – Hallowe'en. The library was festooned with cobwebs, all the employees were sporting costumes, and a vast grim reaper on stilts stalked her way through the reading room before clattering off down a corridor. Elizabeth may have approved of the decoration, disliking as she did 'the very unhauntedness of "functional" rooms'.

The holograph manuscript was bound like a hardback, with gold writing on the spine. Just opening the floral cover and seeing the first page gave me a thrill. The sheets were heavy and brittle to the touch.

The House in Paris by Elizabeth Bowen it read, handwritten, the 'H' of 'House' bleeding slightly into the creamy paper. This was followed by more than three hundred pages in Elizabeth's now familiar loopy hand; the occasional black ink blot; deep nib-pressed crossings out. Only one side of the paper was written on, so the corrections of one page showed through like bruises onto the blank one that followed.

The chilly quality of Naomi's personality was something very apparent in this draft manuscript. Her brittleness was sharpened. The words 'frozen' and 'farouchely' added. There were endless descriptions of Naomi's prominent eyes – Elizabeth, in a letter to a friend, described Madeline as 'pop-eyed with anxiety the whole time'. There were even more references to her glove-wearing hands and her 'touchiness'. Naomi suffered more revision in this manuscript than any other character except the house itself.

As for Max, he moved from the draft into the final novel with far fewer revisions. Physically he is not much like Humphry. Entombed by the house and his situation, Max does not enjoy sunny relationships with women; loving Karen would be a step into the unknown. And Naomi he describes thus: 'Naomi is like furniture or the dark. I should pity myself if I did not marry her.' He is not immediately likeable, but then few characters in the book are.

The bell sounding, I returned the manuscript to the archive trolley. Though I had enjoyed my reading – the freshness of the ink, the weight of the volume, the favourite passages – there had been no unexpected revelation of character. But the day was not over. A discovery did await me, and in a quite unexpected place.

A bus ride across town took me to the independent bookstore on South Congress, Austin's hippest hub. I was hoping for information about some of Elizabeth's American friends, the writers May Sarton and Eudora Welty. There was nothing about either woman in stock but, sniffing a sale of some sort, the assistant recommended two books in the 'biography/memoir' genre. I rejected the anorexia memoir in favour of *When Women Were Birds* by Terry Tempest Williams. Good title, beautifully produced book, intriguing name, and I had never before knowingly read a book by a Mormon.

Shortly before she died, Williams's mother gave her daughter her journals with the strict instructions that she was not to read them until after the funeral. On opening them, Williams found page after empty page. Thinking that she was going to be slipped the key to a fuller understanding of her mother, she instead drew a blank. What follows is a profound meditation on words and memory, on psychic palimpsests, and the ways in which we connect with our dead. It's also a wonderful, unashamedly women-focused book, shot through with a deep love for her mother.

Williams's book did more than relieve me of my search for my grandparents in the echoing rooms of *The House in Paris*. It made me value the spaces in between what I do know of my past. A gathered stone on the journey does not have to be a carved tablet. It can just be a stone.

There remains one further epistolary connection between *The House in Paris* and my family – a letter written by Virginia Woolf to Elizabeth on the publication of the novel. It was in the box I took possession of, more carefully wrapped than all the rest of the correspondence. It was, is, prized.

Elizabeth received it at Bowen's Court just after Humphry's departure in September 1935. She tells William Plomer of a 'very nice letter from Virginia', shortly after filling him in on Humphry's return home to the roofless cottage. Woolf congratulates Elizabeth on her best novel yet, finding less self-conscious cleverness and more depth in the writing: 'I had the feeling that your world unfurled itself in my world, while I read, which only happens when one is being taken in hand by a writer.' In a scratchy hand on sky-blue paper, Woolf's letter runs from her appraisal of the novel to kingfishers and then the visit of T. S. Eliot to her home in Rodmell, Sussex. She signs off in a swirl of initials.

The letter from Virginia was not just from a friend. It was from the best novelist of the day, someone Elizabeth admired. Sharing the flattering letter with Humphry, which probably happened later that autumn, was significant. She was hungry for approbation – not just from Virginia, but also from him.

For those few days in Ireland, Elizabeth had been able to conduct her affair with Humphry in the extramarital hinterland she favoured. Time rewound easily at Bowen's Court. It was 1935, but could just as well have been 1933. But Madeline's telegram shattered this illusion. By calling Humphry back to her and into the present, Madeline shot the bolt of wedlock. She also reminded Elizabeth, forcefully, of a role she had not played – that of a mother. It is this that emerges in Elizabeth's next letter to Humphry, soon after her own return to England. Elizabeth was on a train journey and had to make do with what she had – a scrap of paper she found at the bottom of her bag under her cigarettes and rouge. The words are squished onto the note-paper, and bend at the edge of the sheet to remain legible.

EB to HH

In the train
Wednesday [Postmark: 9 October 1935]

I am feeling better now. I'm sorry if my letter hurt you. You will see that it wouldn't have been written if I had not been hurt myself. Your letter, though dated Friday, must have missed the post, as it only reached me on Monday morning. By which time I really was in rather a state. In view of what I had been through – being ignorant of your movements, I thought your reprimand about what I said about M. uncalled for and unjust. I felt you ought to have seen that it would not have been written if I had not been exasperated by worry. On the whole I am generous to her and about her. I make more allowances for her than, I think, you realize: you must sometimes make allowances for me. It was hard for me to behave well when you had to leave B. Court like that, when that is the only real time in a year we have together. Having behaved well, it was inevitable with a nature like mine that I should have a reaction afterwards, though that reaction could have been averted if you had written one letter more. I felt bitterly, tho' I see it was wrong to be bitter, that because I had behaved with self-restraint you had underrated how hard I had been hit. – Also, you know the whole area is painful when I myself wanted a child so much.

I am sorry to write this on the back of another letter: I have no other paper in my bag. – It does serve one's purpose. I shall be staying with C. D. Lewis on Thursday night at the address stamped on this paper. Will you write me a note to reach me <u>there</u> on Friday morning, before I leave? If you did, it would make a great difference to me.

Elizabeth.

This raw, confessional letter is unlike any other surviving letter from Elizabeth to Humphry. There is no performance, just some painful truths shaken out of her on a train. She is in the limbo-state of a journey, and writes with less self-consciousness as a result. Though Elizabeth speaks of her painful entanglement with Humphry, what she writes also exposes her relationship with Alan, and the expectations of marriage in general.

Elizabeth needed the contours of a marriage – to be, as she puts it, 'held by someone else not only in affection but in their sense of reality'. Her relationship with Alan gave her the freedom to be a writer, as well as the certainty of being a wife. Her childlessness had not been, at first, a problem. She was productive in other ways. Until the advent of Humphry in her life, Elizabeth had not found this framework wanting. Yet since 1933 not one, but two sleeping selves had been awakened in her. Humphry's presence had quickened her sexually. Madeline's condition had brought out her maternal longings. Matriarchal Elizabeth, who had previously described herself as not 'motherly', acknowledges her desire to be a mother when it is too late. Biological time, unlike the narrative in *The House in Paris*, could not be rearranged in a pattern to suit her.

In the last few months of 1935, Humphry and Elizabeth saw less of one another. He found it difficult to get up to London. Her sensual desire for Humphry remained, but the corner he had filled in her life now had new furniture in it. She was embracing the social world of London, developing her friendships with people such as Virginia Woolf and William Plomer. Of Elizabeth's new life Berlin wrote: 'Elizabeth lives in a handsome house in London, and reigns over what might be called Lower Bloomsbury, in the sense in which Keynes & Mrs V. Woolf might be regarded as Upper Bloomsbury.'

Decked out in her suits and pearls, cigarette in hand, she opened the doors of Clarence Terrace to a new crowd of people. These were dubbed the 'Black Hats' by Alan, on account of him coming home from work in the late afternoon and being greeted by a row of visiting hats in the hall. He sometimes retreated alone to the basement study, a space full of golf clubs and decorated with pictures of his favourite cats. Elizabeth meanwhile developed a reputation as a generous hostess, filling her house with artists and academics and plenty of young talent. The alcohol flowed freely – Elizabeth measured her gin in inches. Those who came in contact with her were, according to Charles Ritchie, treated to 'the fascinating flow of E's talk, the pictures of places, people, the continual surprise and pleasure of her choice of a word, the funniness, poetry and brutality of her view of people and events'.

Elizabeth was also beginning to shape a new novel, *The Death of the Heart*, which begins with a walk round the park she could see from her window. The pattern of her working day was well established. A large writing table sat not far from the window; the presence of trees soothing without being distracting. She rolled up her sleeves and wrote, chain-smoking, until lunch. A bite of bread and cheese, a couple of pages of the thriller that she had on the go, a quick turn round the park, and she was back to work. Her refreshment of choice was lime juice, or came in the form of a gramophone record – a song by Richard Strauss or some blues by Paul Robeson. At the end of the day, if there was no party to prepare for she often went to the cinema, one of her great pleasures. (Elizabeth's mark of a truly great film was whether it suppressed the urge to smoke, something permitted in the cinemas of the day.)

As Elizabeth moved into a technicolor phase of her life, Humphry returned to his more monochromatic existence in Devon. Emotionally uncertain and professionally frustrated, he felt a change was overdue and lost no time in looking for a new job. There was the possibility of a teaching post in London, and a more exotic option – as a Professor of English at Presidency College in Calcutta. After his torrid Oxford years and the disappointing spell in Exeter, his CV badly needed a polish. Being a Professor of English for the first time, albeit in India, was a start. His father, at the very least, would be impressed. His wife possibly less so.

As the post was officially offered by the Government of Bengal, Humphry would become a member of the Indian Civil Service (ICS). This institution, though changing in its make-up, was at the heart of British rule in India. The model ICS Englishman was public school and Oxbridge educated – Humphry ticked both these boxes. Being one of the 'heaven-born', as the ICS was nicknamed, meant a decent salary (then 900 rupees a month), a pension, and status. Humphry was never one to wrap himself in the flag – he had earlier failed the 'Patriotism' exam – and the friction between his own political sentiments and the apparatus of Empire would emerge later. Significantly, these feelings did not prevent him considering the job in the first place.

Humphry's reasons for applying for a job in Calcutta have always, in my aunt's version, been reduced to a single phrase – he went to escape Elizabeth. In this family telling, Humphry is absolved of any responsibility for his actions, and Elizabeth blamed. He is a man more acted upon than acting. This explanation identifies a single, external force that propelled him to the other side of the world. Yet Humphry was ambitious, highly intelligent and twenty-eight years old. He was not totally without options in England. There must have been a host of other considerations at play – professional and financial, spiritual and emotional – for him to take such a step. Elizabeth might cast a long shadow, but it could not, surely, stretch to the Bay of Bengal.

Like thousands of young men before him, Humphry imagined going to India alone. This sort of familial separation was expected. Maurice Bowra, whose father worked for many years in China, describes the arrangement, with the wife and/or children staying in Britain, as 'inevitable', and 'the correct procedure for English families'. Humphry had earlier confessed, in the letter to Elizabeth in July 1934, his frustration at the early advent of a child, complaining it was 'settling and domesticating my whole life before I wanted'. Now his new post allowed him to slip the knot of marital and parental responsibility.

Humphry signed a contract as a member of the ICS for three and a half years. Though he did not last this long, his absence meant that my mother was walking and talking before she met her father for the first time.

When Humphry found out that he had been successful in his application for the job in Calcutta, he informed Elizabeth by telegram. She had time at Bowen's Court over Christmas and New Year to digest the information. Despite the difficulties in their relationship, Humphry was dear to her. Elizabeth did not like people leaving her life unless she ejected them first. She must have wondered about how her own emotional life would develop after he left. And in Ireland there was no one with whom she could talk about how she felt, certainly not Alan. So, instead, she threw herself into the house's usual festivities. A hunt ball took place in the house – red velvet curtains were borrowed, a loud band employed, and electric lights rigged up which made the rooms jubilant.

With his departure looming, Humphry planned to be in London for about ten days early in the new year. There were practical arrangements to be made for the voyage, as well as ongoing discussions with his publisher about the Hopkins book. Uncertain of what lay before him, he made a will. He wished to see friends – the Calder-Marshalls, Berlin, and Elizabeth, who was newly back from Ireland.

She was not on top form, and had been spitting up blood. This prompted a fear of tuberculosis – something that a few of her mother's family had suffered from. Alan had been involved in a row at work. Though Elizabeth's success with *The House in Paris* had alleviated her financial anxiety to a degree, she still found herself extremely short of cash. Despite all these strains on her spirit, not to mention the prospect of Humphry's voyage out, Elizabeth hosted a party at Clarence Terrace.

Few houses could have been, for Humphry, a more powerful reminder of what he had failed to secure. Or of what he was losing touch with. The high railings, proud aspect, well-proportioned rooms of the corner house with its view of the park. The guests, intellectuals and ingénues, with their bright faces, complacent pleasures, performative erudition. It was a house in a city that sat in the centre of a world map. Now Humphry saw it through the eyes of a man who was leaving for one of its imperial satellites. And then there was Elizabeth. High-voltage, magnetic. The centre of the room he was passing through.

The party went well, as did a subsequent meeting between Humphry and Elizabeth. He was sympathetic about her illness, interested in her friends, and fun to replay the party with. But his subsequent behaviour towards another guest (female) raised the emotional temperature between them once again. At Clarence Terrace, Humphry had met a young woman called Beatrice, or 'B', the sister of Elizabeth's friend and agent Spencer Curtis Brown.

After the party, Humphry wrote a letter to B which Elizabeth judged as vulgar and misleading. Elizabeth's irritation, possibly spiked with jealousy, coloured their closing exchanges. This culminated in a last, violent argument between the two of them. Of this Elizabeth wrote to William Plomer: 'Humphry and I have had an awful row which is so sad: I am not a quarreller but really I don't think it was my fault. I think the prospect of going to India is upsetting him. Anyway, I'm sorry: I don't like his going off to India under a blight. Who would be young again.'

For Elizabeth, the fact of Humphry's leaving was compounded by the manner of it. She happily described herself as belligerent – she saw no chip on her shoulder, enjoyed high spirits, and a good clean fight. This was distinct from being aggressive, where anger was borne of spite and grudge. She writes: 'A fight, soon over, purifies the air and leaves no one the worse (unless they are dead), whereas a quarrel, unlikely to be ever wholly resolved, not only fouls the surrounding air but may set up a festering trail of lifelong bitterness. That distinction has always been clear to me. I would go miles out of my way to avoid a quarrel.'

What she experienced with Humphry was not a clean break but a painful splintering – a messy quarrel of the worst sort, one that would not be resolved before he left for India. Humphry's reaction to their falling-out was different – he was, after all, more of a quarreller. The letter he sent to Elizabeth on his return to Devon had clearly continued in that combative vein. Elizabeth's reply runs to six long pages. Her hand is firm, the letters large, the nib pressed deep into the paper.

EB to HH

2 Clarence Terrace
Monday [Postmark: 20 January 1936]

My dear, you really must not get into such a stew about all this. (No, I am quite well now, thank you: the flu-cold germ expended itself and a tonic has repaired its ravages.)

[...] I did not feel cheerful, and wasn't. I have a Celtic absoluteness of mood and, very much as I like and love you am not a "man's woman" in the sense of putting myself about when I don't feel like it. To have been artificially cheerful would have been simply, handing you the dope. I thought we knew each other too well for that.

[...] I know I do judge you pretty hardly and harshly. But the fact that I have felt, yes, and known you were worth loving has made me do this.

What cripples you in your relations with people – with a man, I think, as much as with women – is a sort of psychological impotence. Which is as ghastly and humiliating for you as on another plane physical impotence would be. You know something is the matter – a kind of ghastly vacuum – but don't know how to cope, so get rattled to the point of being insane.

Also, you have such awfully wrong, distorted and so, inevitably, often rather vulgar ideas about love.

You still think of it as either snatching at people or battening on them, or both. And you think when people love you they are doing the same thing. Therefore, a muddled panic.

[…] I think one of your difficulties about me has been ignorance. You see so little of me in relation to other people, things, places. Therefore you minimize me to a figure in your personal melodrama. At your best (which happens often) you do realize what an immense power of pleasure, on all planes, in all ways, I have. And how this pleasure is to a certain extent self-generated. But it does connect itself, too, with people, places, objects. There has been so much with you. To this pleasure you, by being you at your best, have added: it couldn't have gone on without you. Can you realize how much of my feeling for you is, therefore, a loving gratitude?

[…] Your last letter, naturally, I discounted. As I have, you know, discounted other distorted ones. One could no more hold it against a badly bilious person that they had vomitted [sic] in one's house. The pain that produced it I was immensely sorry for.

I shall not be writing again before you go. If you would like to write and tell me about Calcutta, when you get there, while impressions are new, you know I should like to hear. I get immense pleasure out of writing to you about New York, Rome, places like that. I hope you'll enjoy the voyage, too. I do. Some do, some don't.

Very good luck to you in what you do.

Elizabeth

Elizabeth had suggested meeting Humphry again before he left London, if only briefly, but the rendezvous never happened. He had not lingered in the city any longer than necessary, and received her letter back in Devon, the quarrel still fresh in his mind. That the events in London further unhinged him in an already stressful month was evident shortly afterwards.

Just days before he left for India, Humphry went out drinking in Exeter. Roaring drunk, he had a car crash – it seems he was alone in the car at the time. He ended up in court rather than hospital. The Principal of the university, John Murray, had quick words with well-placed friends in the magistrates' court. Humphry avoided a charge while Murray accelerated the departure of this slightly problematic member of staff. Humphry left the country under a cloud and with solicitor's costs outstanding.

For Madeline, Humphry's departure came at a difficult time. Still living in the isolated farmhouse outside Exeter, she had one baby in a pram and was pregnant with their second child (my mother). Madeline had given up work to marry. Now she found herself, through parenthood, robbed of both that stimulation and her financial independence. Humphry's limited provision left her with no option but to move back in with her parents in Sussex. Singly, with his treasured crate of books he prepared to sail off; her journey led only to her abandoned past.

Chowringhee, Calcutta, India in the 1930s.
A postcard Humphry sent to Madeline

Chapter 11

East of Suez: *Gone Away*

My mother is setting out on another voyage, sailing majestically into her eighties. Three generations of the House family, and a few lifelong friends, crowd into my terraced house in south London to celebrate her birthday. Most of those born in the 1930s are in the sitting room, catching up quietly with one another. My nephews and their second cousins are in the garden dancing a cancan on a long, wobbly bench.

My aunt has a twinkle in her eye. She cannot wait for Mum to open her present. She asks me very particularly to come through to the living room to see the unwrapping. The present is almost the size of a paperback. But shorter, thinner.

'Lovely paper,' says Mum, as she eases off the rubber band to free the present. It is a photograph album, with a few black-and-white photographs in it. Sitting opposite her, I watch her flick through them, and back, and forward again. She is speechless. Then words spill out. 'It's Did, our father... he's so young... is this when he went to Calcutta?... look at what he's wearing... where did you find these photos?... how have I never seen them before?'

Rachel brims with pleasure. A bullseye, and she knows it.

My mother passes the album across to me. There are several photographs of Humphry, on a low sofa, relaxed. Different poses from the same day. He looks dashing in his crisp, white dhoti and small spectacles. For the first time I appreciate his cleft-chinned charm, his physical attractiveness.

Rachel goes on to explain how she found a stray canister of film among the family junk in her home. A sticker on the outside, possibly in Madeline's writing, said 'HH in India'. Inside was just a single strip of film, no more than six frames. She knew a local photographer, who still had an operational darkroom. Beautifully printed, the images gleam with life as though taken yesterday. In fact, they were taken within a few months of my mother's birth. A photograph pops time like a balloon.

The sisters pore over the albums once more. Both are smiling.

Rachel looks up. 'And this, Julia, is for you.' She dips into her bag, pulls out the canister of film. 'I'd like you to have the negatives.'

February 1936

On a chilly morning in 1936, Humphry boarded the SS *Mulbera* to sail to India. His pregnant wife was on the quay at Southampton to wave him off. The steamer had seen better days; in 1924 she had carried the then Duke and Duchess of York (later King George VI and Queen Elizabeth) to East Africa. Now she plied the Calcutta run, carrying about one hundred and fifty passengers, following the classic route to the East with stops at Port Said and Aden.

The five-week voyage gave Humphry ample time to write letters to Madeline, Elizabeth, and other friends. His letters to his wife, but not to Elizabeth, survive. His feelings about his departure, which he expresses in a letter to Madeline that first night, are clear: 'I don't feel any sense of adventure or seeing the world, but I do feel that it's a mental and emotional adventure which'll be very important indeed: what happens inside me will be what matters.' In this letter there is the acknowledgement that the journey is largely internal, towards a greater understanding of himself. Humphry was conscious, to borrow a Spanish idiom, of 'losing the north'. The compass of his youth had gone awry, and Elizabeth's magnetic presence was one reason for this.

Though there is no mention of Elizabeth per se, she haunts the margins of the letters he writes in the next couple of weeks. Indeed, as the distance of space and time increases between them, he begins shrinking the years in which he knew her: 'I feel already that this whole expedition hitches on more immediately to 1930 than to anything that's gone between.' The Exeter years, he claims, have left no mark. He shifts the marker buoys of this uneasy phase in his life – the years of Elizabeth, his professional disappointments, and his loss of faith.

In her writing Elizabeth often plays with this idea, of life leaking time, of experiences that escape from the linear progress of cradle to grave. In an early short story entitled 'The Parrot' she writes: 'So that was over, and Eleanor could take the parrot home and snap the door of its cage on it, and all that hour of the day would be gone; a nothing, an irrelevancy; a lost hour that had slipped through a crack in her life and vanished.'

From his chest of books, Humphry read literature that spoke of his voyage. *Antony and Cleopatra* carried him past Port Said; 'The Rime of the Ancient Mariner' fitted the bill in a moment of loneliness on the wide waves. Almost inevitably, he chose to read E. M. Forster's novel *A Passage to India*. That novel, like no other, had shaped the British imagination about India since its publication in 1924. One night on board, Humphry was treated to a Hindi song, one also performed in the novel. In *A Passage to India*, Professor Godbole sings to the guests at Cyril Fielding's tea party. The music is the 'song of an unknown bird', which none of the English guests can understand. Forster's metaphor points towards the British failing to perceive the beauty of an indigenous culture, as well as being unable, or unwilling, to communicate in a different language.

Though prejudiced about many things and a man very much of his time, Humphry was capable of insight and of acting on that insight. He was determined to avoid the baffled ears and tied tongue of the Englishman abroad. Dedicating hours of each day to study, he threw himself into the learning of Bengali, the dominant language of Calcutta. His teacher was a cabin boy, a former student of Calcutta University who could find no better job opportunity than his humble employment on the steamer. Humphry's first three nouns in Bengali were garden, book, and girl – 'a summary of a happy life', he writes to Madeline. The studying of it also gave him greater variety of intellectual stimulation – there's only so much Shakespeare, Hazlitt, and Virgil (all packed in his 'wanted on voyage' box) that one man can read at sea.

A geographical midpoint, just east of Suez, occasions one of his most eloquent descriptions about the nature of voyages and their transformative power. He writes to Madeline: 'A change there is over everything in a single night; the arrangements and tempo of life, sea, sky, land, air, clothes, manners, food, all change even on a ship in a night. And a change of spirit, that familiar things are behind, and you are shot out into a place making new demands and needing new approaches.'

After a stop in Colombo, and more than a month at sea, the SS *Mulbera* made her way finally towards her destination. And it is in this letter to Madeline, his last one before mooring, that Humphry mentions Elizabeth for the first time: 'In England I was a tiresome, unproductive adolescent, fretting because I knew I was wasting, and wasting because fretting. I did not tell you before I came away that there had been a violent crisis in my relations with Elizabeth, which made me more than ever anxious to get away from her – which I had wanted to do even before it.'

Some part of Elizabeth and his relationship with her boarded the boat with him, lying in the bottom of his 'wanted on voyage' box. Yet he was now east of Suez, his emotional latitude had changed. Not everything needed to be taken onshore with him. Baggage could be left behind. His revelation to Madeline makes one thing clear: the escape narrative was, initially, his.

From her window overlooking the park, Elizabeth could see snatches of coloured sails on the boating lake. Spring was budding – the leaping spirit of trees palpable. *The Death of the Heart,* her novel suffused with the view from the London house, was well under way.

Elizabeth wrote briefly to Isaiah Berlin about Humphry's departure, telling him she had received 'a moving priggish rather bemused letter from the S.S. Mulbera this morning, all about the new life'. The letter does not reveal how she was feeling but *The Death of the Heart* offers a clue as to how she might view such a separation. In the novel, the narrator muses about absent friends: 'The friend becomes a traitor by breaking, however unwillingly or sadly, out of our own zone: a hard judgement is passed on him for all the pleas of the heart. Willing absence (however unwilling) is the negation of love.' If the absence of any friend could be seen as a betrayal, how much graver the disappearance of someone dear to her like Humphry. Elizabeth would later try, without success, to enlist Berlin's help in persuading Humphry to come back to England.

Her sense of dislocation from Humphry had strange geopolitical echoes. Just as Humphry was pulling away from Elizabeth, so India and indeed Ireland were straining at Britannia's moorings – both matriarchs were soon to see their powers diminished.

Humphry stood outside the YMCA on Chowringhee, the great north/south artery of colonial Calcutta. His accommodation was cheap and in the heart of the action – hotels, clubs, and a famous Italian restaurant called Firpo's were all here. On one side of the road was the Bristol Hotel with its colonnaded verandas, chipped stucco, and layered arches. It sat next to another fine-domed colonial building. The street lamps, droop-headed, would not have looked out of place in a British city. There was a clatter of hand-pulled rickshaws, the smell of heat rising from a herd of bullocks, and an unruly pile of sacks in the road. The contrasts of Calcutta he saw at a glance.

The climate of unrest in the 1930s went beyond Europe to the far reaches of a creaky empire. India was moving slowly towards self-rule, though the passage was not without conflict. The Government of India Act of 1935 introduced direct elections and gave an increasing amount of autonomy to the provinces. Many people saw this as insufficient, others as a calculated attempt by the British to maintain control under the guise of making concessions.

Calcutta had lost its status as India's capital city to New Delhi in 1911. Yet for years it had been the beating heart of the Raj, and this spirit lingered particularly for the members of the ICS who upheld it. The feeling of Calcutta in those years is described vividly by Michael Carritt, a new friend of Humphry's who, like him, was a member of the ICS:

> We still lived in a sort of Barchester atmosphere, cultivating in the far East our fantasy of English middle-class security. I do not remember at any of these dinner parties or other social gatherings any discussion, or even mention, of the economic crisis of the thirties, nor the tragic Civil War in Spain, nor of the rise of Fascism in Europe. What remains

> in my memory is the picture of smooth-swept lawns, the scent of the bougainvilleas, the soft-footed bearers bringing more drinks, the feeling of well-being – as well as the polite and vacuous chatter of men who controlled the destiny of millions.

One of the cities most at odds with its colonial rulers was, unsurprisingly, Calcutta. It was an important stronghold of the outlawed Indian Communist Party, whose influence would last long after India gained its independence. Even before he arrived, Humphry was attuned to the tension inherent in his role as a member of the ICS. With eerie prescience, he writes to Madeline, imagining how being in India will be like living in a Fascist or Nazi country: 'If I'm not very careful I shall be an <u>unconscious spy</u>. If I get to know my pupils and they, being anti-Government, talk freely to me at all; and then in common innocence I mention what was said to another Government official or anyone they suspect for any reason, I shall from their point of view be a spy. I must go around with my ears open but my mouth shut.'

As soon as Humphry arrived in Calcutta, he felt the invasive presence of the state. The letter Humphry sent to Madeline on his second day in Calcutta was the first of many to be censored. The envelope bears an angry, red crayon cross and the words, 'Pol: see letter inside'. The flimsy paper of the first page is half the size it should be. The second page begins with a step-like cut in the middle of a paragraph. He writes to Madeline: 'Will you notice carefully the back of envelopes – the method here at least is to steam open and re-stick one of the four flaps, not necessarily the top one.' Looking at the censored letters, it is clear that they were trimmed of sexual as much as political sentiment.

Despite censorship being a fact of imperial life, Humphry never got used to this invasion of his privacy. He went as far as to take the matter up, more than once, with the Deputy Commissioner of Police, referring to the interception of letters as a 'criminal violation of personal liberty in this particularly mean and offensive way'. He writes to Madeline: 'I trust nobody who has anything to do with the police. They are quite capable of blackmailing my friends. [...] Never write anything about another person – whoever it may be – in a political context.' Humphry advised self-censorship, a conscious editing of their lives, a simplification of their stories.

Humphry's strong feelings about his letters being interfered with make for uncomfortable reading for me. Though I may not 'steam open and re-stick one of the four flaps', I am a spy, an interceptor of letters. I have a metaphorical red crayon and pair of scissors. I am made uneasier still by Madeline and her actions. She policed and edited correspondence, acting as a further wave of censorship.

But it is one thing to intercept and read tangible letters, quite another to 'read' letters that no longer exist. In a memorable scene in *The House in Paris*, Leopold tries to 'thought-read' a non-existent letter from his mother to Naomi Fisher. The absent mother is mirrored in the missing letter: 'Getting up and pushing back the chairs, he began to pace the salon, with his eyes shut, pressing her empty envelope to his forehead as he had once seen a thought-reader do. Then he began to read slowly aloud, as though the words one by one passed under his eyelids: "Dear Miss Fisher," he said.'

Leopold is interrupted by the other child in the book, the slightly starchy Henrietta: 'Oh, you oughtn't to thought-read letters to someone else!' She even goes as far as saying that touching (not even reading) someone else's letters is 'dishonourable', an opinion that Leopold stoutly rebuffs. Leopold's thought-reading is an attempt to imagine and construct his mother, someone who has been no more than a whisper in his life. The shape of the words he 'reads' gives breath to her ghostly presence.

I am faced with the same problems and dilemmas as Leopold as I look at the letters from the India years. Of the correspondence between Humphry and Elizabeth, only her letters survive. His voice in India is heard in what he wrote to Madeline. My grandmother's replies are gone. Then there are the sections of the correspondence that were cut by the police, that did not reach their destination and could only be imagined by the intended recipient. Finally, there are the thoughts and ideas that Madeline and Humphry wished to commit to paper but chose not to – the fear of interception resulting in their own pre-emptive censorship. Words erased between the imagination and the page.

The various gaps in the correspondence are like lines of verse with missing feet – they occupy a space, but make no sound. And so to tap into the spirit of what is lost, to construct my protagonists, thought-reading is required – dishonourable or not.

Calcutta's stifling political climate was matched by a wall of heat and humidity. Humphry arrived just as the Indian winter was ending, and temperatures were starting to rise. His introduction to the city was an evening walk round the Maidan, the huge park in central Calcutta, drinking cool coconut water with the Head of the English Department, Professor Ghosh.

Humphry had already been warned of the low standard of English among the students he was to teach. He was advised to give them composition exercises and 'light talks' to start with, before moving on to more demanding tasks. From Humphry's notes and letters there is no evidence he altered his challenging approach to the teaching of English. The students would be hit with Marvell and Pope before the term was out.

But there was one unpleasant surprise for Humphry as far as the curriculum was concerned: the works of certain canonical writers such as Milton and Wordsworth had been stripped of their possibly seditious or revolutionary content. Students studying *The Prelude* in Calcutta in the 1930s might not have complained that the mammoth poem was now a little shorter, but they were deprived of some of the finest verse Wordsworth ever wrote.

A few days after his arrival, Humphry delivered his first lecture. He was nervous, had ink over his hands, and a shaky voice. The class was huge, comprising more than a hundred students. He called the register by number. Humphry was conscious of being a novelty – for some, he was the first Englishman they had encountered in class. Reading poetry to them was a joy and behaviour, on the whole, was good: 'They listened like angels except the two lounge-lizards at the back.'

Humphry was soon meeting and socialising with the young Bengali professors. One of these new colleagues took him to an 'adda', a feature of South Asian cultural and intellectual life. Addas were informal meetings of educated men, giving them the chance to socialise and discuss the arts. This particular adda was so well known in English circles that it had warranted an article in *The Times Literary Supplement* earlier that year. Many of the men in the group – cosmopolitan, privileged, and left-leaning – had some kind of connection with England. Some had received their higher education there; many more were steeped in its culture. Humphry, with his Oxford connection, was a welcome addition to the group.

At the adda, Humphry met the Bengali writer Sudhindranath Datta (known as Sudhin), whom Elizabeth refers to as 'that particular poet' in one of her first letters. He was in the vanguard of the modernist arts movement in the city, and had begun publishing an influential literary magazine called *Parichay* (Acquaintance) in 1931. Datta would become one of Humphry's closest friends – he was cultured and intelligent, without being threatening. The spectre of class that had compromised some of Humphry's friendships in England was less relevant here. Though Humphry met Datta's wife, social convention kept her largely

Humphry in Calcutta

indoors. The young friends could both enjoy the freedoms that were more commonly the preserve of single men. Meanwhile, far away in England, Humphry's second daughter, my mother, was being born. (Elizabeth commented on hearing the news: 'Yes, I had heard that Rachel had a sister. I do wish her good luck and a good life, -- the dark one.')

The move to Calcutta gave Humphry the chance to find new voices, both literally and metaphorically. Translating Datta's poetry from Bengali to English was one such challenge. He sent his translations of the verse to publications in England and wrote of them to Madeline: 'I'm impatient to see them in print as soon as possible; no nonsense about nine years in a box.'

Another new sound in his life was broadcasting. Soon after his arrival, he was asked to review books for the Indian State Broadcasting Service. It was the beginning of a long and satisfying relationship with the medium. A few months into this employment, the head of the radio station, Mr Fielden, raised a concern that the broadcasts were too highbrow, and would be lost on many listeners: 'the European element [...] does not read, or, if it does, it reads trash.' Humphry was unrepentant, both about his approach and his choice of material: he would speak about Vita Sackville-West's *Pepita* if he wished. And so at ten p.m. every Tuesday, Humphry's euphonious voice drifted out into the steamy Calcutta nights. Political empire might have a death rattle in her throat, but cultural imperialism still had a song to sing.

No letter covered in exotic stamps arrived at Clarence Terrace. Humphry had said he would write on arrival in Calcutta; instead he had been incommunicado for more than two months. The lack of an address stayed Elizabeth's pen, and it wasn't until early May that she wrote her first letter to Humphry. Back at Bowen's Court on her own for a week, she chose to work up in the yellow room at the top of the house, in what used to be Humphry's room. Butterflies batted on the windows. Loud birds sang outside. The gloomy picture of Kilcolman was probably still on the wall.

Her tone is partially one of worry, fearing illness or depression on his part. She misses him at Bowen's Court. Of herself she writes: 'I am loving being in London and am very fully growing into the house. Life has speeded up all round, and I do enjoy speed.' She chooses not to tell him more than that, wanting him to be the one to step forward. News of everything and reassurance that all is well is what she asks of him.

Returning to London shortly afterwards, Elizabeth sent off a second letter to Humphry. She had not received a reply to her first. Her concern for his welfare had given way to something else.

EB to HH

2 Clarence Terrace, R's Park, N.W.1
21 May [1936]

I don't know if this will be my first letter to you or not. [...] The address, got from Gerry [Hopkins], sounded hypothetical; he was vague about it himself. [...] But it amazed me that by not even sending a p.c. with your address you cut yourself off from hearing my news. I really was, and still am, considerably annoyed. What a lot of pleasure you have done us both out of. Your first winter in India, my first in London: neither of them will happen again. And more than half of them – impressions, dreams, pleasures, false starts, excitements, inevitable glooms, exhilarations – have gone down the drain for us both already because we have not written to each other about them. That promised to be the best pleasure of you being away; a better pleasure even, perhaps, than seeing each other. Fool.

Yes, I really do feel remarkably stuffy. I had better work off once for all in this letter what are considerable arrears of irritation and coldness, which made it impossible for me even to miss you as it is right and natural to miss a friend. It's waste of time, all that. […]

I read your letter to Arthur with <u>immense</u> interest. Humphry, it does all sound good. […] I read with pleasure of the temple, the floating bullock-cart on the river at night, the new friends, that particular poet. I like Arthur too immensely myself to resent that you should have written to him first. After all, he is your older friend. But all that is my stuff too. Your ideas of women get so distorted sometimes that I think that you forget what a man I am. You don't need to write me sort of letter-home category descriptions, which are laborious – but I don't think you would. You know I like impressions better than facts. […] I want to hear about people, places, smells, colours, heat, emotions, animosities. In fact, what is current.

No doubt I am overbearing (you said so once). It is the overbearingness of a spoilt woman; I am having lately too good a time – I don't know why too good. I've put in some pretty dull times myself. I enjoy being a personality – I can say this to you because you obviously are being a personality among your new friends. This park is lovely and exhilarating to live in. I love London; living here is like being part of an orchestra. The park now is full of flowering trees, sun and a high wind which blows the trees about madly. The curtains – windows being open because I cannot bear to shut out all this – blow in all over the house, which is exasperating but somehow good.

I don't think I'll write you any of my news (or rather, about what is current) partly because you haven't yet asked for it (another small twinge of stuffiness), partly because I don't want any of your first letter to be taken up with commenting on it: I want to hear about you. And please write often, then I will.

A certain degree of love (peppered with indignation)
from
Elizabeth

You see, writing to me isn't one of your duties. It is one of your pleasures, my good man. […]

Why make me so cross? Why should I have to paint myself such a spoilt, unpleasant character? After all, if I were a prima donna or an actress, no more gifted on their lines than I am in my own, I should be allowed to scream and throw chairs about. I do hope being with good Indians will unlock your dread of what you used to call demonstrativeness; what I call spontaneity. They sound to me good and great people because they are unlocked. No wonder the English are so discountenanced by them. But you can be so much more than English yourself.

What is Chowringhee? Where are you living?

Elizabeth's desire to reprimand Humphry (he was not, under any circumstances, to treat her simply as a woman) was coupled with a wish to reconnect. To do this she needed to locate him in both psychological and physical space. Her love of travel and her penchant for word-pictures were further reasons for requesting him to colour in his surroundings. As Arthur Calder-Marshall wrote to Humphry after meeting Elizabeth for the first time in the spring of 1936: 'She combines being intelligent with the curiosity about people that only novelists and washerwomen have.'

Though Elizabeth had not seen India, she had ventured across its terrain in her imagination. As a child, she had devoured the jingoistic interpretation of Indian history to be found in G. A. Henty's adventure stories (ones aimed firmly at boys). The idea of the country crops up throughout her fiction: it is a convenient place for deaths, past friendships, and absent characters. The edgeland of India is used powerfully in the short story 'The Girl with a Stoop', which was published in 1941 shortly after Humphry's years in Calcutta. The story centres on a young woman, Tibbie, who is betrothed to a man working in India. As she walks the promenade of a seaside town, she is spotted by a rich invalid, Francis, and his cousin, Geoffrey. They invite her to tea. When questioned about what she writes to her fiancé, Tibbie confesses she has very little exciting to say. There was more tennis played than kisses landed in their courtship. Tibbie exposes her ill-preparedness for adulthood, marriage, and sex by not writing the right sort of letters to India.

Humphry's stop on the way to Calcutta had included the dusty pleasures of Port Said – the knife grinders, the sellers of dirty postcards, and a warm beer in a faux-French café. My trip east of Suez saw me sprinting through Doha airport to make my flight before collapsing into my seat with relief. This was the furthest point on my map, an emotional and geographical outpost. It was the journey that most excited me – anti-malarial tablets, the sound of crickets at night, food fried at the roadside, all spoke of adventure and reminded me of my childhood in Africa. Elizabeth's spirit had powerfully inhabited other locations; she had dominated my imagination on previous journeys. But Calcutta did not belong to her. If I was to meet Humphry as an individual, this was surely the place.

My first port of call was Presidency College itself (now Presidency University). Its fine old building, dating from 1875, sits amid dense trees just off a busy thoroughfare. Arched hallways, quadrangles, a

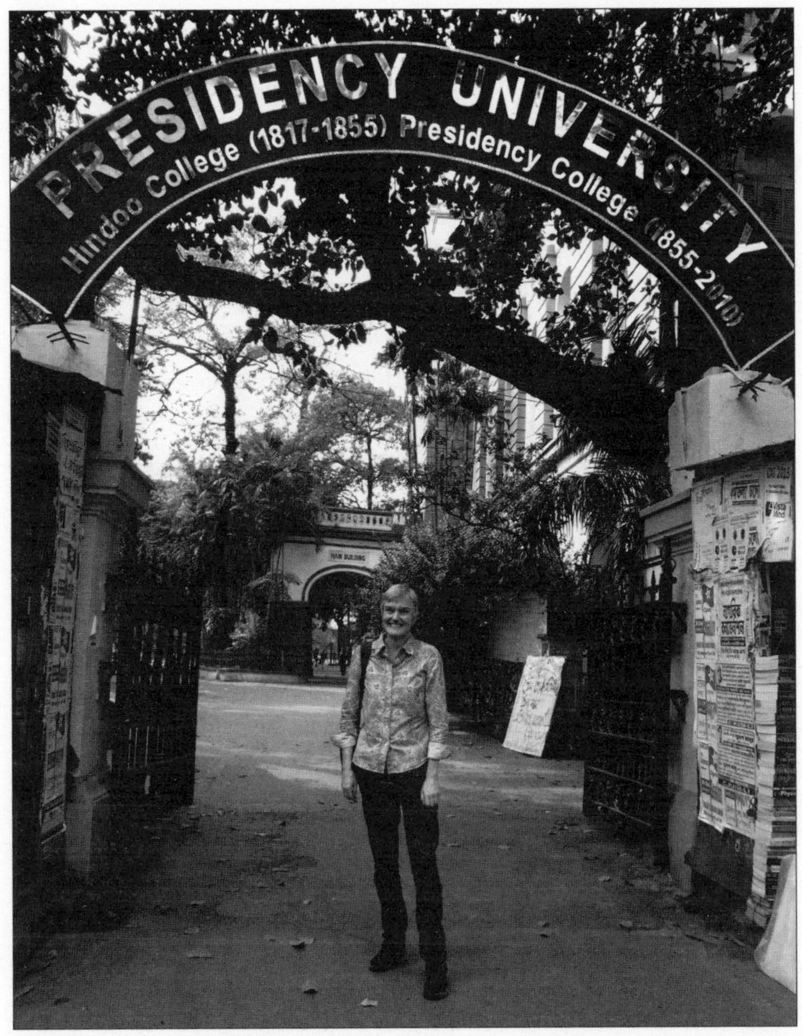

The author at Presidency University, Kolkata

mighty statue from the early nineteenth century of one of the founders, David Hare, are as they have been for generations. Yet inside: posters and student graffiti, a large mural, 'Do I Dare Disturb The Universe?', a plastic-chaired café with cheap dhosas and cans of Pepsi. And women, everywhere.

In Humphry's day, the students were all men, and there was not a single female professor. Now there are many, including the current Head of English. Over a cup of chai, she told me that there might be college magazines dating back to the 1930s, as well as books written by Humphry, in the college library. His book on Aristotle's *Poetics* is still on the reading list. 'No one explains tragedy better,' she said simply.

Half an hour later I was sitting in the library, my request for the yearbooks taken noiselessly into the stacks behind me. The room was stuffy – its tired blue paint had sweated through generations, uncooled by remote ceiling fans. Hanging askew were portraits of name-lost dignitaries from the cobwebby past. The librarian returned with several ancient volumes, tied together with fraying string, and placed them on my desk. Bound in crimson leather that crumbled at the touch, were the college magazines from the 1930s. The covers of some of them had been eaten away by weevils.

There was Humphry: his appointment announced, and an essay listed in the index at the start of the 1936 volume. 'House, Prof. A. Humphry: The Poetry of W. B. Yeats.' I turned to the page but the piece was gone; his wild swans of wisdom flown, presumably, into the twilight of some student's homework. All the other essays from 1936, on topics ranging from vitamins to Kipling to the Bengali peasant in debt were there in damp, yellowing splendour. A second piece written by Humphry about modern verse had also walked.

I then constructed as consolation a plausible reason for the essays' vanishings. Humphry had a reputation as a brilliant lecturer, and therefore, my tale went, the plagiarist had specifically targeted his contributions, rather than those written by anyone else. My spin on Humphry as a professor in Calcutta was not far from the truth. He did make a lasting impression on his students, none more so than on a young Satyajit Ray, who went on to become an outstanding figure of Indian cinema in the twentieth century.

In Andrew Robinson's biography of the film director, he describes Humphry thus:

> Of the British staff at Presidency College, Humphry House, who had written books on Dickens and Gerard Manley Hopkins, was quite an influence on his students at this time. Like a handful of other renegades in the last decade or so of the Raj, he rebelled against the colonial establishment. […] A few of his mock-exam questions are worth quoting for the peculiar flavour that they give of the last decade of the Raj in Calcutta:
>
> […] 2. Compare the Wife of Bath and Mr. Pickwick as bourgeois types. […]
>
> 4. Which is better, a code or a cipher? Give examples from other people's letters.
>
> 5. Expand the following statement to about twenty-five times its original length, bringing out the implications in such a way as to show that it is seditious: […] 'My faith in the People governing is, on the whole, infinitesimal; my faith in the People governed is, on the whole, illimitable.' (Dickens)
>
> One can see why House's students, Satyajit among them, liked him.

Elizabeth's attempts in early May 1936 to restore epistolary contact with Humphry were finally successful. A flurry of correspondence flowed between them in the next couple of months, though only Elizabeth's letters survive. On receiving news from Humphry one morning, Elizabeth replied by return. She was beginning to learn to type, despite a slight aversion to the typewriter: 'a clattery steel hedge between myself and half my faculties.' There is a sniff of indignation about his recent uncommunicative behaviour: 'Silences don't matter, but their quality does.'

Then she is on to telling him about friends, her reviewing, and a chance encounter with an old flame of hers, John Anderson. Nice enough, she feels, as being with him 'is like being in the sun'. But she prefers slightly 'savage' people with interesting things to say. Ever the storyteller, Elizabeth revisits Humphry's departure and writes a new version of this scene: gone is the 'terrible row' between them to be replaced by an assertion that they had parted on a good plane. Humphry's position further from Elizabeth's heart is evident throughout, and especially in her valediction: 'Very good luck to you, my dear, in all your undertakings.'

Elizabeth's next letter (12 June) is wildly different in tone. Their letters had crossed in the post and misunderstandings were refreshed. As a character explains in *The Death of the Heart*: 'Nothing arrives on paper as it started, and so much arrives that never started at all.' This letter describes Humphry in his friendships as 'suspicious as a Scotsman who feels his pocket may be picked'. She views his wish to blame sex for any problems in a relationship as 'a mean and muddled device to cover a deficiency of your own nature'. She tells him not to lecture her as she is 'not a bulliable person', and accuses him of bunk, priggishness, and falsity of feeling. Finally at the end, Elizabeth strikes a more conciliatory tone: 'Humility is, surely, becoming to both of us.'

This was the last time that Elizabeth scrutinised Humphry's character and conduct in such detail. And the last time that she spoke of the ways in which they had engaged with each other, and might continue to do so. Her liking for savage people did not stretch to them lacking civility. The letter was another attempt on Elizabeth's part to set the record straight, and so make sure that her version stood.

But these two letters – one friendly, one furious – mark not so much an ending, as a transition. Humphry's departure had irrevocably changed their relationship, and brought into being new, liminal positions for both him and Elizabeth. The crossing of a bar, be it of sand or emotion. But one crucial thing would always remain between them.

In one of her letters to Humphry in the early summer of 1936, Elizabeth writes: 'I see now that though feeling may be suspended it never dies or terminates -- that there is in a sense no past in it. I said more than I knew in the House in Paris when I said that the past was simply a present elsewhere. Feeling, throughout life, seems to me to be continuous -- the same, or almost the same towards people or objects -- turned, simply one way or another, but seldom or never turned off.'

Feeling would endure, in some shape, in years to come. The electric charge that I sensed when I first read the letters was just another manifestation of it. Their past is my present – felt here, there, elsewhere.

While Humphry and Elizabeth were exploring new worlds, Madeline was shrunk back to remembered rooms. She returned with one-year-old Rachel to her parents' house in Eastbourne having given up the cottage in Devon for good. She was seven months pregnant with their second child. Her taut horizon was stretched by one possibility – that of joining Humphry in India. The issue was something the couple had clearly discussed before his departure. A letter to her from Humphry in March 1936 reads: 'This is no country for a wife. The idea of you coming here with Rachel and x seems now wildly ridiculous: the social objections I foresaw are doubly applicable from closer quarters and domestic objections heap up every day, […] keep then in mind as a serious possibility that you should come here alone when you think Rachel and x can be left.'

Madeline's desire to go to Calcutta showed both her love for Humphry, and an adventurous spirit undimmed by parenthood. The trip would also give her the opportunity to claim Humphry back, once and for all, from Elizabeth. The practical arrangements for childcare in such an event could surely be made. The trip was the perfect and possibly only opportunity she would have to go back to Asia. Her compass already swung East; it was the place of her birth and childhood. The dream of a return – to a land of heat and glare – must have made her chilly walk along the seafront with the pram that much more bearable.

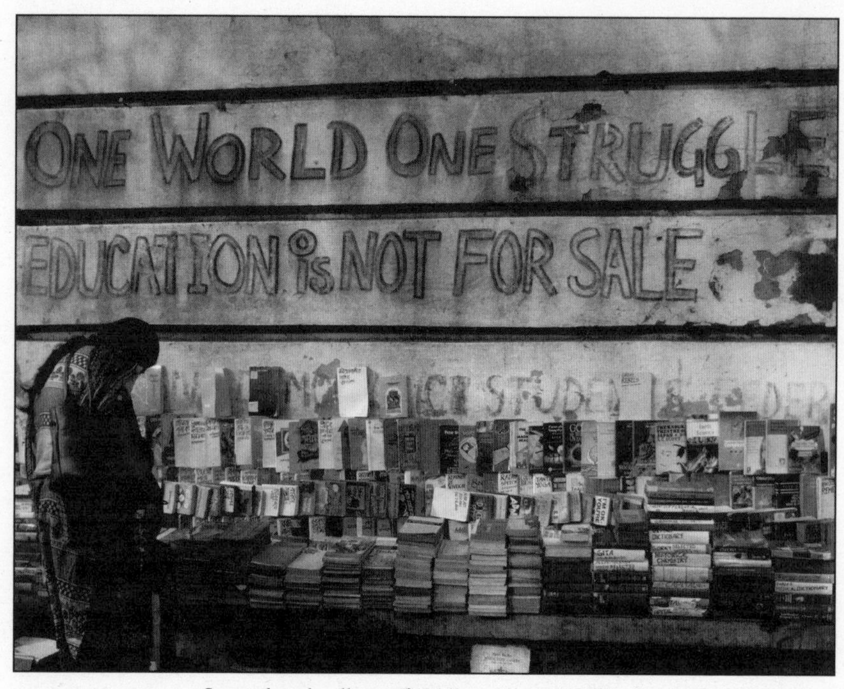

Street bookseller, off College Street, Kolkata

Chapter 12

Calcutta: *The Heat of the Day*

A cluster of bookshops lines College Street in the heart of Kolkata's university district. Das Gupta Booksellers ('125 glorious years' beam their plastic bags) is thick with books – in glass-fronted cabinets, in open shelves, in piles. These rise to a ceiling stuck with flies and sorry-looking fans. A counter meets the visitor, behind which a slow flow of ageing gentlemen, bespectacled and balding, drift about their task of finding the requested books. Into the bowels of the shop, up improbable ladders, or round a spiral staircase that disappears into the floor above. The student in front of me requests a book on prestressed concrete; another buys *The Wise World of English Proverbs*.

I have the names 'Elizabeth Bowen' and 'Humphry House' written on a scrap of paper, which I show to the quiet man serving me.

His eyes graze the first name. He shakes his head, 'Elizabeth…' Her surname in his mouth rhymes with 'cow'. 'No, I do not know her.' Then seeing Humphry House's name, he lights up, 'Yes, very famous author! We have one, maybe two, of his books.'

He turns and has a short conversation with a colleague who disappears up the perilous staircase. A few minutes later, his colleague comes down, empty-handed. A few words pass between them. Looking up, he catches my eye, nods, 'Wait for Humphry House. He is coming.'

June 1936

Humphry lay in a hospital bed, thin and feverish. There was no breeze to cut through the air of illness that hung over the ward. The attack of dysentery had come upon him quite suddenly on his return to the city from the cool hills of Darjeeling. Like many expatriates, he had gone north for a few weeks to escape the worst of the summer heat. Now he was almost too weak to feed himself and the thin soups he was given he found impossible to digest. It required a huge effort to move and his hand trembled across the page in the few letters he wrote.

His illness marked more than a physical low point to his time in Calcutta – it heralded a further shift in the relationship with Elizabeth. Her letter of 12 June, which had chased Humphry across India up to Darjeeling with indignant stamps being added to the envelope at every post office, was the last hectoring letter she wrote him. Like a monsoon wind, she had blown herself out. Elizabeth's redrawing of the epistolary boundaries between them saw a quite different letter two weeks later.

She had just received a letter from Humphry, written shortly before his illness. She glanced at this briefly before a sensational day of cricket at Lord's between England and India with Alan. Then she reread the letter twice whilst luxuriating in her pre-dinner bath. Finally she sat down to reply. It sees her, probably unwittingly, sticking the bucolic knife into Humphry as he lay in his sweat-drenched bed in Calcutta.

<u>EB to HH</u>

2 Clarence Terrace
29 June [1936]

I got back from the country on Saturday afternoon to find your very very good letter of June 15th – 16th, with the picture of Calcutta and various other things. [...]

You make me see Calcutta very plainly -- how correctly, of course, I shall never know. But you make it vivid: I almost experience it. How odd, this business of constructing a picture inside oneself, according to some one else's directions -- which is what a description amounts to -- is. I mean, what a scrap-drawer of images one draws on -- images come by in the queerest ways. In this case -- water-colours in drawing rooms, lantern slides at missionary lectures, illustrations to missionary magazines, uncharacteristically concrete phrases in Anglo-Indians' talk, rather crude descriptions in Anglo-Indian novels, travel circulars, snapshot-albums of travelled majors' wives. It is like ransacking everything from rare editions to shop catalogues to make a Surrealist <u>collage</u>. [...]

I've been to a good many places since I wrote last -- Hythe, then Norfolk the week-end before last. Stayed with some Anglo-Irish relations, Hubert Butler's uncle and aunt, in a very lovely Georgian red brick house, with a P. G. Wodehouse, Blandings Castle garden with expanses of mown lawn, a vast blue cedar, two showering patriarch copper beech. Cousin Bertha Clarke is unnaturally rich -- as my family go -- positive, punctual, domineering but immensely [sic] kind, and gives one a lovely time. There's something refreshing, I find, about formality sometimes, when it's combined with a high degree of comfort -- a sort of 'whose service is perfect freedom'. The bland beauty of the surroundings, the really idyllic weather and knowing exactly what to do, and that what one might say was of interest to nobody made the week-end restful. I bathed off a sandy shore in the morning -- Sunday -- and spent the afternoon on the broads in a motor boat -- conducted by Cousin Bertha with immense decision. How magnificent, bright and narcotic the Broads are. I should like to be back on them. A sail, a Perpendicular church tower, a fishing rod, or a human head appearing with equal beauty, oddness and lack of reason against the blue air above the rushes.... The reflections translate everything: I mean there is a sort of democracy of strangeness. A young woman in a sky-blue satin dress walked past along the bank, by a row of poplars, while we were having tea, like a Renoir figure. Nothing could have been better than that triumphantly inappropriate dress, which was long and swept the ground. [...]

Then last week -- it was still very hot and fine -- I went to Dorset: Abbotsbury. Do you know it? It's lovely. Austere but smiling, as all Dorset is. It has a swannery to visit, and an exotic garden -- a sort of island garden, with no house, in a warm fold of the otherwise bare hills, just inland: lush and dark and trickling, with palms and water-lilies, waxy vermilion sprays of things and arum lilies growing above their reflections out of turgid dark-green pools. The Abbotsbury inn is small and excellent: candle-lit, with a small bosky garden behind, matted with yellow roses, with a small fountain dripping over a slimey [sic] green statue. I got back from their [sic] on Saturday, the day I found your letter and saw the match.

[...] We drove John Hayward down to spend the day at Buttinghill yesterday. The weather again was perfect, the house

its best. They gave me a big bunch of roses and sweet williams to take home, which was very imaginative. John Hayward is fun to motor with as he goes out so little that his observation and curiosity are immense. Alan says we chatter, as we no doubt do. We drove home through that Cudham-Westerham country, which is quite lovely, isn't it -- I remember you saying you thought of living there, and I do see why. Those untrodden-looking valleys slipping liquidly past in the evening light were a dream, and those steep deep light-shot woods.

I must stop now.
My love, my dear
Elizabeth.

If Elizabeth had written a list of things to make Humphry feel homesick, she could not have done it any better. This letter is richer in sensuous description than any other Elizabeth sent him – it reads like a page from her best fiction. Different also is her approach, with its focus on the exterior, the natural world, rather than psychological, internal spaces. And though she addresses Humphry, she seems to look beyond him. Here is a letter for which posterity-conscious Elizabeth might have imagined the afterlife of publication.

Elizabeth had strong relationships with pens, tables, rooms, as much as with people. In this letter she explains that her writing could not be done without her 'almost erotic fondling of the pen'. This shapes and stimulates what is to come. Typing is more mechanical, less a part of her: 'A sentence becomes not me the moment it is on paper, and the unsympathetic clatter of keys has something astringent about it.' Humphry's position further from her heart is evident both in what and how she writes. This letter is typed – no more erotic fondling for him.

That Elizabeth was moving on from Humphry emotionally was

evident soon afterwards. The summer of 1936 saw a shift in her relationship with Goronwy Rees. Charming, excitable, and flighty, Rees was, like Humphry, a younger man of modest means. A journalist and novelist, he was later associated with the Cambridge Five spy ring through his friend Guy Burgess. However, Elizabeth's romantic interest in Rees was blindsided by fellow writer Rosamond Lehmann during a house party at Bowen's Court in September.

Bowen's Court in the 1930s

Elizabeth wrote a vast, fuming letter to Berlin about the episode – how poor cousin Noreen had been forced to hear the nocturnal shenanigans between Rees and Lehmann as the wall that divided her room from Lehmann's was 'no more sound-proof than a paper screen'. The young, virginal girl lay frozen with embarrassment throughout. Elizabeth says, possibly as much about herself as about Noreen: 'we Irish are squeamish and those two nights were trying for her.' Indeed it is not Elizabeth's wounded sexual pride but the violated house that lies at the heart of the letter. The couple had 'crashed across the sensibility and dignity […] which the house creates and imposes on me as it does on everyone else'. She concludes: 'This is no house to go creeping about at nights. We have had all sorts of crooks and sex-maniacs here but it's never happened before. I feel those two outraged something.'

Yet Elizabeth's aversion to a man tiptoeing through the house in the dark is partly about his destination: the young lover did not stop at her room. In her letter to Humphry of 12 July 1933, written at the emotional height of their affair, she said how much she wished he had knocked on her door in the night. Indeed, she thought she heard his particular step on the landing, got out of bed, and went to check if he was there. This sexually awakened Elizabeth could imagine throwing off the blanket of propriety that the house tucked in around her. But that night, as during the Lehmann/Rees episode, Elizabeth lay in her chilly bed alone.

In the autumn of 1936, once his illness was behind him, Humphry moved to a new home. This was on Lord Sinha Road, within shouting distance of Calcutta's Anglican Cathedral, St Paul's, with its beautiful Burne-Jones stained-glass window. There he shared a borrowed flat for a few months with John Auden, the geologist and brother of poet Wystan (W. H.). John Auden worked many years for the Royal Geological Society of India. Just a year later, he would join an expedition to the Karakoram area of the Himalayas undertaking the most comprehensive mapping of the area ever attempted. One of the men who accompanied him, Eric Shipton, was to write *Blank on the Map* (1938) about the trip, a classic of early mountaineering writing.

Though largely undertaken for scientific reasons, these adventures mirrored the involvement of some members of the Auden generation in the Spanish Civil War. (Stephen Spender's brother, Michael, was also involved in some of the Himalayan expeditions.) Both allowed an expression of heroic masculinity, a return to the pre-war pages of the Henty novels they had all read as boys – tales of British triumph, male bonding and derring-do. Though Humphry would have preferred to sit at the bottom of a mountain with a cigarette and a book, his time in Calcutta was similar in several ways. A trip into the unknown, it also facilitated a return to the homosocial worlds in which he felt most comfortable – the patriarchal framework of empire and Indian traditions both positioned women firmly below men. Here he was not going to be threatened by a woman with a big personality like Elizabeth.

Humphry and John were almost the same age, with similar backgrounds and sensibilities. They became good friends, sharing both 'pro-Indian feelings', and nights on the town. In an ironic echo of King Duncan in *Macbeth*, he wrote of Auden: 'He is a man on whom I would build an absolute trust.' The young men lived in a modernist flat which came with a Boulestin cook and had paintings by Duncan Grant and Ronald Dunlop on the walls. Here was civilised style: the colonial good life, which Humphry loved for its comforts and despised for what it represented.

This tension was a feature of his time in Calcutta; he struggled with where and how to fit in, an echo of his feelings when he first went to Ireland to visit Elizabeth: 'I am rather lost among all the people I meet: I see quite clearly that it's to be either Bengalis or Europeans. Feet can't be kept in both camps.' John was better acclimatised: 'He's off bathing at one of the clubs I won't join', laments Humphry sitting in the flat alone, opposite a statue of Molière.

The prospect of a swim at precisely this sort of club was the perfect end to a hot day in Kolkata for me. A few stops on the metro, a short walk past the vendors of guavas and potato balls, and towards the green calm of the Tollygunge Club. Thanks to the energetic organisation and contacts of my travelling companion, I was staying at one of the three clubs that formed the nucleus of colonial Calcutta, at one of the clubs Humphry refused to join. The coincidence was pleasing.

I had arrived at the Tolly (as it is affectionately called) in the middle of the night; I had noticed nothing more than tall trees, and a water feature. Coming out of the room the following morning, I was greeted by blush bougainvillea and birdsong. A few early golfers strolled up the heavily watered course. Huge trees cocooned the clubhouse. There were pink hollyhocks redolent of the Cotswolds. Inside, a bridge room, chandeliers, quiet footfall. If John Auden had walked past on his way to the pool, woollen trunks under his arm, I would not have been surprised.

The pool that afternoon was a delight. It had something of the Victorian baths about it, high roofed metal work, and wooden, saloon-style swing doors in the changing rooms. A light film of laterite on the surface, the chubby children of the affluent bobbing in the water. I did a few lengths and then had a Kingfisher beer in the open-sided bar which debouches straight out onto the lush golf course. My fellow drinkers were mostly Indians riding the success of the country's economic boom. The mood was complacent, the pace slow. It felt lazy miles away from the palpable present of Kolkata earlier that day.

Back in England, Madeline was making plans for her trip to Calcutta, filling her trunk with books and contraception. The two young girls (my mother only a few months old) stayed with the Church grandparents, with a nanny to look after them. While Humphry had worried that the presence of two infants in India might be problematic socially and domestically, Madeline may well have considered other issues more important in the decision to leave them behind. One of these would have been the health of the babies. A long voyage followed by a harsh climate and the possibility of illness must have been factors. Humphry himself, a man in his twenties, had recently been bedridden with dysentery. The risks were that much greater for children. Madeline could comfort herself that her time away from the children was only going to be for a few months. It would not be years of damaging separation such as that experienced by six-year-old Rudyard Kipling and his three-year-old sister Alice.

Just before she sailed for Bombay in October 1936, Humphry wrote to her of the 'mission house in the slums' that would be their home for most of her stay: 'The street outside is full of lepers and beggars and people at the point of death, and cows of course.' At least they would have a flat to themselves. Trees and gardens surrounding the bulky colonial building gave the mission a more genteel feel, despite its location. Today it still acts as a Christian college – its porticoed facade and cool, arched corridors quite unchanged. Above the main door, in firm lines of crimson paint is the following quotation from St Paul: 'I press toward the mark.' One wonders whether Humphry, the one-time deacon, passed under the words every day on his way up to the flat.

Madeline followed a different route to the East; her vessel a grander one than the one in which Humphry had sailed. There was an on-board band that struck up for evening dances, a swimming pool, and a 'cinema apparatus' that was rigged up in the dining room. Her table at dinner included the ship's Assistant Purser, a munition maker and a 'great flopsy bunny of a woman' who suffered badly from seasickness. The vessel docked at Bombay, after which she caught a train across India. She arrived in Calcutta full of vigour and having already made friends en route, with an Indian high court judge and his wife. Other new friends followed, including Minnie Bonnerjee, reputed to be the first Indian woman to learn to fly. Madeline hesitated for only a moment before she too went up in a tiny aircraft and flew across the city, its outlying villages, the plantations of mango and banana, and the Ganges blood red in the setting sun.

Freed of all domestic duties, Madeline could enjoy Humphry's company anew. Elizabeth's presence in their marriage was dissipating, and Madeline was no longer in an environment that demanded she act principally for the well-being of others. It was a happy time for the couple. She and Humphry and his friends spent evenings at Firpo's with its fine food and pseudo-French furniture. After dinner, the glittering chandeliers were dimmed, and coloured spotlights splashed across the revellers on the only sprung dance floor in the city.

Cultural offerings varied in quality; T. S. Eliot's *Murder in the Cathedral* was performed with more enthusiasm than skill by a group of missionaries; the Gonsalez Italian Grand Opera Company, which performed seven different operas in a single week, was very accomplished. The fading pomp and ceremony of empire saw the couple dress up (Humphry in borrowed tails and an ill-fitting white topee, Madeline in a blue and white georgette frock) to welcome the Viceroy of India. They endured a display of troops followed by two hours sweating in the sun as the band played on. Madeline noted indifferently: 'I have done my bit as wife of a Government official.'

A black-and-white photograph bears witness to her lively pleasure in India. It shows Madeline, Humphry, and John Auden sitting round a camp fire at Rishikesh, in the foothills of the Himalayas, over the Christmas holiday. (They took a plum pudding to eat on the day itself.) On the right is John, quietly folded, fingers knit, legs crossed. He wears little round spectacles, a shirt buttoned up to the neck, a tweed jacket. He couldn't look more like a prep school Classics teacher if he tried. He gazes into the fire, as does Humphry, who sits in the middle. His hands are similarly together though his pose is more unkempt. There is a slight smile on his fine, square face. But the energetic centre of the photograph is Madeline, head up, relaxed in her chair, cigarette in hand. She looks beautiful and content – her dark eyes aglow.

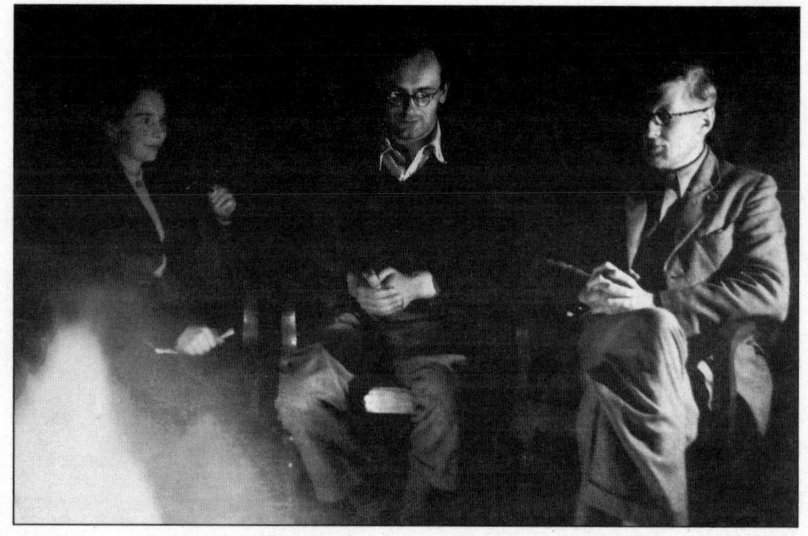

Left to right: Madeline, Humphry and
John Auden in the Himalayan foothills, 1936

Madeline was very popular with Humphry's friends – Sudhin Datta, in particular, was smitten with her. He wrote her passionate letters on her departure, describing himself as 'unbalanced as a schoolboy experiencing his first infatuation'. He had her horoscope prepared and sent her the results. The fortune teller, he writes, 'emphasized your goodness and generosity and remarked that it was your unfailing sympathy and candour which made you most attractive to people. [...] He spoke of your accomplishments and artistic leanings and thought you might achieve some sort of a name as a writer'. At the time, Madeline must have dismissed such a future for herself. But the prediction proved to be far more accurate than she could have imagined.

Madeline was similarly taken with Sudhin – Calcutta giving her the freedom to enjoy an intense bond with a married man. Humphry was not aggrieved or surprised at this development; he, too, admitted to being half in love with Sudhin. Besides, he was enjoying a flirtation of his own – with the actress and dancer Sadhona Bose. She starred as the protagonist in a performance of *Savitri* by the Calcutta Art Players in May 1937 shortly after Madeline's departure for England. The programme of the show reveals more than the shapely figure of Sadhana Bose. Underneath her name, in Madeline's writing, is the following: 'On whom H. had a great crush, 1937.' She seems unperturbed by his wandering eye. Neither an Anglo-Irish novelist nor a Bengali actress would threaten the marriage.

After five months away, it was time for Madeline to return home. On the voyage, the steamer stopped off at Colombo. She went to the house she had lived in as a child, revisited the fragrant garden of her childhood. Then it was back onto the SS *Domala* for the long voyage to Europe. (The steamship would become famous three years later – on a voyage from Antwerp to the UK in March 1940 the ship was bombed by the Luftwaffe and sunk. This was the first naval action of the war in the English Channel and resulted in more than a hundred fatalities, most of them Indian seamen.)

Madeline's homecoming suitcase was full of saris, ornaments, exotic tales. These fascinated her eldest daughter in particular. Rachel was determined, when she grew up, to go to India. Years later, she was to meet a young Anglo-Indian man and marry him. The family compass swung East once again.

Elizabeth's personal life in the wake of Humphry was as colourful as the park through her window. It seemed that now a more complex emotional and sexual self paced the rooms of her heart, one open to adventure. Following the death of the affair with Goronwy Rees, her quick-settling eye fell on a quite different person. This was May Sarton, the American poet. A naive twenty-five-year-old, Sarton fell for Elizabeth, 'this extraordinary woman', with the same wide-eyed zeal with which she fell for many others. Elizabeth liked young, clever, sexy people – being admired she did well. Sarton writes in her appreciative essay of Elizabeth: 'I understood that earlier in her life she had loved at least one woman, but I gathered that that period was over.' The time-slipped contradiction of this sentence is typical Elizabeth – she tells Sarton her sapphic days are behind her, while she soaks up the adoration of a young woman.

The similarities between Humphry and May are numerous – they were very much the same age when they met Elizabeth; they were bright and spirited; occasionally immature and selfish. They were both insecure wordsmiths who engaged Elizabeth in their work and were desperate for her endorsement of it. Humphry wrote to her about his plans for a novel set in the villages of County Cork. May sent her poems, including one called 'Portrait by Holbein' which was dedicated to Elizabeth and is a barely disguised description of her.

Of this Sarton later wrote:

> It took me years to understand that the poem that one writes out of love and brings to its subject as a present is not always as delightful to receive as it is to give. For poems of this kind are always pleas and must, often, be warded off out of kindness. It was one of Elizabeth's graces that she could accept them quite simply as gifts, and allow herself, momentarily, to be carried on their stream.

May lived for a few months in a famous building in Rye called Jeake's House which, in the 1930s, was owned by Conrad Aiken, the American poet and critic. T. S. Eliot, Radclyffe Hall, E. H. Benson all came through the fine wide door. May's room 'looked out over the roofs and chimney pots to the wide lonely marshes, misty in the moonlight'. It was here that the two women spent the night together. A full moon, a big bed, an attic room in Rye – Sarton's description of the night with Elizabeth leaves no romantic cliché unexpressed. But that was where it ended; it was just one of the 'sudden irrational attachments' to which both women were susceptible.

The morning after the night before often gives birth to a letter. Elizabeth wrote to May telling her 'the truth', possibly of other preferences and attachments. A final letter about the affair came to Elizabeth a few months later from Virginia Woolf, who asked drily whether she had 'despatched that goose May Sarton'.

Yet even as she flirted with Sarton, Elizabeth carried the germ of another attraction in her heart. She would shortly change direction again, and sail across a body of water to meet a young man. This new liaison would bear fruit that summer and would dominate one of the most unusual letters she wrote to Humphry.

A photograph of Elizabeth taken at Bowen's Court in 1937 sees her lounging on the lawn, face shielded from the sun. The tall trees surrounding her home are visible in the background. Snaking across the grass towards her is Sean O'Faolain, a young Irish writer with whom Elizabeth had a brief but intense affair that took hold in that summer. O'Faolain, like Humphry, was clever, creative, and married. The men were also similarly framed – both in physique and in style of spectacles.

Apart from a short note at the beginning of 1938 asking him when he is coming home, this is the last of Elizabeth's surviving letters to India. The numbered pages indicate that the first half of the letter is missing, though who acted as censor on this occasion is not clear. Added later on the back of the paper, in a different hand is, 'Fragment: 1937'.

EB to HH

Undated [Summer 1937]

I have no news, except news of a very personal sort: England seems almost as far away to me as it must to you because I am, we are, someone and I are, very much in love. It doesn't feel like a love affair, it feels like a marriage. I tell you, partly because you seem to be the only person I can tell, partly because it may account for a sort of newslessness and vagueness in my letters about life in general, and I should hate you to think that arose from any apathy about writing to you. Indeed, my dear, this only makes me feel a stronger affection for you, both retrospectively and in the present. This seems to be the completion of everything I ever saw shadows of before. He is Irish, and lives in Ireland. He is the best (I think, without prejudice) of the younger Irish writers. I only read any book of his last summer, for the first time: then I thought, I must meet this person and nearly wrote him a fan letter, then didn't. Then this last April, when he was in London for a week, staying at the Thackeray Hotel and working at the B.M., he wrote me a fan letter, about my books. We met at the end of that week. Since then we have always met in Ireland, at B. Court or in Dublin. He was fighting with the Irish in the Anglo Irish war, then with the Republicans in the Civil War. He is not at all like anybody's idea of an ex-gunman, he is a very gentle person with fair hair – or hair, at least, about the colour of mine. We are the same age – and doing such very different things in the same years of our lives. Nothing is easy; he has a very nice wife he has been married to for ten years, and they have got one little girl of five. He would hate to upset her just as much as I should hate to upset Alan. So we are trying to pay for our happiness by being very good. We are both, also, by nature extremely secretive, which helps. This, as you can imagine, makes me more homesick for Ireland than ever: I feel wedded to the country, and rooted there.

That is the story. I do hope the police need not read this letter. I must stop now, or this will be overweight. Don't be cross or hurt that I scold you about that letter; it's a testimony to affection (however annoying a testimony) as you will surely see. Write again soon, Humphry dear. Nothing would ever make me not want your letters.

I do hope it's not too hellishly, hellishly hot. I wonder if you're in Clacutta [sic] at the moment.

My best love.

Elizabeth

Thousands of miles away, Humphry must have felt a tang of bitterness – it is never easy to hear one has been replaced in the affections of a former lover. A glimpse of Humphry's reaction to the news of Elizabeth's new love surfaces in a letter to Madeline in July 1937: 'By the way, I had a letter from Elizabeth the other day, after a long interval, which has eased – in fact abolished a difficult situation there: you have nothing now ever even to ask yourself questions about.' If he felt jealous of O'Faolain as he read the letter, he does not reveal this to Madeline. The information about receiving Elizabeth's letter is tossed out casually, its contents not discussed. Madeline is told to feel safe, but stay silent. One way of controlling a conversation is not to let it happen.

It might seem odd that the person Elizabeth chose to tell of her new affair was Humphry, a recent ex-lover. There was, of course, the simple, acknowledged need to tell someone, anyone, and he was conveniently far from the action. She might also have wished to taunt him with the information – even if her pen was not raised with vengeful intent, one senses a hint of pleasure in the tale.

Another reason for telling him lay in Elizabeth's feeling, evident in both her fiction and non-fiction, that experience means nothing until it repeats itself. Elizabeth's affairs were not simply different chapters in her life: in each new one, there was a fundamental part of the last relationship that was filtered and re-experienced, which added shape to the current one. Furthermore, with what happens in the present, you can add colour to the past. That was why she both feels a 'stronger affection' for Humphry now, and why she states: 'This seems to be the completion of everything I ever saw shadows of before.'

With O'Faolain, Elizabeth was having the type of affair that was impossible with Humphry – one that existed in the wings, wholly outside matrimony. Yet the diction of marriage is central to the letter. Though they are both bound to other people the quality of the connection makes it feel 'like a marriage'. O'Faolain's presence in her heart has burnished her feelings for Ireland; she is 'wedded to the country'. The Irishness they had in common, although wildly different in nature, 'rooted' her. Their shared idiom was the vowel-memory of the land, as well as the more prosaic language of love.

With Madeline back in England, Humphry embarked on a new chapter in Calcutta. He hadn't suddenly become a saint but he was more settled in the wake of Madeline's visit. He writes appreciatively to her: 'You have given me what I wanted in my rages as a child. You used to take charge of them, of my horridness. I've remembered several times lately that night in Charlotte Street when I rolled over naked on the floor and you poured water over me.' It is an intriguing glimpse of their shared past and of Madeline's no-nonsense behaviour towards him.

Now at a distance both in time and space, Humphry can reflect on the qualities of his wife, and crucially, tell her about them.

Meanwhile in England, the Hopkins book had finally been published. Elizabeth wrote to Berlin about it, saying she was 'so glad' the work was finished and being well-received, though she wouldn't be reading it in a hurry: 'G. M. H. fills me with horror and claustrophobia. As far as I am concerned, he utterly destroys sensation of any kind. And what does he mean by "inscape"?'

Though relaxed in his dhoti at home, Humphry was finding the starched collar of the government servant increasingly uncomfortable. He found that his political sympathies and sense of outrage at police tactics could no longer be squared with his job. As a result, in April 1937, he resigned from Presidency College. He received from 'his loving students' a piece of cloth printed with a valediction: 'You won our hearts the day you came: an Englishman, you never made us feel for a moment that you belonged to a different race; and we found in you a most inspiring teacher, sympathetic and kind, whom we learnt to love in return. It was a pleasure to read under you: a greater pleasure still to know you and have you as a friend.'

Though Humphry's employment with the ICS was at an end, this did not alter his feelings about the way the corrupt system worked. Beyond the interception of his correspondence, it was manifest in more sinister ways. At one point, there was a rumour that he was a Communist agent (like his friend Michael Carritt), a notion that both amused and irritated Humphry. He was sometimes followed round the city, and would come out of his home to find a man idly sitting on a wall, waiting, watching. When in Kolkata myself, I could not escape occasional uneasy feelings of spying on him, of tracking his footsteps. It was a sensation heightened by the knowledge of what Humphry wrote as soon as he left the ICS – a satirical pamphlet about spying.

As Humphry was writing *I Spy with My Little Eye*, he maintained an almost paranoid secrecy about the project. In his smoke-filled letters running up to publication, he refers to it as 'the other thing', or simply '*I*'. The pamphlet attacked the systemic surveillance of the time, drawing both on Humphry's experiences in Calcutta and on his erudition – there were numerous esoteric and literary references. Published in November 1937, the pamphlet was well-received. One newspaper, the *Amrita Bazar Patrika*, called it 'brilliant', and a 'modern little classic'. (*I Spy with My Little Eye* has, in fact, just been reissued in India after more than eighty years; an acknowledgement of its unique importance as a record of the last days of Empire in the city.)

In the publication, Humphry dealt playfully with the very sections of literary texts – passages by Wordsworth and Milton – that were deemed possibly seditious by the government. For Humphry, the text as it originally appeared was sacrosanct. Whoever takes up the scissors to edit, and for whatever reason, is guilty of a crime.

When he left Presidency, and until his return to England in 1938, Humphry taught at Ripon College, a private institution. Though it was less prestigious, it had the key benefit of being independent. He was no longer one of the 'heaven-born' – he was an English professor, pure and simple. Here the classes were bigger, the standard lower. In the photograph of Ripon College, staff and students, which hangs on the landing in my parents' house, Humphry sits right in the middle of the front row. His is the only white face among almost fifty others. He looks relaxed, and pleased with life; here is importance, but not self-importance.

Nowadays, Ripon goes by the name of Surendranath College. Its slightly dreary looking main building rises a few steps from a chaotic side street in Northern Kolkata. Here are no tall trees or Victorian

Humphry with staff and students of Ripon College, Calcutta, 1937

statues. As I watched the students spill out from the narrow doorway, I was approached by a man in his sixties who asked me why I was there. When I explained Humphry's historic connection with the college, he immediately offered to show me round.

We wandered past huge classrooms, with steeply raked rudimentary benches and blackboards full of equations. Then down corridors cramped with students, up steps, then more steps, and finally to the library where there was nothing of Humphry to be found. Throughout our tour, my guide, a Professor of Bengali, regaled me with stories of great Bengalis who had passed through the halls. Did I know Hiren Mukherjee? I had to admit I did not. I was filled in on the renowned politician, a tale which led to another story, more history being told, then time rewound further, back to the era of Humphry, 'a true son' of the college.

At my departure, the professor clutched his heart and said, 'I am so proud of you. You are being so good to your grandfather.' This was a reaction I had encountered several times in Kolkata. Being there, finding information, was showing care for Humphry the person, my relation, rather than just interest in House the historical figure. I had not, before the trip, thought I was coming to 'find' Humphry, let alone Madeline, in Kolkata. It was my eyes and head, not my heart, that I intended to use. To see where he had lived and worked would help me understand context, climate, colour.

In her book, *A Time in Rome,* Elizabeth describes exactly what I was hoping to do: 'In Rome I wondered how to break down the barrier between myself and happenings outside *my* memory. I was looking for splinters of actuality in a shifting mass of experience other than my own. Time is one kind of space; it creates distance.' Finding splinters of information in the teeming mass of life that is modern Kolkata; bridging the gaps of space, time, distance: those had been my aims.

However, when I spoke of my grandfather's bond with the city, my trip was inevitably seen as a voyage into the heart of the family: it was all about my relationship with him. The barriers I was being asked to break down were not just between myself and Humphry's imagined past, but between myself and my constructed version of him. I found myself being forced, gently, kindly, into a reappraisal of my grandfather. Just as Humphry had imagined transformations taking place in India, so I too had experienced them. The light in which I viewed things had changed. East of Suez, the light was brighter.

P. & O. R.M.S. "STRATHNAVER" 22,500 TONS.
INDIA AND AUSTRALIA MAIL AND PASSENGER SERVICE.

Homecoming: the postcard Humphry sent to friends and family telling of his return

The cottage on the fringes of the forest in the 1930s

Chapter 13

Ashdown Forest: *The Last September*

I visit an uncatalogued archive, my mother's memories of her childhood. We sit together in my parents' kitchen, topping and tailing gooseberries. From their high perch on the cupboards, a row of Staffordshire figures watches, blandly. There is a rack of Welsh love spoons and an African carving on the pale blue wall. A broken dishwasher stores onions and potatoes from the allotment. The smell of fish pie, the blurring of an ill-tuned radio, fill the air.

Speaking in her clear strong voice is my mother. 'It was a red-brick cottage in Sussex on the edge of Ashdown Forest. The closest village was Maresfield, about three miles away. That was where we were living when Did came back from India. He came up from the lane, then up a steep flight of stone steps to the front door, box hedges on either side. Instead of coming in, he first looked through the window into the sitting room. It was a lovely room – a big fireplace and coconut matting on the floor. I was scampering about saying "Helen running fast! Helen running fast!" That was his first sight of me. How strange to think I was walking and talking before I knew him.'

My mother sighs. The crack of memory closes over. We lapse into separate silences, while our hands continue to pick in unison at the pale green fruit.

May 1938

The P. & O. RMS *Strathnaver*, all 22,500 tons of her, chugged up the Thames Estuary towards Tilbury Docks. It was May 1938 and Humphry was returning home. Ill health, the savage climates of Calcutta, and homesickness, had all played their part in his early departure. The Britain he saw from the deck seemed the same to the eye but lay differently, askew. Major political storms crackled across Europe.

Three months after Humphry's departure in 1936, the Spanish Civil War had broken out. Many saw the war not only as a question of ideological differences between socialism and fascism, but also about the future of civilisation itself. Politicised by the crisis, active in their response, were many prominent figures in the literary world – from George Orwell to Virginia Woolf, E. M. Forster to Christopher Isherwood. The poet Stephen Spender, a friend of both Humphry and Elizabeth, became involved in the war, going to Spain twice in 1937. He wrote: 'The struggle of the Republicans has seemed a struggle for the conditions without which the writing and reading of poetry are almost impossible in modern society.'

Elizabeth was not, like Virginia Woolf, organising fundraisers for the citizens of bombed Bilbao. The shocks of Spain did not crash into her home as they did into her friend's: Woolf's nephew, Julian Bell, was killed in the fighting. Elizabeth's horror of Mussolini, apparent in her letter of 1934 after her visit to Rome, she felt most powerfully when she was in Italy. When back at home, she seemed less engaged with foreign affairs.

In June 1937, the *Left Review* published a pamphlet entitled *Authors Take Sides on the Spanish War*. Nearly a hundred and fifty British and Irish writers expressed their opinions of the conflict (the overwhelming majority supported the Republicans). One of the organisers of the enterprise was Elizabeth's friend Stephen Spender, and many other people she knew well, from Cyril Connolly to Sean O'Faolain, contributed their opinions. Though there may be a simple explanation for it, Elizabeth is conspicuous by her absence in the publication. Her seeming lack of political involvement at this time could be seen as apathetic unconcern on her part or simply the desire, evident in so much of her life, to compartmentalise its different elements. At the heart of this were her feelings about the purpose and nature of writing.

Looking back at the writers of the thirties in an essay written a decade later, Elizabeth identified the 'vehemence' of writers politicised by events in Europe, such as Spender, Auden and Day Lewis. However, she was unconvinced by what they wrote: 'The obvious absence of creative pleasure impoverished their work – at least for numerous readers. [...] During the Spanish Civil War, very few people thanked the poets and their brethren novelists for fanning the flames of partisan feeling, which already burned high in England.' What readers wanted, she felt, was entertainment and diversion. For Elizabeth, not engaging with the burning issues of the day seemed almost a writerly virtue. Tellingly, she also identified another dimension to the political earnestness of her peers: 'Younger writers claimed that the novel should serve serious purposes; in particular, they meant that the novel should be wrested from the hands of women.'

These sentiments may go some way to explaining the absence of the Spanish struggle, or other political developments, from the letters Elizabeth wrote to Humphry in India. Instead, the conflicts that stiffened the pages of Elizabeth's letters to him were largely domestic – ones played out in front of her eyes and within her heart. She delighted in telling him about literary dogfights and squabbles. There was also the wrestling she engaged in with Humphry himself – her final, indignant exhalations as their romantic relationship ran out of breath.

European politics are not discussed at any length in the letters Humphry wrote Madeline from Calcutta either. Of course he was away from the action and had his own obsessive interest in the corrupt colonial administration in India to write about. Nevertheless, he did discuss the rise of Fascism in Europe both in the adda and with his English friends, Arthur Calder-Marshall in particular. As for Madeline, the absence of surviving letters from this period leaves unheard the voice of a woman whose political engagement began in the slums of Deptford in the twenties and saw her a lifelong member of the Labour Party.

Though Humphry had been conscious of Nazism before his departure in 1936, its menace was incomparably greater on his return. As Humphry docked at Tilbury, Hitler was paying a state visit to Mussolini's Italy. The British Prime Minister, Neville Chamberlain, was continuing a policy of rearmament while trying to prevent the escalation of tensions between Germany and Czechoslovakia. In Humphry's years away, the mood had changed: he knew little of appeasement and its popularity, and the shifts in public discourse about war in general.

It was not long before German bombers would fly over the quiet cottage where the House family lived. Not long before war came to Elizabeth's adopted city, terrace, doorstep. Not long before loss, birth, and death would come to Madeline, Humphry, and Elizabeth.

Shortly after his return, the dust of Calcutta still on his shoes, Humphry met Elizabeth again. She was enjoying a fulfilling London life in her house overlooking the park. Her affair with Sean O'Faolain continued. *The Death of the Heart*, her tale of lost innocence, was close to completion.

In the novel the teenage protagonist, Portia, arrives in the brittle London home of her stepbrother and his wife. Here she meets a spineless chap called Eddie and is powerless to resist a puppyish infatuation. The narrative is pierced with the sharp thorn of disappointed first love – it is not her hand Eddie wishes to hold in the darkened cinema. Portia's diary, which Eddie sees as a 'horrible trap', is a crucial device. Words written in private are never, in Elizabeth's world, safe from prying eyes.

Just as she had in *The House in Paris*, Elizabeth raided her own life, and those of her close acquaintances, for the novel. Reading *The Death of the Heart* a few years after publication, Charles Ritchie noted:

> It is an exact description of her house and of her husband. The position of the sofa in the drawing-room, the electric fire in his 'study' are all described exactly as they are. What is alarming is the husband is an unsparing portrait of A [Alan]. […] She took that from here, she copied that turn of speech, that must be so-and-so, these thoughts go through my mind as I am reading. It is like eating an elaborate dish after seeing the materials of which it is made up lying about in the kitchen, or being so near the ballet that you can see the make-up.

This sensation of purloined verisimilitude stretched to the character of Eddie. He, it seemed, was based on Goronwy Rees, a young man freshly in focus for Elizabeth. But even if she did write part of Rees into Eddie, it requires readers to make that link explicit. Rees himself was so incensed by the characterisation, so sure it was him, that he threatened to sue Elizabeth for defamation of character.

Yet on reading *The Death of the Heart* Madeline later confessed to worrying that there were streaks of Humphry in Eddie's make-up. Where did Madeline see the similarities between Humphry and Eddie? Perhaps in his charm, his casual cruelties, or in his thinking that all of Shakespeare was about him. I, too, want the novels of the Humphry years to be as revelatory as Portia's diary. And so in my unpicking of the stories, in my appraisal of the characters, I inevitably follow in my grandmother's thought-steps.

Tucked away down a narrow lane on the southern fringe of Ashdown Forest sat a small cottage, the home Madeline had lived in with two small daughters since the summer of 1936. The cottage was paid for by Madeline's father who was eager to see her resettled and closer to family after Humphry's departure for Calcutta. Christened 'The Steps' by the Houses, it was to be the family home until after the Second World War. The garden was huge and tiered, with a flower bed at the top and an expanse of lawn below. The land fell away into a nettle patch, then an apple orchard, before ending at a lane. Through a central front door you were met by a staircase. To the left was a dining room that sloped backwards into the kitchen, and further to a well. The sitting room was painted bright ochre by Madeline.

Shortly before leaving Calcutta, Humphry had written to Madeline about his return: 'I am rather worried about the next year in England: but mean to stick to my determination not to teach – for a year at least: after that I think I may be the sort of person to whom jobs are offered instead of one of those who has to apply.' There was no recognition of the fact that he had dropped from view and conversation in the universities where he wished to work. Or that the political uncertainty of the times made getting a job more of a challenge. Or that, with a young family, he was really not in a position to embrace joblessness and book projects and, in his words, 'damn the debts'.

The din of Calcutta was replaced by English birdsong, a classroom of two hundred pupils by a garden shed where Humphry chose to work. His first summer was taken up with getting his bearings and re-establishing contacts both personal and professional. Inevitably, he asked Elizabeth for assistance, particularly for securing work at the BBC.

In a letter written within a fortnight of his return, Humphry wrote to Alan Cameron, then Secretary to the Central Council of School Broadcasting: 'Elizabeth wrote me a note the other day saying she had mentioned to you that I was wondering about the possibilities of doing some broadcasting, and that you hadn't turned an altogether deaf ear.' Alan recommended Humphry to both the Schools Programme and the Talks Department, thereby facilitating the start of Humphry's successful broadcasting career for the BBC. If there was any lingering awkwardness between Humphry and Elizabeth it did not prevent him from appreciating that she, successful and well connected, could be useful to him. Alan's generous assistance, to a man he might have suspected had played an emotional role in his wife's life, is noteworthy.

Humphry's other major task was to get to know his children, particularly two-year-old Helen, my mother, who had only been real to him as a name on a page during his years away. One photograph from that summer has the two little girls sitting on the lawn in vast white bonnets. Another shows Humphry, with a cigarette stuck to his lip, trying with one hand to fasten the gate of a playpen. In the other hand he holds a book.

An early visitor to the house on the edge of Ashdown Forest was William Plomer who told Elizabeth about the visit. Humphry was in good form and had asked his friend about a book on India he wished to write. Plomer's advice was clear: 'it should be unified, and as personal, & as much like a story, an autobiographical story, as possible, and not too intellectual.' Plomer also met Madeline for the first time and shared his impressions of her with Elizabeth: 'I don't make much out of her, do you? There seems to be something tense & unresolved about her. She doesn't make me feel uneasy, but I think she feels uneasy.'

A few days later Elizabeth replied:

> I'm interested to hear your impression of Madeline House – she looks pop-eyed with anxiety the whole time, poor little creature: I always feel at once sorry for and depressed by her. I thought Humphry much set up by India, really very sweet, now he's back, but I agree with you that I don't think he's more than half digested anything he found there. When he went out there, he was a person of so little experience (except of the most hectic and bemusing kinds) that I feel he had too few terms of reference – really no means of sorting anything out. He had, in fact, a rather inadequate stomach, and I feel it's been given lately (in India) too much to digest. It will be interesting to see how he shakes down in England now. I do hope well – he's so nice. I do hope to God he'll take your advice about his book. He's been rather ruined, so far, in what he's written, by the tendency to over-intellectualize things – a form of indigestion (like acidity) I suppose.

Then at the beginning of August 1938, Elizabeth herself went to spend the day with the Houses. For Madeline, the memories of Elizabeth's painful visit to Greenslinch must have flooded back. She could probably feel Elizabeth casting a critical eye around her home as she poured the tea; the low ceilings and child-smudged walls were a world away from the airy style of a Regency terrace. Elizabeth wrote to Plomer afterwards about 'that queer little claustrophobic house of their's [sic].

It's really rather touching, that little anxious blond woman and those plain blond babies and the little husky blond nurse – something between a dolls' house and a rabbit hutch'. Her feelings about Humphry himself were revealing: 'I felt rather unhappily uncertain that Humphry would thrive there for long – he seemed to me a bit claustrophobic. Poor incompetent angel, to miss you again.'

The contrast in how Elizabeth sees Humphry and Madeline is stark. Bug-eyed Madeline remains pitiful, an ongoing reflection of Naomi in *The House in Paris*. The only addition is her unlovely children. And they are very much hers – nothing is mentioned of Humphry's parental responsibility. Yet Humphry is re-seen. Nice, sweet. Both Plomer and Elizabeth identify the considerable challenges facing Humphry on his return – that the foreign air clinging to him will complicate his reabsorption into English life. That his ambitions as a writer, focused that summer on a book about India, will not be realised.

Like Humphry's mooted *The Book of Ruth As a Novel* in 1933, the book about India seems never to have been written. There is no evidence in the age-bitten boxes under my mother's desk of any such work. Though that idea did not come to fruition, his first autumn back brought another exciting possibility – this time a collaboration. He was going to work with Elizabeth.

Elizabeth's trip to The Steps took her into a family home, with children underfoot and a wife at its heart. Soon afterwards she extended an invitation to the Houses, as a couple, to visit Bowen's Court in September 1938. They were not the only guests – cousin Noreen was there and various other friends. Perhaps Elizabeth was giving herself a last opportunity to gauge Humphry's emotional availability. On all Humphry's previous visits to Bowen's Court, she had been able to tie him into her life very successfully. If those sparks were to be fanned into life once more, then Bowen's Court was surely the place. Humphry's infatuation with Bowen's Court and Elizabeth's Irish life would have meant a happy acceptance of the invitation Elizabeth extended.

For Madeline, the trip must have been very difficult. She knew little of Elizabeth's recent romantic attachments, but she was very conscious of the power Elizabeth had exerted over Humphry before he went to India. And now here she was in the ancestral lair of the other woman, possibly even staying in the yellow room with the picture of Kilcolman on the wall. One day during their visit, Madeline was encouraged to spend a day in Dublin being shown round by Stephen Gwynn, the politician and writer, who was also the brother of Elizabeth's stepmother. The day away might have been a relief for her, though she must have guessed the reason for it – Elizabeth wanted some time alone with her husband.

The awkward feeling of the holiday, at least for Madeline, is captured in a series of strange holiday photographs. Taken in the library, the photographs include several groupings of the people at Bowen's Court that autumn. All of the shots are taken from the same point in the room – the high marble fireplace is on the left, there are glass-fronted bookshelves thick with leather-bound volumes to the rear, a small sofa to the right of the frame, and in the middle a large armchair. Of the five photographs I have, one stands out.

Perched on the right of the armchair, knees together, is Elizabeth. She is attired in a dress with wide lapels and a cinched waist, a neckerchief, court shoes. The omnipresent cigarette is in her right hand, her hair tightly waved. She sits neatly, upright, and has a slightly startled expression on her face. On the left arm of the chair is Noreen, her cousin, handsome, slouching, carelessly clothed. On the other arm, directly behind Elizabeth, is Madeline. She looks unimpressed and wears a fashionably tight top. She belongs more to Noreen's generation than to Elizabeth's. All of the women are looking off to the left; none of them is smiling. Behind the chair stands Humphry in jacket, tie, and spectacles. He is the only one looking at the camera. There is no discomfort in his eye as he stands above the three women. Having more than one woman in the frame at any one time was not, after all, a problem for him.

Left to right: Elizabeth, Madeline, Humphry, and Elizabeth's cousin, Noreen Colley, Bowen's Court, 1938

In a letter to Isaiah Berlin (with whom he never truly re-established his pre-Calcutta intimacy), Humphry briefly reveals his feelings about the visit: 'Yes, this place is pleasant; and Elizabeth's talents and resources as hostess unfailing. She is having to sign 400 Book Society book-plates and they blow about the library.' The book in question was *The Death of the Heart*, Elizabeth's sixth novel which had just been published. Humphry jokingly asked Berlin if he knew of any job opportunities as 'teaching in England except in Oxford or Cambridge is The Death of the Heart indeed'.

The novel's title was apt – Humphry and Elizabeth might well have flirted with one another but there was no replaying of former intimacies, even in a house where time stood still. When the Houses finally left Bowen's Court, their suitcase included a copy of the novel inscribed, in Elizabeth's looping hand, to both of them. (I now have this copy; between the black boards the heavy cream pages are liver-spotted with age.)

The holiday at Bowen's Court included an outing to Annesgrove, as well as the usual daytime walks and alcohol-coloured evenings. There would have been ample opportunity for Humphry and Elizabeth to discuss their joint enterprise – a book of essays about Charles Dickens and the social history of his day. Indeed, one of the other photographs is of the two of them talking in the library, Humphry leaning forward eagerly in his chair, Elizabeth caught mid-sentence. Madeline may well have been in the room but she was out of the picture.

The vision for the book of essays seems to have been Humphry's – he wished to come 'at history from the literary end', so that a more enlightened reading of the novels and their context would ensue. Having Elizabeth as a co-editor would raise the book's profile enormously, particularly if she were able, as she hoped, to get Virginia Woolf to contribute an essay.

The attractions of the project are less immediately obvious for Elizabeth. She had, in 1937, acted as the editor of a book of modern short stories, published by Faber and commissioned by T. S. Eliot. Though she had found the job tiresome (she complained to William Plomer of the 'absolute mediocrity' of most of the stories she had to wade through), it had furnished her with experience for this type of work. Furthermore, she respected Humphry's intelligence and had earlier enlisted his help with an essay on Jane Austen while visiting the Houses in Devon in 1935. She knew that her involvement would be a help to Humphry; throughout her life she was generous in her professional support for those whom she believed in. And then there was Dickens himself.

Despite saying later in life that reading too much Dickens as a child curtailed her enjoyment of him as an adult, Elizabeth's appreciation of him as an artist did not waver. In her slender volume *English Novelists* (published in 1942 as part of the *Britain in Pictures* series), she writes: 'His linked senses of threat and of friendliness make him second to no other writer in penetrating the atmospheres of landscapes, houses and streets.' She would write an essay about the uncanny in Dickens; Humphry about the broader social context of the novels.

There are, perhaps, more obscure psychological reasons for Elizabeth agreeing to work with Humphry. These lie both in her feelings for him and in her relationship with her own work. Like many authors, she saw her books as her offspring. On the publication of a later book of essays she wrote: 'I hadn't realized myself that I've once again become a mother – I mean, got another book out.' But for Elizabeth this idea ran deeper. Though the childless author birthed her books she saw them shaped, fathered, by the men in her life. Of her 1948 novel, *The Heat of the Day*, she wrote to Ritchie: 'Short of there having been a child there could be no other thing that was more you and me.'

Madeline's presence at Bowen's Court reminded Elizabeth of her trip to Maresfield, and meeting the 'plain blond babies'. That sort of issue would never be hers. But by joining forces with Humphry the young father, she came close.

On their return from Ireland, Humphry threw himself into the work, travelling up to London for his research. He writes modestly to Madeline: 'The Dickens books I've had a look at are short, amateurish, and won't need much reading: so I shall try to read 4 in a day.' At the same time, he was pitching two further books to the Oxford University Press – a short biography of Samuel Bamford, the nineteenth century radical and writer, and a longer life of Gerard Manley Hopkins. Though he received an advance of £70 from the OUP this money would not go far to support his wife and family, particularly if he was spending weeks at a time in London staying in hotels or lodging houses in order to do his research.

With his nose deep in the papers of the past, Humphry seemed hardly aware of what was happening outside the walls of the British Museum Reading Room. No letter back to Madeline in Sussex made any mention of the fact that London's contours were changing. Writing to her sister Vanessa Bell at the beginning of October 1938, Virginia Woolf described the city as full of the talk of war, with sandbags being piled in the streets and men digging trenches.

Elizabeth was aware of this shift in mood, writing to Isaiah Berlin as the Munich Conference was called: 'London yesterday morning was horrible – overcast, sluggish; all the poor people so gutted-looking, they didn't seem to have any reactions at all.' Her own response to the National Emergency was to do 'nothing but eat figs, read the A.R.P. [Air Raid Precautions] handbook, read my own book with considerable anxiety, listen to the wireless, go to a movie, try on a gas mask and have my hair shampooed'.

Her work continued much as before – a few short stories were published in periodicals; there were more reviews. Then in the early summer of 1939, shortly before their affair came to an end, Sean O'Faolain encouraged her to write a book about Ireland. The subject was not just close to her heart: it was her heartbeat. She was to write one of her most personal books, a history of her family and their Irish home.

Gingerly, I open my copy of *Bowen's Court* being careful not to damage the dull green dust jacket. It is inscribed: 'To Humphry love from Elizabeth, 1942.' Her writing is childlike in its roundness. With the copy, Elizabeth enclosed a photograph, a superb landscape portrait that catches her seated at the long table in the Hall of her ancestral home. Persian rugs cover the floor, the temperamental grandfather clock is to the left, the marble fireplace to her right. Looking down at her from two sides are the paintings of her ancestors, dark in their heavy frames. Elizabeth looks directly at me as I prepare to walk through the damp leaves of her home.

My sense of an uncanny correspondence with Elizabeth takes many forms. I feel it in our shared obsession with letters, journeys, ghosts. But there is also a sense of being a pupil under her tutelage, inevitably influenced and inspired by her as a writer. This is at its strongest in her discussion of the craft of family storytelling, something that lies at the heart of *Bowen's Court*.

Her approach is refreshingly dynamic, direct. She cannot help being a bit disappointed in an ancestor who proved to be touchy. She admits that she is far more interested in some Bowen traits, such as spontaneity, than others. Speculation, for her, is a form of illumination, a torch shone down a dead end, even if a way through is not to be found. One thing she values in the telling of a family narrative is personal response: 'it seemed to me more honest to leave my reactions to history their first freshness, rather than to attempt to evaluate.'

As is inevitable for Elizabeth, there are important influences at work that are beyond her control. She talks of a frame of family history made up of facts and oral records: 'Inside this frame, I have written about the Bowens out of what I do know but do not know why I know. Intuitions that I cannot challenge have moved me to

Elizabeth in the Hall at Bowen's Court, watched by her family

colour their outlines in.' Writing my family story, I too have felt this friction between actual and emotional knowledge. What cannot be challenged are the things that tie us to our past and shape us unawares. My literary inheritance is as powerful a connection with the past as the paintings of her forebears looking over Elizabeth's shoulder in the photograph.

Even in the structure of the tale I have chosen to tell is an echo of hers, in the interleaving of family accounts with other history. She explains: 'My family, though notably "unhistoric," had their part in a drama outside themselves. Their assertions, their compliances, their refusals as men and women went, year by year, generation by generation, to give history direction, as well as colour and stuff. Each of the family, in their different manners, were more than their time's products; they were its agents.' In a few sentences, Elizabeth validates the telling of the histories of the uncelebrated, of people like Humphry and Madeline. My story, she says, should not be all about her.

There is, however, one phrase in *Bowen's Court* that stands out, that has been a talisman for me. Elizabeth writes: 'Like all stories retold with gusto, it has its variations: every Bowen tells it as seems to him or her best. I will give the version that most appeals to me.' A more liberating and exhilarating line for a person writing biography is hard to imagine. And like a good girl, I do as teacher says.

Elizabeth's enthusiasm for her family history and its sudden all-consuming place in her life had an immediate effect. Other work fell by the wayside. Humphry's brainchild, the Dickens collaboration, was stillborn.

<u>EB to HH</u>

2 Clarence Terrace, Regent's Park, N.W.1.
9 July [1939]

My dear, I do not know how to begin to say how sorry I am for for [sic] the bother and the worry amounting to pain that my dilatoriness and silence and unprogressiveness over the Dickens book has caused you. It simply has been a case of procrastination – not, I must say, owing to idleness, but to a growing absorbtion, while and since I was in Ireland, in this other thing I am doing, the Bowen's Court book. [...]

The same reason accounts for my hopeless incompetence as a fellow-editor – not letting you know how things stand. [...] V. Woolf, whom I thought I was certain of for an essay, became, when I last asked her, totally irresponsible, vague and whimsical and said she'd forgotten she'd said she would do a Dickens essay. I said no one else had. I asked her again, and she said she might do one in the future, but couldn't possibly say when.

[...] I support strongly the suggestion you make yourself (I do hope seriously, with a wish behind it, and not in either anger or irony) that you should write a book on Dickens yourself, to take the place, with the O.U.P. of our proposed collection of essays by different people.

[...] I shall be very sorry if you feel you can't forgive me, and we're not friends any more. On the other hand, I can't help thinking how happy it would be if we could go back to being friends <u>without</u> any project, as we were when you first came back from India, without any project or any matter to cope with. [...] I am really only any good as a friend when my relations with the person are completely foot-loose and irresponsible. I

> *can't be friends "about" anything. The sheer pleasure of knowing someone seems an end in itself. [...]*
>
> *This is no time, here, when I am deliberately discrediting myself, to write to you the appreciation of your essay that I feel. Its scope and solidity, and what I can only call its importance, astounded me. [...]*
>
> *I hope your illness is better?*
> *Love from*
> *Elizabeth*

No doubt disappointed, Humphry did not weep at the death of the collaboration. Instead, with his own determination burnished by Elizabeth's encouragement, he decided to write the whole book himself.

When *The Dickens World* was published in 1941, one of only three author's copies given outside the family went to Elizabeth. If Humphry's gift acknowledged her initial role, it also showed him looking for approbation and marked Elizabeth's continued importance in his emotional and professional life. The book was an instant success both commercially and critically. A second edition was issued the following year. Elizabeth's absence from the cover of the book was, in some ways, a godsend. Humphry was seen in his own right as a scholar and writer. The book did more than just raise Humphry's profile – it established him as a new authority on Dickens. The novelist, and the Victorian Age in general, would form a major part of Humphry's critical output for the rest of his life.

Elizabeth's wish, that she and Humphry could be friends in an uncluttered way, was fulfilled within a few weeks of her backing out of the Dickens book. They spent a day at the seaside in Brighton. Of the outing, Elizabeth wrote to Plomer:

> We went into a most nerve-racking pier entertainment called "1001 laughs for 2d", which included syren [sic] screeches in a dark room, and being biffed on the head by a sudden skeleton arm. I don't react at all well to that sort of thing, and it gave me palpitations. Humphry was nice, and seems to be expanding after a winter and early summer of nervous gloom and tension, brought on, I imagine, by over-domesticity, war-fears, and, as you describe it, "living among all those bushes".

Shortly after their visit to the seaside, she wrote to Humphry.

<u>*EB to HH*</u>

2 Clarence Terrace, Regent's Park, N.W.1.
Sunday [31 July 1939]

My dear, that was a most lovely day. No words for how good it was and how happy I felt. In fact, except for wanting to write to you, I really hardly want to write about it now. The whole day has become one of those permanent things that are the capital that one lives by – in fact only on that goodness does one go on living at all.

I have still got your comb and am keeping it. I hope you have another – I say ruthlessly. That one I took off you is a very nice comb, just the right mesh for my hair.

I won't begin to ennumerate [sic] the things I remember constantly about Brighton – and non-Brighton, the top of the downs and that fantastic hotel where we had tea.

I cross to B. Court on Friday next, 4th, night. Will you post Finnegans Wake here before then as I rather want to read it again in Ireland and it might be stopped in the post if it went straight there.

I very much hope you will be going to search through that dead Dublin Jesuit's mattress for Hopkins papers – I mean, I do hope you may possibly come to B. Court. Let me know, as time goes on, what the chances are. And do write to me at B. Court anyway.

My love. May I say, diffidently, how very much I love being with you.

E.

A brisk walk, a fine tea, a kept comb. Some of the malevolent spirits that had swirled through the relationship left in the tunnel of the ghost ride. A day to remember, which produces from Elizabeth a letter of sated finality. And yet, in it is the sense that such simple pleasures are being threatened.

Though Elizabeth, in her letter to Plomer, imagined Humphry to be suffering from 'war-fears', Humphry himself attempted to stand apart from what was unfolding across the country. In August 1939 he wrote an essay entitled 'National Service' which included almost identical sentiments to the ones Spender had expressed in *Poems for Spain* – that creative expression was a crucial component of political freedom. The essay finished: 'I would rather be damned with Milton than go to Heaven with the Unknown Soldier.' The *News Chronicle* chose not to publish the essay. If Humphry's belief in the potency of peace was one reason for not joining up when war was declared in September 1939, just as important was his desire to continue with his various academic pursuits. In rural Sussex, the family was safe and isolated – from news, shortages, and the outside world. He could sustain the belief that his duty did not lie beyond his work or home. In this, he was following his own definition of a patriot – as someone who lives, not gives, his life for his country.

The extent of his teaching in the first 'phoney' year of the war was an occasional lecture for the Workers' Educational Association. His subject was *The Growth of Modern England Seen Through Literature*. Paying 6d. a lecture, anyone interested could gather at Mrs Wickham's house on Maresfield High Street to hear Humphry speak. There was discussion and probably a cup of tea and a slice of home-made cake afterwards. Then in the dark he would return to the silent cottage a few miles away where his daughters slept. This was a long way from his nights of well-oiled high jinks in Calcutta, where dance music swung out under huge chandeliers, waiters picked their way barefoot through broken glass, and a six-foot tall blonde bandleader called Ilsa belted out popular tunes on her saxophone.

In October 1940, Humphry left The Steps for Oxford and more research. He had just received a much needed professional fillip, being awarded the William Noble Fellowship by the University of Liverpool, which he hoped would give him enough money to finish the Hopkins biography. The trip away came as a relief, as he admitted to Madeline soon after he left. He felt weighed down by the 'fixed, close, narrow, unbroken routine' of family life. He needed to get away from all those bushes.

Once beyond the forest's margin, Humphry was shocked by what he saw: 'the atmosphere everywhere is of a society being deeply changed.' By the autumn of 1940, Churchill had replaced Chamberlain as Prime Minister, and the war had intensified. Unable to reach Oxford by train in one day, he spent a night on a camp bed in a stranger's sitting room in Reading. Oxford itself was full – airmen, soldiers, Londoners. He eventually found a room as a paying guest on the Polstead Road. Mrs Pollock charged two guineas a week with breakfast and dinner included. These he had to eat, rather to his chagrin, with both her and the other guests, a Tasmanian and a water engineer. At least Mrs Pollock brought him a cup of tea in bed in the morning.

In an unsent letter to Madeline, he confessed to earlier considering becoming a conscientious objector, but the raids on Southampton, food shortages, and endless air raid warnings began to soak into his spirit. He decided that he had to do his duty and join up. Because of his more privileged background and education, there was the possibility of a comfortable job at the War Office. However, Humphry failed the entrance IQ test and instead became a Trooper in the Tanks Corps of the Royal Armoured Corps.

He spent Christmas in the barracks on Salisbury Plain filling gun belts with ammunition while listening to the King's Speech. A man told stories about putting up stockings at home, another unwrapped a package from a distant sister. The soldiers, who called him 'Professor', pulled Humphry's leg part of the time and then asked him how to spell words. From their wallets, all brought forth snippets of their other lives – newspaper cuttings, photographs of children, and precious letters, their pages softened by loving touch.

Old Forge Cottage, Maresfield, Sussex

Chapter 14

Old Forge Lane: *A Day in the Dark*

I describe the bridge over the stream, the curving lane with huge trees pressing in on either side. And the flight of stone steps that rises from the lane to the house. A cup of tea with my mother after my visit to her first home in East Sussex, where the family lived during the war. I show her some photos – the triangular garden, the house with its half-tiled cladding.

Mum's face looks blank. 'But this doesn't seem right. Which way is the house facing? I don't remember there being a row of trees directly outside the front door.'

I press on with my description, willing her memory to chime with my mine. 'It's now called Old Forge Cottage. You said that was the original name, didn't you? And there are,' I add slightly desperately, 'steps. You said there were steps up from the road.'

'No, Julia, this is not the place,' says Mum firmly. 'I can't picture it properly anymore, but I know this isn't the house.'

'If you can't remember, how can you be so sure?' I am suddenly conscious of the fragmentary unreliability of memory and of knowledge.

'Rachel went down to see the cottage recently,' Mum says. 'She walked up from the lane through some tall security gates. There was no one in but she walked round the outside. Only when she turned to leave did she realise the gates had closed behind her and that she was locked in. She threw her walking stick under first and then had to roll out!'

Mum and I laugh together. 'As for you, I think you just visited the neighbours.'

1940

Just inside the door of Clarence Terrace lay a tin helmet and a pair of sturdy shoes. Elizabeth had volunteered with zeal as an air raid warden clumping round Marylebone on nocturnal patrol in the sharp darkness.

The febrile atmosphere of war, the shattered streets, chimed with her psyche. The city's life-in-death is vividly described in her essay 'London, 1940':

> It is a fine morning and we are still alive. This is the buoyant view of it – the theatrical sense of safety, the steady breath drawn. We shall be due, at to-night's siren, to feel our hearts once more tighten and sink. Soon after black-out we keep that date with fear. The howling ramping over the darkness, the lurch of the barrage opening, the obscure throb in the air. [...] Around three sides of the Park, the Regency terraces look like scenery in an empty theatre: in the silence under the shut façades a week's drift of leaves flitters up and down. At nights, at the end of my terrace, I feel as though I were sleeping in one corner of a deserted palace.

The war appealed, among other things, to Elizabeth's sense of drama. She could play new parts, don different costumes. Her gin-drinking, glove-wearing self still inhabited Clarence Terrace, but she was more muted than before. Elizabeth now wore both the visible uniform of a warden in London and the clandestine cloak of a spy.

Volunteering her services at the outbreak of the conflict, she sent reports, on her visits to Bowen's Court, from neutral Ireland to the British Ministry of Information. As she had little access to politicians, these despatches instead described local sentiment and the movements of specific individuals. Having a home in Ireland gave her the freedom and opportunity to undertake such a role. Having a personality attuned to conflicting loyalties made her ideally suited for it. She could pass on information to London while maintaining her support for distinctly Irish interests, such as the neutrality of their ports.

Elizabeth was not alone in thinking the Allied cause worth fighting for: thousands of Irish men and women joined up to fight for the British. What sets Elizabeth apart is that her activities were concerned with her neighbours, not the Nazis. For some, Elizabeth's wartime activities forever took the 'Irish' out of her descriptive tag as 'Anglo-Irish'. One Irish historical society, based in County Cork, refers to her as Elizabeth 'Espionage' Bowen on its website. For Elizabeth there was less of a conflict; she inhabited two worlds, and belonged exclusively to neither. She commented, not entirely in jest, that she was only really at home on the sea between.

Another role that she assumed in 1941 was as the lover of Charles Ritchie, the man who would be her emotional bedrock for the rest of her life. Ritchie was a cultured Canadian diplomat, younger than Elizabeth, whose career took him to positions in both Europe and North America. Like other lovers of hers, he was a man open to several attachments at one time. Elizabeth's relationship with Charles Ritchie was more visible than the affair with Humphry. He was a regular visitor to Clarence Terrace, where his photograph sat on the mantelpiece. Ritchie and Elizabeth shared qualities of being outsiders, observers, while moving easily between the worlds they inhabited. Elizabeth referred to them both, almost inevitably, as 'spies'.

The war energised Elizabeth, emotionally and creatively. She embraced the battered city – as buildings fell, so did walls of class, age, background. Everyone in London during the war lived, according to her, in a state of 'lucid abnormality'. Sensations were raw. The half-dead and unburied were as real as anyone else. Her short stories from these years, rich in the rubble of consciousness and memory, are some of the finest of her oeuvre.

In one of her most chilling wartime stories, 'The Demon Lover', the unfortunate Mrs Drover returns to her shut-up house in blitzed London. (It is, without doubt, my favourite story of hers to teach – eerie, beautifully paced, and with a devastating ending.) A letter from her sinister fiancé, presumed dead in the First World War, flies across a room, across time, to await her on the dusty table in the hall, at 'the hour arranged'. Missives choose when to arrive, when to be read, when to exert their power. Only when the sensibilities of a reader are in tune with the contents of a letter, will they reveal themselves, physically and psychically.

Several years ago, I first read the correspondence between Humphry and Elizabeth. Since then, these two people have filled themselves out as individuals, as writers – using their own words. The almost total absence of Madeline's letters from the 1930s has left me with their versions of the affair and of her. Their reconstructions, projections, fictionalisations. Yet I cannot escape the feeling that Madeline has been consciously waiting in the wings, choosing with care the right moment to take the stage.

I have a pile of Madeline's letters in front of me, written to Humphry throughout the war. They never seemed important before.

Yet the letters have 'insisted on forcing their own way out' as they tend to in Elizabeth's fiction. My grandmother was vividly present in my dreams the other night, walking towards me down a corridor saying something I did not quite catch. I got up and wrote down what I could of the dream in an attempt to keep her with me. Rereading my midnight scribblings now I struggle for their meaning. But what is clear as day is the knowledge that I was spoken to by Madeline. She has crossed the threshold of my consciousness, entered my dreamscape. A more benign presence, I hope, than the ghost in 'The Demon Lover'.

> You've read in the papers, I expect, that Wednesday night's raid on London was the biggest of the war: and we realised it very clearly while it was happening. Planes started coming over before 9 p.m., and there wasn't a moment's pause till 1.30 a.m. It wasn't just that as the sound of one plane faded away to the north another could be heard coming up from the south, but that the whole sky seemed full of them the whole time. I've never heard anything like it. It was horrifying. I hadn't any real fears for our own personal safety, for it was obvious the bombs weren't intended for us; but the horror lay in sitting helpless under that roaring stream as it went northward to work destruction and death. And all the next day seemed blackened and awful. But I've recovered now.

So writes Madeline in April 1941 in a letter to Humphry who was then stationed at Perham Down on Salisbury Plain. When the air raid warning whined out, Madeline bundled my four-year-old mother and six-year-old aunt into the cupboard under the stairs. As the sinister sounds of war continued, the family waited, tense and fearful. Occasionally they did jigsaws by lamplight to take their minds off the situation. Then finally, the all-clear filled the loaded darkness, and it was back upstairs quietly to bed. When the new day dawned, it swirled with activity.

The war turned the garden into a vegetable plot, flowers wilting under the patriotic sun of digging for victory. Madeline thinned carrots, grew marrows, potatoes and cauliflowers. She buried tins of food in the ground in case of invasion. In the summer of 1941, she wrote to Humphry of the family's self-sufficiency being increased further:

> Darling, the hens have arrived! I'm terribly excited. Chatfield has been busy all the evening with wire netting and tarred string, and made for them what the woman who sold them me called 'a perfect little garden of Eden, Madam, oh I can see they'll have a happy home.' [...] They're a breed I've never heard of, – Barn Velders; dark blue-brown hens decoratively speckled. I am prepared to love them, and Rachel and Helen have names all ready for them in advance. Rachel's special three are to be called Stringy, Scrag and Erb; Helen's special three Stitchwort, Bluebell, and Pimpernell [sic]. [...] Tomorrow my troubles begin.

As well as running the home, a large part of the day was given over to the education of the girls. A village school sat a few miles away, but it was too far to walk at their age and the journey was potentially dangerous. Madeline wanted to keep her chicks close. There was 'geography, history, and nature-study', and any number of creative pursuits: 'And today in lessons ("handwork") we started making models of tanks. They're fun: corrugated cardboard for the tracks, cheese-boxes for turrets etc. But heated disputes now about the number of wheels and how they go.' They made on a tray a great three-dimensional map of England in plasticine of different colours.

Sitting at the heart of Madeline's educational programme was poetry. Into hand-stitched, cloth-bound books the children copied out vast narrative poems: 'Horatius at the Bridge' by Lord Macaulay, 'The Jackdaw of Rheims' by Thomas Ingoldsby. My mother still bursts into delighted recitation: 'Never, I ween, / Was a prouder seen, / Read of in books, or dreamt of in dreams, / Than the Cardinal Lord Archbishop of Rheims!' On her first day of school, aged seven, my mother was unable to recite the Lord's Prayer. Yet diffidence permitting, the one hundred and fifty lines which describe a robbing jackdaw becoming a saint would have presented her with no such problems. The young girls were also writers, and each composed *The Adventures of the House Family* complete with illustrations.

Madeline's lively letters detail numerous outings with the children – at first by car, and later by bus when the car was laid up due to petrol rationing. They went to Knole Park, to an opera matinée, to see the plaque of Edward Gibbon in Fletchling Parish Church. But the war was never far away as Madeline realised powerfully on a visit to Humphry's father after a firebomb had destroyed his home in Kent. More of the fine old house was intact than Madeline had expected. She could see the space where the bed she had shared with Humphry had been, and the shape of chairs gathered round the hearth. Piles of scorched, sodden papers and photographs lay on the ground among broken china and bits of bath and bedstead. Spotting a small, undamaged engraving of Tonbridge Castle, Madeline fished it from the debris to keep. Then on the way home, she drove to the castle itself, still solid and standing, where the children fed the pigeons with stale toast left over from breakfast.

Independently, Madeline kept up a social life beyond the family. She had friends to stay and was the Literature Secretary of the Uckfield Labour Party. Boxes of pamphlets (recently unearthed in my aunt's attic) attest to her active political involvement: there are titles such as *The Communist Party and the War*, and *You're Young: Here's Your Biggest Job* by Clement Attlee, and a whole series of Labour's *Reconstruction Pamphlets*. She took in occasional evacuees, sharing her home with people from London forced to flee their homes. These were most commonly young mothers with a single child. The house also became an unofficial lending library with soldiers from a local camp coming over to borrow books.

The contact between Humphry and Madeline in the early part of the war was fitful – Humphry sometimes managed to get home for a couple of nights. On other occasions Madeline met him at hotels near his camp before driving a fair distance home afterwards:

> I was trying to race the fading day-light, – crouched over the steering-wheel like Toad of Toad Hall with eyes glaring. And I didn't like a wood I had to drive through about 5 miles out of Winchester: it was high on a hill and very dim and brown, and quite 50 great army lorries, camouflaged and sinister, stood waiting in its shadows. But the other side of Petersfield darkness settled in, and I stopped worrying about speed and time and everything. Near Midhurst a policeman jumped out at me from a hedge and said my lights were far too brilliant: the side-lights should have had paper over them as well as the black paint ring. But he was a charming policeman with a face like Jack Hulbert and an Oxford accent and he said he'd "hate" me to be reported, so we tied up the lights in coloured pocket-handkerchiefs and parted with expressions of mutual esteem.

The verve, humour, and independence of Madeline is everywhere in these letters. Yet despite all the descriptions of family bustle, Humphry chose to imagine her leading a more prosaic life. She had to correct his erroneous impression: 'You know when you write "You're in the old setting, with the old things, doing almost the same as before" you are stating part of the attitude that baffles me. For to hell with the old things and old jobs; they don't matter a damn. Feeling and thinking can be fresh in spite of them. So please don't identify me with furniture!'

Madeline's sentiment is an uncanny echo of one expressed by Elizabeth, who bristled at Humphry trying to reduce her to her 'setting' at Bowen's Court. Both women saw themselves as far more dynamic than they appeared in Humphry's imagination. Both of them were attracted to a man who couldn't help putting them in their place – or the place that he felt women should occupy. Her heated reply to Humphry also has a psychological edge. In *The House in Paris*, Naomi (the Madeline character) is described as 'like furniture or the dark'. By resisting the wooden association Madeline unconsciously swats away Elizabeth's domestic metaphor for her. Neither her husband, nor Elizabeth, would reduce her to being merely a woman of hearth and home.

The novelties of army life – parading 'spat on and polished up, in proper battle dress', or spending an evening peeling potatoes with twenty other men – soon faded for Humphry. Within a year of joining up he lamented: 'I am not a soldier, and oh how much I want to get to work again.' *The Dickens World* had just been published, and it brought a sharp reminder of his erudition and ambition. Working on his wireless exams and improving his woeful Morse code skills held neither challenge nor imaginative appeal. He was asked to give the odd lecture, but this was about tank tactics rather than Tennyson. He writes: 'Only Jane Austen is getting me through this very nasty week.' He did, at least, have a new friend, a commercial artist called Brett. When they were allowed to leave the barracks, they would walk to the pub, have four pints of beer and a pile of tongue sandwiches, and then amble back blearily through the dark.

'Tanks.' Humphry, a Trooper in the Tanks Corps of the Royal Armoured Corps

Returning to camp from visiting his family in May 1941, he witnessed the effects of some of the most destructive bombing of London. He told Madeline of the 'appalling chaos' of the capital. Escaping gas hung thick in the air, fires crackled brightly under the arches of Waterloo Station. Nearby, rows of shops and houses lay flattened. Shredded wallpaper tousled with underwear on the pavement in front of a draper's; clods of plaster and ceiling joists buried a row of new bicycles. The quiet of devastation was broken only by one or two hysterical people weeping beside their ruins. As smashed plate glass crunched like gravel under his boots, Humphry, for the first time, understood what war meant.

Humphry received his commission as an officer in October 1941. This gave him far more flexibility – not just to pop out drinking in Salisbury with his new friends, but to return home more frequently. Yet in the early months of the following year, his army career ground to a halt – Humphry suffered an attack of lumbago, a severe lower back pain. Initially he was in a nursing home in plaster of Paris from the neck down, totally immobilised. Afterwards he convalesced at home for several months. The back problem finally put paid to the slim chance he had of seeing active service in the war.

On his way back to Perham Down after his convalescence, Humphry stopped in London to have lunch with Elizabeth. Her standards had not slipped – she frequented the Ritz, Claridge's and the Café Royal during the war, despite being, apparently, short of money. Elizabeth lived beyond her means throughout her life, spending in a way that she felt a lady should. If Humphry felt that the arts were the pillars of civilisation in times of crisis, Elizabeth saw the same pillars holding up the dining rooms of grand hotels. The luncheon, which Humphry described as a 'great delight', concluded with Elizabeth inviting him to stay a night at Clarence Terrace, sometime in the near future. This in itself was evidence of her reconfigured relationship with Humphry – friends, not lovers, came to stay under the roof she shared with Alan.

Humphry promptly informed Madeline of the invitation. Ever the master of the backhanded compliment, he wrote: 'I think it would be best to go this very next weekend; for after being with you continuously for over three weeks I shall miss you less just now immediately than I would if I didn't come home for a later weekend. So I am writing to Elizabeth saying I shall come for this very next Saturday night, and will do so unless you urgently protest that I mustn't.'

An urgent protest was not forthcoming. Humphry went ahead with the visit, writing to Madeline afterwards: 'Saturday and Sunday at Elizabeth's were splendid. Good talk and good company I do need.' One of the party was Charles Ritchie. Humphry writes of his energetic hostess: 'She is a really great woman, and there is now no possibility of anything in my friendship for her affecting relations with you in any way. She suggested that when it's possible we should take the children with her to the Zoo and then to tea at Clarence Terrace. A great plan for my next seven days' leave.'

A family outing – enjoyment for all. At least in Humphry's opinion. Long forgotten is the evening of 'spiritual dumbness and numbness' the three of them had shared in Exeter. Nor does he consider that Madeline might not leap at the idea. Indeed by not even consulting her about the zoo plan beforehand, he acts as he always has done where Elizabeth is concerned – as a lone player, if not a single man. But things were different. The affair between Humphry and Elizabeth was over. And the presence of children would shift the lines of vision: to hands held, penguin slides, and animals that roared.

The outing to London Zoo came and went. I would love to say that my mother remembered Elizabeth, but she doesn't. Nor does my aunt. The day did not settle into their quick-sifting young minds. For Madeline, the visit came during a dissonant few months in the marriage. This tension went back to Humphry's lumbago-enforced presence at Old Forge earlier in the year. It continued into a weekend the couple had in London immediately after the trip to the zoo.

Back home on the Sunday night Madeline sat down to write. She was in good spirits. It had been a beautiful afternoon to drive home. She had given lifts to relays of optimistic young soldiers. The contrast between them and her own soldier needed to be addressed directly. She writes of the events of the previous evening with Humphry: 'Last night too, after walking for a good half hour more after you left me, I realised I wasn't deeply hurt or shocked. When I came to think about it then, and now while I write about it sitting here, the fact that you told me what a completely uninteresting person you find me didn't, and doesn't, worry me in the least! Walking around Bedford, Gordon, Russell Squares last night was a very different affair from, for instance, an anguished late-night walk I remember well in Exeter – I'm just not hurtable in those old ways.'

Without flinching she reflects on the 'bloody week' he spent at home: 'your desperate gloom sitting over the supper table here in the dusk while I cleared away the dishes: (incidentally, why shouldn't you have cleared them? I know no good answer to the question).' She corrects his impression that she had really been looking forward to his stay. And then describes how the tension between them spilled into the day at the zoo: 'Often I've met you with keenest joy. At the Zoo I didn't – What followed was a good deal my fault. But, please note, I don't mean "my fault" in the "Oh yes I am a poor stupid creature" tone of voice. What I mean is that if I had gone about it in the right way I could have controlled, or even entirely got free of, my fears.'

Another letter followed soon after, sent from Norfolk where she and the children went for a few days' holiday to stay with an uncle of Madeline's, the vicar of a small village near Norwich. In it, Madeline reveals her feelings about Elizabeth in greater detail than anywhere else in her surviving correspondence.

MH to HH

Winfarthing Rectory, Diss, Norfolk
Wednesday [Postmark: 28 May 1942]

My dear,

[…] What I really want to write about is how lovely it is here, and how and why lovely. But there's that tiresome quarrel of ours which has to have something more said about it first: I've got to answer your letter to me. But I don't mean to do it at length; for of the week before last I'm already beginning to feel "How interesting, and how long ago"!

First about the problem of coping with my "double position", my moods seeming so much dictated by yours. I think we complicated the problem by over-simplification. For your depression is not communicated to me directly and almost inevitably, as measles is by one child to another. It is rather that we both make mistakes in behaviour. You when depressed snub and crush. I respond by rolling up into a ball like a wood-louse. You get more snubbing and crushing. I waste all my energy wondering whether to quarrel at once and deciding, – No, partly out of sympathy for the cause of your depression, partly hoping things may clear without quarrelling, partly because quarrelling over little things approximates to bickering. […] Quarrels clear the air: and when I read your remark "We must plan in future to quarrel directly we meet" I said Yes! licking my lips in pleased anticipation – for I had still quite a lot of quarrel left in me. But quarrelling to clear the air only takes us half the way, doesn't it? We've got to try to be consistently better and wiser people. And I do believe that when we are at our best (whatever best may mean!) we can be really happy together.

Next about Oxford and Elizabeth. Here indeed I find in your letter the "old pattern" cropping up! I do not regard either

O. or E. as my rivals: and your use of the word "rivals" suggests that you are thinking of the situation in a queerly ungrown-up way. (Rachel would add a "conceited" way!) For of course there's no reason why you shouldn't be on good terms with Oxford, Elizabeth and me. I've not taken steps to see Elizabeth in the last six years for the simple reason that I've not had the slightest wish to nor supposed that she had the slightest wish that I should. This last meeting with her was the first I've ever really enjoyed. And I enjoyed it because I had got out of the old pattern in my ways of thinking of her. I admire her a lot; but I don't consider her faultless; and I know where I get on and off in any relations I may have with her. Yet you talk as if I were a simple, impressionable, flatterable child who is bowled over by another woman, just as soon as the other woman wants to bowl her over, – (not that that was at all E.'s intention). I did like seeing her that Zoo day. But your remarks on the meeting belong to the sort of attitude which buggers things up.

My hands next! I know they must have upset you: in fact I thought about it at the time. They are the first thing I neglect when things are going wrong and I'm feeling bad. Neglect of them's a sign not a cause of there being trouble about. My hands are always uphill work. For weeks I'd been rubbing cream into them at bed time: but I deliberately stopped doing that or anything else to them while you were here.

Yes, I see your point about not helping carry away the supper things!

Oh my dear, the whole of this suddenly makes me laugh. Fools indeed.

Love, darling

Madeline

Madeline's strength and dynamism sing through this letter. She manifests a trait she shared with Elizabeth – the liking for a good clean fight, particularly with a man who did not feel she should even enter the ring. Over the years, she had chipped away at Humphry's patriarchal presumptions and carved out a fairer place for herself in their marriage. Only a few battles remained, piled like unruly plates in the kitchen.

Elizabeth elected to stay in London during the Blitz. Clarence Terrace rode its luck, remaining largely unscathed throughout the early years of the war. Scars of damage were visible in the surrounding streets. In the park beyond, debris from stunned buildings was piled high on the lawns. Until the penultimate year of the conflict, the house stood firm.

Then in the summer of 1944, a new menace fixed its sights on London – the V-1 flying bomb. In early July, the terrace was hit, and the house rocked in its shoes. Ten days later the windows blew out and the ceilings collapsed. Reluctantly, Elizabeth and Alan moved to a different flat nearby. The location was no safer, but at least the spine of the building was still straight. In this new home Elizabeth wrote 'The Happy Autumn Fields', one of her most extraordinary short stories. It is, inevitably, another narrative of dream-journeys and ruined houses.

That summer, the whining cry of the flying bombs was the soundtrack to sleep all across south-east England. It was heard by Elizabeth in her temporary flat, and by Madeline and the children in the lonely cottage in Sussex. Madeline was worried, justifiably so. The launch sites for the bombs were along the French and Dutch coasts – the family was in the line of fire. She took the decision to evacuate the children to the countryside, going to stay with friends in the village of Beguildy on the border between England and Wales. The head of the household was Mabel Hopkins, the wife of Humphry's editor and friend Gerry.

Madeline described the house in a letter to Humphry as a 'stern little cottage' from the outside, long, low, and grey. Inside, its white-washed walls and pleasant furniture made it a welcoming place. She writes: 'We look across a valley, through which runs a stream in which the children bathe, at a wide hillside, chess-boarded with small fields. There's nothing rugged and typically Welsh about it. It's comfortable country, and friendly.'

Madeline paid £1 a week for herself, and 10 shillings for each of the girls to join a motley collection of other evacuees. There were two teenage lads who went out haymaking, a girl with learning difficulties, two boys – one Swiss, the other, 'an incredible little tough of 10, who seems hardly possible outside an American low-life film: he is immensely fat, and curly-headed and exhibitionist'. Helen and Rachel adapted without fitting in, being sent on various errands by Mabel. One of these trips to the village to buy bread ended in disgrace. With one of the boys, perhaps the hefty hoodlum, they sat in a cornfield and polished off a loaf and a half between them. Mabel's ire was matched by that of the local farmer whose corn they had damaged.

The family stayed in Radnorshire throughout the summer and harvest season until the threat of the flying bombs had fizzled out. By October 1944, the launch sites in Northern Europe were in Allied hands. With skies clear of danger, and their peregrinations at an end, the House family prepared to go home. They returned to The Steps; Elizabeth and Alan to Clarence Terrace.

For the two women, the latter part of the war had been vivid, varied, vibrant. For Humphry, now working for the War Office and stuck in subterranean bureaucracy in London, this had not been the case. His administrative job anchored him to a desk above which the frantic footfalls of Londoners passed every day. From 1943 to 1945, he had twenty-five clerks working beneath him, all burrowing through the tedious logistical elements of the conflict.

Though Humphry played his part in the Second World War, the fighting for the values he treasured was done more actively by his wife. Madeline's adherence to his definition of a patriot – someone who lives their life for their country by keeping alive the good things of peace – was practical where his was theoretical. A devoted, inspirational mother, it was she who grew the vegetables, filled the minds of her children with poetry, and threw the hoop of safety round their home. The war also allowed this newly flexed domestic power to spread into her relationship with her husband – though committed to Humphry, she would not put up with any nonsense from him. Madeline comes out of the shade in these years in the most compelling fashion. Generous, determined, clever, resilient.

Hearing my mother's stories of her childhood (which I had never been curious enough to ask about before) makes me appreciate intergenerational ties afresh. I am continuing her lost tale of the House family; there remains the love of learning poetry. On a French campsite with my young nephews, I task them with learning a Shakespearean soliloquy. My mother, inevitably, rehearses them before their final performance. The eldest performs 'All the World's a Stage' from *As You Like It*; the second is Caliban and emerges from a cave of deck chairs to speak of an isle full of noises. Then, with his fringe in his eyes, the youngest recites Macbeth's 'Tomorrow, and tomorrow, and tomorrow'. The past is a present elsewhere.

Pendine Sands, South Wales

Chapter 15

Pendine: *The Disinherited*

'Our father wasn't part of our daily life,' says my aunt crisply. 'But we did go on holiday to the seaside as a family every year, for a fortnight.'

'Every year,' my mother echoes, 'we went to stay in guest houses. In Hunstanton, Charmouth…'

'And Pendine,' says Rachel, brightening. For my benefit she adds in the schoolteacher voice that is a feature of the family, 'It's in South Wales.'

'Do you remember Mr Giardelli?' says Mum.

'Oh yes,' replies Rachel, and the words and memories of both sisters tumble out simultaneously.

'He played the cello…'

'Beautifully…'

'In the evenings to all his guests…'

'It was wonderful…'

'Yes.'

Then like a slide suddenly replaced in a projector, a fresh image falls across the face of my mother. 'The beach. We played cricket on the beach.'

Rachel sees the same. 'And our father spent hours with John who was about five then. They built, right down to the last detail, a cathedral made of sand.'

1945

After the war, the friendship between Elizabeth and Humphry thinned to an occasional lunch in London. Elizabeth had new people in her life and Ritchie to fill her emotional horizon. Humphry had a family and a life outside the capital. Yet even as their lives diverged, there were strange echoes and correspondences in their creative and professional lives. And for the Houses there was a new addition to the family, my uncle John. The boy child was not, in the end, christened Gerard.

His arrival, a few months before the end of the war, left Madeline in a convalescent home for more than a month. She was forty-one years old, the child weak. But Humphry had a son at last – one to treasure and keep close. He confessed to Madeline: 'I am really excited by him; for I have wanted a son more, I think, than I have let you see.' This pleasure spilled over later into Humphry's educational programme. In a move that mirrored the teaching Hartley Coleridge received from his poet father, John knew the Greek alphabet by the age of two.

Humphry's delight in his son was matched by a major breakthrough in his Hopkins research. The Liverpool fellowship at an end, Humphry submitted an incomplete biography of the poet. In his covering letter to the Professor of English Literature at Liverpool, he explained that, though he knew his written submission was substandard, there were extenuating circumstances – both thrilling and unexpected.

The last surviving sister of Gerard Manley Hopkins was, according to Humphry, 'a bit difficult and silent and did not seem to like intruders, and she claimed to have searched herself everywhere for all GMH MS etc'. On her death, Humphry got back in touch with the family and was invited down to their home by a surviving brother – ninety-two-year-old Lionel, a renowned Sinologist: 'we got on together like old friends and he had a very real devotion to GMH indeed. It seems that he had been suppressed and kept out of the business by his sisters for all these years, and now released came into a new life. He has been incredibly good and helpful, and none of these discoveries could have been made earlier.'

A quick look round the house and library convinced Humphry that 'the house might contain untold treasure'. He returned for a second visit, this time with Gerry Hopkins, and in a very superficial search of just two rooms of the house they did, indeed, strike gold: 'We found not merely many more family things of great interest but four new GMH letters, seven new GMH drawings, including his only known water-colour and the most complete autograph MS piece of his music yet known.'

As a result of the finds, a letter was attached to the will of Lionel requesting that Humphry and Gerry Hopkins be consulted about the books and manuscripts in the house, as 'sort of literary advisers'. It was, as Humphry concludes, 'very like *The Aspern Papers*'. In a surge of emotion Humphry wrote about the discoveries: 'I do honestly think I have been one of the luckiest men under heaven this last few months. Astounding coincidences have occurred in all directions, and bits of information have clicked together while I have been asleep.'

Humphry's excitement is so infectious I cannot resist him. He is an enthusiast, a lover of literature, someone on a quest. Someone, finally, connected with me – through blood, ink, ideas. My familial songlines have not always been this vibrant. Indeed, it is Elizabeth's world view – of subtle hauntings, knowing houses, vital journeys – that has sat more comfortably at my side as I write.

But here it is his spirit that strides towards me. He feels the privilege in the discovery of unknown papers. He understands his responsibility towards them. He knows that, in order to interest others, he needs a certain approach: 'I want it to be a book that the ordinary reader will delight in, not just a thing for scholars. Therefore you will find few footnotes to the text. I am keeping all notes on sources and the bibliography to the end, so that ordinary chaps won't be scared.'

The House family was now settled in a house in Cambridge that backed onto the Botanic Garden. Madeline's family was again instrumental in them securing their new home; it had been leased before the war by Madeline's parents for their curate son Geoffrey, before being requisitioned during wartime. In 1946, and with only twenty years to go on its lease, the Houses were able to secure the fine house for a minimal rent.

Humphry returned to reviewing and broadcasting as he looked for a more permanent position. He became a regular contributor to the Third Programme and the Far Eastern Service of the BBC, speaking mostly about the Victorians. Then in the summer of 1948, there arrived the possibility of a job he really wanted – a lectureship in English at Oxford.

He wrote to Bowra who acted as a referee: 'I am truly feeling rather frustrated by my failure since getting out of the army to get a job of any kind I want and think I ought to have! Near misses and kind words don't keep a family or even provide cigarettes.' He highlighted the importance of his broadcasting career, one that began with Elizabeth and Alan Cameron opening the door to the studio: 'If it hadn't been for the starting of the Third Programme and the lucky chance of having a sellable voice I should have been on the rocks in the last two years. As it is, the B.B.C. work ought to be taken into account as evidence of lecturing technique.' (Sadly, there are no surviving recordings of his broadcasts. My mother attests to the beauty of his voice.)

In July, Humphry went to Oxford for the interview, and stayed at Wadham, his old college. Bowra invited him to dinner as usual. Another guest was Elizabeth. She was in Oxford teaching on a lucrative summer course for American students. Fifteen years earlier, Humphry and Elizabeth had met at Bowra's table. Now they reprised the occasion, with wine in their glasses and water under the bridge.

Peacetime Britain had not been entirely kind to Elizabeth. The fever of wartime excitement was over; her range of disguises reduced. There was a new prime minister, Clement Attlee, whom Elizabeth did not care for, and financial concerns bit more powerfully. No government compensation was given for war damage to houses in London and Bowen's Court continued to leak funds. The months leading up to seeing Humphry again had also been difficult emotionally. Alan had taken early retirement due to his faltering health. Then at the beginning of 1948, Charles Ritchie had married his cousin. Elizabeth described as a 'deformity' her inability, on occasion, to accept the fact of Ritchie's marriage. As well as the envy she felt for the new wife Sylvia, there was a renewed sense of her solitude.

The year saw Elizabeth finishing a new novel, *The Heat of the Day*, after a lengthy gestation period. She had written sections of it during the war, sending completed chapters, like evacuated children, to a friend in the country for safekeeping. Set in a wartime city of fractured terraces and souls, it describes another love triangle hingeing on betrayal. It is a world in which secrets tick like watches under your pillow, rooms have the look of no hour, an eyelid comes down on the day. The book is seen by many as her finest, one in which she explores the fragmentation of self both emotionally and syntactically. In response to early reservations expressed before publication about her style she wrote: 'In some cases I <u>want</u> the rhythm to jerk or jar – to an extent, even, which may displease the reader.' Only then could a sentence make 'the exact psychological impact' that she desired.

Elizabeth travelled extensively during the year, lecturing for the British Council in Europe on various aspects of literature, both for financial reasons and possibly also to mitigate her increased loneliness. Being in Oxford for her was an interlude, a pleasurable earning opportunity among friends. By way of contrast, Humphry was hoping for a return to his spiritual heartland – a prodigal's welcome from a city he both loved and feared. He wrote to Madeline that he felt the interview and 'particularly the long stay in this College will have set many emotional ghosts about Oxford to rest'.

Despite feeling that he had underperformed in the interview – 'I made myself rather a trivial person, as indeed in some respects I am' – Humphry was offered the lectureship. He celebrated at home in Cambridge with several bottles of IPA beer. The job began a few months later and with it a weekly commute from Cambridge to Oxford on Monday mornings, returning at the end of the working week. Numerous letters to Madeline mention laundry – shirts, socks, handkerchiefs – which he sent home and which his wife duly washed and posted back.

Humphry's involvement in family life was limited but, more often than not, revolved round literature. He read *Oliver Twist* aloud, adopting a range of voices for the different characters. But one memory of Humphry from this time stands out in my mother's mind. Helen went upstairs to her father's study with his cup of tea and, as usual, knocked on the door for permission to enter. Her father asked her in and read Wordsworth's 'Ode: Intimations of Immortality' aloud to her. He became choked with emotion at the end and said, 'Tears are not very far from the surface.' Helen's shock at seeing her father cry was huge – he never cried in public. Yet the thoughts that lie too deep for tears had burst through Humphry's defences. The loss for his daughters was that his passionate engagement was more with literature than with them.

Within a year of Humphry receiving his post in Oxford, Madeline was turning her hand to more than parenting and laundry duties. A hugely ambitious plan, a definitive edition of the letters of Charles Dickens, was proposed by the Pilgrim Trust, with Humphry at the helm. Before long there was an advisory board and a couple of associate editors. And this time Madeline was more than the shadowy support figure, German translator, and typist of previous years. She had a proper role – as assistant editor. The position brought a fresh bloom to her relationship with Humphry, and gave Madeline's considerable intellectual gifts a garden in which to grow.

Humphry's approach to this colossal task was determined by two main factors – his feelings about the art of biography, and the quality of previous editions of Dickens's letters. These had been neither comprehensive nor sufficiently scholarly. The first was compiled by Dickens's sister-in-law, Georgina Hogarth, and his eldest daughter, Mamie. They left out all intimate family matters and on occasion fused together sections from different letters. John Forster, Dickens's friend and earliest biographer, also took considerable liberties with the originals. In *The Life of Charles Dickens*, Forster added sentimental and dramatic flourishes, altered the spelling of words and pretended letters were written to people other than the original recipient. A more successful selection was included in the vast Nonesuch Press edition of Dickens's work, published in 1938. But as part of a pricey set, the letters remained out of reach for the ordinary reader.

The new edition, taken over and eventually published by the OUP, would present all extant letters of Dickens as they appeared. It would double to more than eleven thousand the number printed by Nonesuch. All letters would be, if possible, transcribed from original manuscripts, microfilm, or photostat. The Houses and their team would start from scratch. As Humphry explained in his 1951 broadcast about the work: 'It is a *sine qua non* of proper biography that the letters should all be brought together in print, properly indexed and annotated; and the filling of the gaps will contribute also to the social history of the century.'

The house in Cambridge became the headquarters of the project. The old lodger's room was given over to Dickens. Occasional guests had to squeeze past him into the small divan bed pushed up against a wall. Over the mantelpiece hung a framed key and index to their filing system. Tall as an eight-year-old and nicknamed 'The Bible', its typed pages were stuck onto a large piece of card – a murky sea of letters, numbers, codes, categories. Later tweaks to the key were just stuck onto the glass. As well as a big writing desk with a typewriter, there was a kitchen table whose cutlery drawer housed the microfilm of the letters. A magic lantern of a projector threw Dickens's words onto a small screen of card in the eyeline of the transcriber. This person, particularly in the early days, was Madeline.

Her excitement about the venture fills her letters to Humphry in Oxford. There is a growing assurance in her own abilities springing from her immersion in the work – the tone of her correspondence changes. Early on she writes: 'I feel I am getting into the swing of the Dickens business and that there's masses I could do.' A couple of years later, she describes to Humphry a fragment of an early Dickens letter she has been sent. The sender thought it was a forgery; Madeline, confident she could recognise Dickens's writing more accurately, was convinced it was authentic. Instead of waiting for Humphry's confirmation that she was right, she confidently acted on her conviction in a bid to save the letter.

There was a gap, however, between the work Madeline was doing and her reward for it. Though assistant editor, she was not being paid as such. Several years into the edition, Madeline fretted whether the '£3 a week to offset housekeeper expenses' was 'a firm understanding' with the publisher or not. This amount was paid to a succession of young German women who looked after the house, thereby leaving Madeline free to devote her time to the edition.

Though effectively working for nothing, Madeline never complained of this. Instead she was full of the work's delights. She was always on the hunt for new, unpublished letters and spent hours chasing down every possible contact. She wrote to Humphry of nights sleepless with excitement about a newly arrived manuscript. Of a particular letter being a 'beauty'. Of how a previous editor had missed a crucial comma in a letter, and how its absence changed the sentence utterly. She was a tireless sleuth, looking at subtle changes in Dickens's signature and handwriting, in the spelling of words, in the colour of paper, to help date letters.

Humphry, too, was caught up in the positive spirit of the Dickens letters. This time of greater intellectual equality between them was one of the happiest periods in their marriage. After one trip home, Humphry wrote Madeline a love letter in the voice of Dickens himself.

HH to MH

Wadham College, Oxford
6 March 1951

Dear Mrs. House,

I am writing very promptly after my return to thank you very much for a most delightful week-end. Your generous hospitality in bed and at board was such that I shall treasure the memory of it when much else has begun to fade; and in particular the supper-party on Saturday evening will remain, with all its attendant circumstances and consequences, for many years a source of revivication and delight. Your charming family, too, did so much to enhance the pleasure of which their mother was the more charming centre.

My dear Mrs. House
Ever most faithfully yours,
Charles Dickens

That I have become, like my grandparents, an editor of letters is a joyful connection across the generations for me. However, they might be appalled at my treatment of their letters. Their purpose was a definite edition of all extant letters written by Dickens reproduced in their entirety. I, meanwhile, leave letters out, chop bits out of others, string them into a narrative paper chain thereby altering their original shape and intention. But my defence would be something that we all share – the sheer excitement of correspondence, the getting to know someone almost as if you know them in the flesh. The ink on the page a kind of lifeblood.

Hanging on the wall of my study in London, just at the edge of my vision is 'The Bible' – the index to my grandparents' extraordinary filing system for the Dickens letters. It is flanked by two paintings of Spain – the leaping limbs of a village fiesta a sharp contrast to its dense print. 'The Bible' charted not only how Humphry and Madeline looked at letters, but also eyed them doing so. Of my grandparents together I have nothing tangible except this vast frame of fading yellow papers. A record of joint epistolary endeavour, a record of their love.

In contrast to the Houses, whose Dickens work made one little room an everywhere, Elizabeth was heading for narrower straits. *The Heat of the Day* gave her an autumnal glow of success, both critically and commercially, that she would never repeat. (It sold 45,000 copies in Great Britain alone.) The novel, published in 1948, looked backwards – not just in its wartime setting, but also in its consciously stylised writing. The early 1950s saw the advent of a different sort of prose – sparse, direct, shocking. Elizabeth's London was invaded by triffids. Novelists such as Graham Greene and William Golding pointed towards the darkness within rather than the superficiality without. When her next novel, *A World of Love*, was being prepared for publication in 1955, Elizabeth asked her agent to rein in her stylistic excesses. She knew, as well as anyone, that tastes change.

Though the first few years of the decade did not see the publication of a novel, Elizabeth was hugely busy. She became a Member of the Royal Commission on Capital Punishment, travelling to prisons on both sides of the Atlantic, and making pertinent recommendations on a range of issues. The affair with Ritchie, which continued despite his marriage, saw her snatch time in Europe or North America to see him. In 1951, she published a short history of Dublin's foremost hotel, *The Shelbourne*. She continued to review and broadcast. She also contributed to women's magazines, such as *Harper's Bazaar* and *House & Garden*; 'they pay handsomely' she had written to Humphry many years earlier. Her association with *Vogue* dated back to the 1930s; in 1936 she wrote an article about the 'aesthetics of aquatics' for their holiday issue. In 1956 she contributed a piece called 'How to be Yourself – But Not Eccentric'.

With Alan ailing, and financial considerations to the fore, the Camerons took the decision to move properly to Bowen's Court at the end of 1951. This followed a minor heart attack that Alan had suffered when Elizabeth had been away in America earlier in the year. Together in Ireland they enjoyed a last few quiet months before Alan died peacefully in his sleep on 26 August 1952.

A few weeks later, almost twenty years after they had first met, Elizabeth wrote to Humphry. This is the last surviving letter she wrote him.

EB to HH

Bowen's Court
16 September 1952

My dear Humphry,

Thank you for your letter: I was comforted by your kindness (no other word for it) and your understanding. Yes I do feel lost, and am in pain. What is good is that everything had been so good: it has been a great thing to have had these months here. And Alan, though he had a gently detached and stoical attitude to death and its possibilities, did so very much want to live – I am glad of that, too.

In these days, I feel ghostly; he seems realler than ever. But the pain left by torn-off happiness has – do you find? – a sort of living substantiality.

Yes, as you say, if this had to happen, this was the place: London would have been terrible, with its unreality. There is a dignity and fitness about things here. Everybody inside and outside this place has been so good; and what's most healing is that here its [sic] natural to weep. Nobody is so ignorant as to say "Forget it."

I hope to live on here if I can afford to. It will mean a hard-working and hard life. I shall be in England from time to time, and I should like very much to see you. Just yet I don't feel much like going to Oxford, though the place does hold some of my best friends. But when I know what my movements are, may I let you know?

It's nice to think of you walking – if you are still doing so? – about Regent's Park. I always liked it best at this time of year.

Love from
Elizabeth

Elizabeth and Alan had been married for almost thirty years. Despite looking for sexual satisfaction and intellectual stimulation outside the marriage, she loved and treasured him. She wrote to Berlin on Alan's death that he was 'not only the anchorage of my life but also the sort of assurance of moral good in it'. Now alone, she felt the weight of having, both legally and psychologically, no next of kin. What she felt she had lost was 'really the feeling of home and of being protected from winds that blow'. The big house remained at her side, but it provided a different wall of solidity. Cold air would seep in at the windows; there was no one to pour the first drink of the day. Loneliness, something she absolutely dreaded, stared her in the face.

Elizabeth's increased isolation was in sharp contrast to the well-peopled world Humphry was enjoying in the early 1950s. Younger than Alan by thirteen years, Humphry was finally receiving the professional recognition he had so long craved. In 1950, he had been made a Senior Research Fellow in English at Wadham, the very Oxford college he had left as chaplain nearly twenty years earlier. Madeline was thrilled: 'Darling, it was a great joy, even though not unexpected, to hear the news from you yesterday afternoon. To me it seems better than any other Fellowship or any other appointment anywhere could be, this coming full-circle back to Wadham, – even if you start off later on yet another curve!'

Her delight at his success was not always mirrored by positive feelings on his part. Humphry was occasionally overhung with morbid thoughts, a despondency he had suffered throughout his life. He confessed to Madeline: 'The love of my family, the affection and good opinion of my friends, which I have evidence of, day in and day out, ought now, when outward things have become so much better than ever before for me, to make me a happy, contented, active person. But they don't: I still have this restless, and sometimes evil, spirit in me that seems deliberately to sour and foul what could be sweet and fair.'

A small scribbled note from the end of 1950 reads: 'Death and deadly illness everywhere in the last two years.' His father had just died. His older brother had been given six months to live. His own health was suffering from the bruising schedule and commute – he was overweight, and admitted to feeling 'done in' by any sort of physical activity. He was still smoking and conscious of occasional chest pains. His response to this, expressed in an unfinished letter to Madeline was: 'I hate the idea of being a hypochondriac even more than the idea of being ill. [...] At the moment I'm not ignoring it, but trying to get used to it.'

Despite these concerns, he continued to work flat out. Building on his reputation as an inspirational lecturer, he was awarded the Clark Lectureship at Cambridge for the academic year 1951–1952. This series of lectures on Coleridge would be published as a book which he dedicated to Madeline and the children. He embarked on the preparation of two publications about Hopkins, one of which was a new biography in place of the one he did not complete during the war. The work on Dickens's letters was expanding in scope and ambition. By early 1954, Humphry imagined eight volumes of seven hundred pages each. He devised a work schedule for the letters mapping out the next three years for himself and Madeline. For both of them, it would be the project of a lifetime.

In the middle of a February night in 1955, Humphry woke up screaming, his heart on fire. The pain in his chest was so severe Madeline rushed downstairs to telephone the GP. Breathlessly, she requested an immediate house call – yes, this was an emergency. The doctor arrived and administered a thrombolytic to try to save him. The injection came too late. Humphry was dead before dawn.

Crossing the upstairs landing a couple of hours later, Madeline went into my mother's bedroom. Helen was about to grumble about the unnecessarily early wake-up call when Madeline told her simply that her father had died in the night. There was no school that day for either Helen or nine-year-old John. Rachel, by this time at Oxford studying History, was called home.

Humphry was laid out in an open coffin in his study, surrounded by his books. Regarding him from above the mantelpiece was the Dickens Bible – the map he had imagined would guide his feet through years to come. Rachel, entering the room on her return, was struck by how young he looked. And when she kissed him, how cold. My mother remembers nothing more than being conscious, for the first time, of the sweet smell of death. In the days that followed, Helen would long for something that she could not remember her father ever having given her – a kiss.

Elizabeth's reaction to the news of Humphry's death is recorded in a letter she wrote to Charles Ritchie from Rome on 25 February: 'The only thing that is making me sad, and very sad, is that I suddenly saw in the Times that Humphry House, that friend and long-ago former love of mine, is dead. At 46. The announcement just said "suddenly". I've written to Maurice Bowra to ask the details. How people come alive, almost unbearably, when they're suddenly dead. And he was a darling, and a great, though an odd, character.'

Bowra, the person who had introduced the couple, replied to Elizabeth:

> Humphry's death is an appalling blow. He was my most intimate and distinguished colleague, of a strength and integrity never at all common and certainly not common now. [...] My only comfort is that this College, after treating him disgracefully in 1932, had made amends and treated him well for the last few years. He had a great hold on my colleagues, who liked his sudden thirst for blood and his genial way of telling them that they were no good. Poor Madeleine [sic] is left with about £200 a year and three children. We shall have to see if the university cannot help. Rupert Hart Davis has been exceedingly kind and helpful and will probably find a job for Madeleine, who is broken in to editing Dickens' letters and is well qualified to go on with them.

Shortly after Humphry's death, a photographer arrived at the bewildered house full of letters. A portrait of Humphry lying in his coffin was taken, his face firm but frozen. The photograph would lie in a box at Madeline's bedside for the rest of her life.

She began to deal with Humphry's papers, the most urgent of which was his will. Made in the frantic weeks before his departure for Calcutta in 1936, it left his estate to his 'dear' wife. Three other people, central to his life at the time, were also left some of his personal effects. One of them was Elizabeth. To her he bequeathed several items, most notably an etching done by Pablo Picasso, an illustration of Ovid's *Metamorphoses*. There were also a couple of books about Aristotle's *Poetics*, a facsimile of the Trinity College manuscript of John Milton's early poems, and his copy of the same poet's works, bound in red leather.

With his will, Humphry seemed to be forcing the two women together again just as he had tried to do twenty years earlier. Whether they met, and whether Humphry's wishes were carried out is not known. Neither is the fate of the Picasso etching.

What Madeline felt in the barren days after Humphry's death she expressed in a letter to Isaiah Berlin.

MH to IB

61 Bateman Street, Cambridge
22 February 1955

My dear Isaiah,

I am so glad to have had this letter from you, and I want to see you more than I can say. What you can do, I don't know. There may be things. The problems, both literary and personal, are vast.

I know well that Humphry loved you. – I write that in the past tense with an effort: for still – though I was with him when he died and he lay dead in this house for four days – I can't really believe any of it. You write of his "noble and in some ways tragic life" – Yes, Isaiah, those are the right words. And it makes me cry so much if I try to write what, after years of marriage, I know to be true – of his goodness and greatness, that I am grateful for these words you give me.

I've got to tell you about his Will – because you are mentioned in it. He made it in 1936, before going to India; and lately it had become a stock family joke. It leaves you any of his books on Medieval and Indian philosophy that you might care to have. Since about 1938 Humphry has known this was nonsense. The Indian books are worthless: they lie in the attic here, deep in dust. The books on Medieval philosophy? I think he believed he had nothing you would want. But I should be fearfully glad if there were any you wanted.

Yes, I'm coming to Oxford on Thursday, and am half (but only half) pledged to have tea with Rupert Hart Davis, who will be coming from London. Do you know him? He is being good past description in involving himself in the two unfinished Hopkins books. (In the Dickens project he was already involved.) Would you care to see him?

There's no time for you to answer these questions. But I shall see you. Love and gratitude, dear Isaiah

Madeline

This anguished letter is the piece of correspondence that, of everything I have seen, has squeezed my heart most. I had spent the day in the Bodleian Library in Oxford reading the letters that

Humphry had written to Isaiah Berlin. Confident I had seen everything of note, I dawdled through the 1940s when the friendship between the two men was less close than before. Expecting little of note in the 1950s, and with my time nearly gone, I flicked through the final few years. Suddenly I caught sight in the index of the words: 'Madeline House, about the death of her husband Humphry House.' In the folder were a couple of blue pages, still crisp, in my grandmother's straggly hand.

Before I had got to the end of the second paragraph with its awful shift of verb tense, I was in tears. I now saw properly the depth of her love, the quality of her devotion. And the future she contemplated for herself, shrouded in loss. I read the letter several times, the tears flowing freely. Then as quickly as I could, I transcribed the letter and returned it to its home.

Haunted by the image of Linny sitting beside Humphry's body for four days, I left the library and walked across Oxford to meet a friend. Together we entered a cramped little theatre for a student production of Lorca's *The House of Bernarda Alba* and sat on a squeaky bench near the back. A former pupil of mine was playing one of the daughters of the house, caught in the stifling hold of family mourning. A house. Its death. A woman dressed in black.

Some years later, Madeline received a volume of poetry from Humphry's old friend Stephen Spender. Written inside the collection, entitled *The Generous Days*, is the following: 'To Madeleine [sic] House as for Humphrey [sic] (see p. 16). Stephen Spender, Feb '70.'

On page sixteen is the following poem, the sixth in a sequence of eleven bagatelles:

'For Humphrey House'

When you became a christian, mocking (not mocking), I said
"Then, bless me!" You growled: "Kneel!"
So I knelt down there in the High.
I carry this like an amulet always. You know –
If you watch from bright air under earth where you lie.

Elizabeth's final home (the white house), Hythe, Sussex

Chapter 16

Hythe: *Requiescat*

'I always say the house chose us, rather than the other way round,' says the dignified woman deliberately, her fine eyes meeting mine across the room. She wears no jewellery, is dressed in a long skirt and a plain grey top. She sits on a white sofa, above which hang several floral oil paintings. French windows open onto a lush garden. There is a caw of seagulls, a slight breeze. I take a bite of shortbread and return my coffee cup to the marquetry table at my side.

'We weren't even looking for a house but the agent called us... we wanted to move because of my husband's health... it all happened very fast. I knew of Elizabeth Bowen, of course, and had read some of her books. Then I did some more research and found out her second name was...'

'Dorothea!' I interrupt, unable to suppress my delight in coincidence.

'Yes, we share the same name. And so, we are here for now because it just feels right.'

'Elizabeth would have loved that,' I say smiling.

'I know,' says Dorothea, and the space between us, in Elizabeth's former home, shrinks perceptibly.

'This bit of the town is called Front-line Hythe. They are very proud of the War here. I am Prussian, born in Königsberg. My father died in the Battle of Stalingrad, or starved to death as a prisoner of war. I saw the sky red over Dresden. We suffered too…' She stops, deep in the past. 'Reconciliation is so important. That was something Elizabeth understood. You see it in her Nativity play. She was very brave.'

I am shown the house. The living room and the upstairs study both have windows on two sides, something Elizabeth loved. One looks out to sea, the other across towards Rye and the Dungeness peninsula. The view from the kitchen is of St Leonard's church and its graveyard. 'You can see the lights of France, like jewels, when you are washing up.' Dorothea tells me that cuts to council funding mean that Elizabeth's novels are no longer to be found in Hythe library, and of her decision to get the house blessed when she and her husband moved in. There are, she claims, no ghosts.

'You know Hythe means haven in Anglo-Saxon?' asks Dorothea. 'I love Gerard Manley Hopkins and especially the poem "Heaven-Haven". It is about the search for a peaceful place. That was what Elizabeth was looking for when she moved to this house, and I think she found it.'

Before I leave, Dorothea gives me some photographs of the house, a booklet about Hythe celebrities (all men apart from Elizabeth), and her business card. On a blue background is a single figure, a woman. She is seen from behind, walking alone.

1956

'Why, then, fear new chapters in our personal being? Each decade is, surely, a fresh beginning – a challenge, yes: but also an invitation to adventure further, to experience more.' In an essay entitled 'The Beauty of Being Your Age', Elizabeth discusses how people, particularly women, approach the uneven pavement of later life. Face powder cannot hide the wrinkles; bones creak in the morning. She is speaking of herself but also of Madeline – only three years separated the two women. To thrive in your fifties and sixties requires elasticity of spirit as much as body. Her outlook is one of measured optimism: 'For women who learn how to live them, or know instinctively, these ages hold unforeseen treasure.'

The agility of soul and intellect common to Madeline and Elizabeth meant that both continued to 'adventure further' in these years. The contours of their emotional lives were changed – they shared the status of being widows – but their energy and productivity were undiminished. And there remained a frayed thread of contact between them – Humphry, though dead, was not gone.

Elizabeth's schedule in the 1950s and early 1960s was relentless. There were lecture tours to Germany for the British Council, frequent trips to Rome, summer visits to Bowen's Court, the conclusion of the Royal Commission on Capital Punishment. She was awarded an Honorary D. Litt by Oxford University to follow the one she had received earlier from Dublin University. Two novels were published in this time: *A World of Love* (1955) and *The Little Girls* (1964), as well as her travel book *A Time in Rome* (1960). They are works written looking over her shoulder, at the past, at history, and how it is recorded.

Elizabeth was enjoying a fresh burst of popularity and society – this time in America. Since her first visit in the 1930s, she had revelled in the speed and shininess, the welcome and laid-back feel of the USA. Now she had a social circle in New York, as well as friends further afield such as May Sarton and Eudora Welty. Though cocktail parties were always welcome, Elizabeth's reason for being there was more mundane. She badly needed the money. Her dwindling coffers were pleasingly replenished in her latest role – as a teacher and lecturer.

In Elizabeth's fiction, teachers are always desperate, stunted women; some even fantasise about killing their pupils. Her final novel,

Eva Trout (1968), features a teacher called Iseult Arble who has to rank as one of her most shipwrecked characters, and there is plenty of competition for that crown. These lonely, often unmarried women – all tweed skirts and shrill demands – seem an easy target. Now Elizabeth, widowed and in reduced circumstances, joined their ranks – ones that comprised Madeline's peers from university, and the plumbers' daughters Humphry had lectured in Exeter.

A photograph of her class at Vassar College in New York State in the 1960s, sees Elizabeth seated majestically on the left of the frame. Spread across the floor, eyes up in admiration, is a group of young women. They feel they are in the presence of a star; Elizabeth glows in the knowledge. But being admired as a teacher is one thing – teasing out the talents of your students quite another.

As a third generation teacher, after Humphry and my mother, I could not help wondering how good Elizabeth was in the classroom. The clues to her performance lie in her teaching notes, which form part of the Bowen archive at the University of Texas in Austin. Of all the original documents of hers I have touched these excited me most. Two ring-bound student exercise books, covered in doodles, contain her planning for a short story course taught at Vassar in 1960. At the back a list of her pupils, a little memo to remind her to attend a staff meeting, and a note to herself about where her reserve shelf in the library was to be found.

Every sentence of each class was written out in continuous prose, lecture-like. Though possibly a way to minimise her stammer, it showed clearly the points she wished to highlight. Full marks for preparation. The course itself was extremely well organised; a wide range of writers used each week to illustrate various aspects of the short story. About each there were detailed biographical notes. Full marks, too, for homework.

Week one introduced the short story as a form. Her opening remarks are these: 'Form is the <u>servant</u> of subject. [<u>Not</u> a rigid container into which the subject – having been poured – must adapt itself.]' Week two was the short story as 'a unique expression'. And the writer chosen to illustrate this point? Elizabeth chose herself, of course.

As the course progressed, her questions became more interesting and her notes less formal. Rather than the lecture style of the first semester, there were bullet points (all teachers have been there). These are two of the questions she asked when the class was studying the American short story writer, O. Henry:

1) What would Chekhov, Joyce, Maupassant, Hemingway develop onward from an O. Henry opening?
2) Who are O. Henry's descendants? Conscious or unconscious?

What she was interested in as a teacher was helping students explore how stories may change over time and are shaped by it; how narratives that start in one place can have a variety of endings; and how a writer's spirit may be carried forward in the work of others, even unconsciously. Creative reinterpretations in the best and broadest sense. That is what Elizabeth asked of her students. It is what she and my forebears ask of me. It is what I ask of mine.

My A level English Literature class filed in smiling. A baking hot day in Madrid. Their last week of secondary school before their final exams; their last lesson with me. The group were a lovely mix: four boys and five girls; some native English speakers, some Spaniards; a reflection of the dynamic international school in which I taught.

I felt a pang, not just for this particular group, but also for myself. Within two weeks, I would be gone. My reason was simple: Elizabeth, Humphry, and Madeline required more attention than I was currently able to give them. And so I was leaving my lovely, noisy flat in the city centre, uprooting myself, and heading back to London.

I was slightly embarrassed about the text I was asking the pupils to look at. It was something I had written, the account (now much changed) of reading the correspondence between Elizabeth and Humphry for the first time at John's house in Catford. I hoped the students would not see this as an appalling act of vanity on my part, a fishing for compliments. I felt it was a way of trusting myself to them, in much the same way that they had trusted themselves to me over the years.

I read the passage to them and then gave them about fifteen minutes to write. Their responses were wonderfully varied and perceptive. Some focused on the use of language, particularly on the metaphor of the box. Others on the way the story was told. All, without exception, gave me suggestions about how to improve. One wrote a full page entitled, 'What I would change'. Another commented: 'That first sentence has to go!! LOL :).' A third advised: 'The writer must write about her explorations, but must definately [sic] avoid saying how she "found herself" (sorry for the cliché, Miss) in India, for example.'

The hour was soon over, and the students bundled themselves noisily out of the room. 'See you, Miss!' Only then did I realise that the passage I had given them was a kind of letter, a goodbye to them, the school, and my life in Spain. I picked up the students' replies – so funny, so clever – and got ready to leave. Those I would treasure. Teaching, at its best, is a joyful correspondence.

I turned off the air conditioning and packed my bag. Then I left the classroom, closing the door behind me. The sense of an ending, but also of a beginning.

The pace of America could not chase the clouds from Elizabeth's sky. Her married lover, Charles Ritchie, had a wife to put first and a diplomatic career at its height. Elizabeth tried, just as she had with the Houses, to make Ritchie's marriage an irrelevance in their affair. She met with only limited success. Her letters to Ritchie in this period are increasingly shrill and clingy. (Though many of these letters appear in Victoria Glendinning's fine book, *Love's Civil War*, about the correspondence between Ritchie and Elizabeth, the originals have not been so lucky. At the time of writing, they sit uncatalogued in a back room of the archive in Texas, out of their spatial and emotional context. It seems a sad fate, not just for these particular letters, but also for Elizabeth, with her keen sense of rootedness on the one hand, and dispossession on the other.)

A further strain on Elizabeth's emotional health was something that had been a mainstay in her life – Bowen's Court. When Alan died, Elizabeth wrote to Humphry that she was going to try to go on living in the house. Each year this proved more difficult, without adequate moral support or financial means. The old house was becoming a troublesome parent. Finally, in 1959, Elizabeth decided to sell Bowen's Court, placing it in the hands of a local estate agent. Elizabeth told no one of her plans to sell, not even her family. One story goes that her cousins, the Gilbert Butlers, came dashing down to Bowen's Court in a bid to buy it when they finally received news of Elizabeth's intentions. The house was important to them both and they could have kept the family home alive. The Butlers were told they were too late – the sale of the property to a man called Cornelius O'Keefe could not be reversed. There was, the story concludes, a large brown envelope of money involved.

That O'Keefe had been saying the right things to Elizabeth in the run up to the sale is not in doubt. She fancied that his children might fill her home in the future. In fact, he was primarily interested in the land and timber. And so the box-shaped house, full of memories and history, passed out of the Bowen family. With the sale of Bowen's

Court, Elizabeth severed a crucial cord, both with the land and within herself. When it was demolished the following year and the trees of her ancestors felled, she was spiritually homeless.

The early 1960s saw her living back in Oxford for a while, within shouting distance of her old home. She tried to rekindle the spirit of the 1930s, but the university and the town had spun away from her. She wrote to Ritchie of an encounter with Miss Lucy Sutherland, the Principal of Lady Margaret Hall: 'When we were introduced she said, oh, was I staying in Oxford for the weekend? Hardly, I replied somewhat icily, as I live here – in Old Headington, next door to the Berlins. Really I think these women's colleges (with the exception of St. Anne's) are the limit. I'm quite a credit to my, the female, sex in a small way, but where all these women are concerned I could die and rot.'

When she left Oxford for the last time, she did not even pack up her possessions properly. Boxes of papers were left in the cellar – old bank statements and, more importantly for me, all Humphry's letters to her. These were the ones returned to my uncle John many years later.

Their survival is all the more surprising given Elizabeth's feelings towards letters as she got older. Her literary executor Spencer Curtis Brown described her in later life as someone who hardly ever kept letters, preferring to reply swiftly to correspondence and then dispose of it. But there are some possible theories as to why Humphry's letters survived beyond the first flush of epistolary importance. The clues lie in the fate of other letters that Elizabeth wrote to Virginia Woolf.

When Nigel Nicolson began editing the Woolf letters, he got in touch with Curtis Brown hoping to track down the letters she had written to Elizabeth. He was informed that none of Woolf's letters to Elizabeth survived. Then a few months later, Curtis Brown contacted Nicolson to say that some of Woolf's correspondence had been discovered by a great nephew of Elizabeth's in a chest in Ireland. This seems to indicate that some letters written to Elizabeth survived in spite of her, not because of her. Humphry's letters, like those of Virginia Woolf, seem to have been kept by chance rather than carefully hoarded. They ended up in the cluttered attic of past experiences, just like the letters in *A World of Love*.

In 1965, Elizabeth finally found her way back to Hythe in Kent. There was no more family silver to sell to fund the purchase of her small red-brick house, so instead she sold something just, if not more, valuable – her literary archive. On this strip of the coast she had lived as a child with her mother after her father's breakdown. Her affection for it was enduring, and a return to these grafted roots brought her some of the centredness she had been lacking in recent years. She loved Kent's wide views, dramatic coastlines, and late-blooming villas. Hythe itself had appeared in her fiction, playing a crucial role in the affair between Max and Karen in *The House in Paris*. The Kent coast also features in her final novel, *Eva Trout*, published in 1968.

The eponymous heroine, with a fortune as large as her self-delusion, buys a house in North Foreland. Just down the road is Broadstairs, the seaside town so well known to Dickens. The cottage he used as inspiration for the home of Betsey Trotwood in *David Copperfield* now houses the Dickens Museum. In one scene, Eva meets her former teacher Iseult Arble at Dickens's house. Iseult has, after a becalming marriage, refound her intellectual edge and is hard at work translating a French re-evaluation of Dickens: 'She was now in a state of total immersion in his works, and letters.' (The uncanny parallel with Madeline's life is impossible to ignore.) When Iseult enters Dickens's study, she is most struck by the empty chair in which the great man used to sit. Eva is not so reverential – she has, on previous occasions, sat in the chair for fun.

In the scene, Elizabeth quotes not just from a biography of Dickens, but also from his correspondence. By the time Elizabeth wrote *Eva Trout*, the first volume of Dickens's letters, with Madeline a key player, had been published to considerable acclaim. It is tempting to imagine Elizabeth with Madeline's edition in front of her, poring over her scholarship, reading her perspicacious footnotes, the empty chair sitting squarely between them.

Elizabeth, after the death of Alan, imagined grief as a geographical state 'with a climate and landscape of its own'. To this place of squalls and crags Madeline was brought when Humphry died. Young John loomed larger in her emotional life as a result of his father's absence. My mother, on completing secondary school, went up to Oxford to read English. To this day she speaks with regret about having missed Humphry as one of her lecturers. (She was at Somerville, one of the women's colleges that Elizabeth found so awful.) The fatherless family continued the tradition of the two-week summer holiday at a coastal guest house. On one occasion, there was a more exotic destination – Madeline took the family with her to Switzerland when she went to work on the Dickens letters owned by the Comtesse de Suzannet.

Madeline was always a private person, and her letters to her close friends, the Calder-Marshalls, speak only briefly of her own feelings of loss. She writes just as much about her anxiety for her children. Arthur reassures her:

> Don't rack your heart so much. I'm sure that both Rachel and Helen regard you as an utterly managable [sic] Mum. Far more predictable than Humphry was. You have got their love. […] Obviously both of them have got your combined abilities. And as you know, I always said that intuitively yours were straighter than Humphry's though you did not dare to trust them. You went by your star, Humphry by his map and compass. He was always able to tell you the route by which you had reached where you were.

Beyond the personal, were the literary problems Humphry left behind for Madeline. There were two incomplete Hopkins books and, more importantly, the Dickens letters. Knowing that someone with a university post was crucial to the edition, the publishers enlisted the assistance of Graham Storey, a fellow of Trinity Hall. Madeline, despite not having an academic position or reputation, was seen as vital to the success of the Dickens project and continued in her role as editor. It was a remarkable vote of confidence in her abilities. Humphry's prophecy, in an early letter to Elizabeth, that Madeline had the 'capacity for interest and intelligent work' which might 'develope [sic] her into something quite big' had finally come true. It was just as the Calcutta fortune teller had predicted. Now with a different man at her side, Madeline went back to work – there were eleven thousand letters in need of careful attention.

The first volume of the Dickens letters was published in 1965, ten years after Humphry's death. Madeline's major share in the work was recognised by the award of the Rose Mary Crawshay Prize of the British Academy, given annually for a critical or historical work connected with English Literature written by a woman. Calder-Marshall was effusive in his congratulation: 'Gratters, old girl. You deserve it. A hundred smackers not just for slogging, but for being the continuity between a pipe-dream and a performance. Have you ever thought, lovey, how impossible it would have been for Humphry to carry through the Dickens letters at the same time as acting as a don? He would have gone scatty. Or schizo. The only way he could help you was the way it happened.'

How strange it must have been for Madeline to return home with the prize. Conscious of Humphry's role as the founding father of the edition. Conscious too that Humphry's sudden departure had done more than facilitate her own success – it was an essential ingredient in it. The house now became even more centred on her scholarship, and that of the new team working on the Dickens letters. 'The Bible' still hung on the wall, his original design was still largely followed. But neither the study, nor the prize, was his.

Elizabeth had enjoyed a life of rude health, despite all the cigarettes smoked and gin drunk. But the smoker's cough that had rattled throughout her life developed ominously into bronchitis in 1970. The following year she required treatment in a nursing home for a bout of pneumonia. As a result, she left the sea-fretted house in Hythe for a warm hotel annex in Woodstock, Oxfordshire.

The warmer months of 1972 resulted not in a restoration of spirits, but a loss of one of her most treasured assets – her voice. Now speaking in whispers, she went to see a specialist at University College Hospital, London. The diagnosis was lung cancer, for which she underwent brutal radium therapy. Despite feeling that the treatment had affected her mental sharpness, she zealously read entries for the Booker Prize which she was judging that year. She also watched hours of televised tennis from Wimbledon, the rallies top-spinning through her dreams. Once out of hospital, she continued to see friends as much as she could, played Scrabble at home, and reread all her own work. A last trip to Ireland for Christmas to stay with friends finally took the wind from her sails. Shortly after returning to England, she was admitted to hospital in London. She did not leave again, and died with Ritchie at her side on 22 February 1973.

She was buried beside her husband in the churchyard of St Colman's in Farahy, County Cork. Theirs is a tall, straight memorial on raised ground, its apex a simple cross surrounded by curlicues. Behind the tomb lies a band of trees and the ivied wall of her family's former estate. Alan's name is above Elizabeth's on the single gravestone, his military cross remembered. She is described merely as 'his wife'. Her writing is not mentioned – the words 'Elizabeth Bowen' appear in parenthesis under her full married name.

Elizabeth Bowen's grave, Farahy churchyard, County Cork

The church itself, a short walk across the fields from Bowen's Court, was where generations of her family had worshipped, sitting in their pew at the front. An unused Victorian schoolhouse is tacked on the side, reached through the church's main door. There are still newspaper cuttings about Elizabeth on its walls, and a large black-and-white photograph of Bowen's Court over the fireplace. There is also a plaque. It reads: 'In memory of Elizabeth Cole Bowen of Bowens [sic] Court. Wife of Alan Cameron. Born 7 June 1899. Died 22 February 1973. She left in her writings a proof of her genius, a reflection of her personality, and a history of her home.'

Losing Elizabeth was a devastating blow for her cousin Audrey. And so she reached out to Rosamond Lehmann, a keen spiritualist, asking about how to get in touch with Elizabeth beyond the grave.

Soon afterwards, Audrey wrote with delight to Rosamond:

> The news is not only good but electrifying. I wrote to Lady Sandys as you suggested; she wrote back and asked for something like a letter from Elizabeth, which I sent her. She must have dealt with it soon because yesterday I got a lovely message via the "writer", which she said came through very easily. It was short; ("power" apparently limited) but so loving and so delighted. Utterly thrilled with her present life, and urging me to "unblock" and communicate as we always did.

Audrey's 'contact' with Elizabeth was triggered, inevitably, by a letter. Its electric charge pierced the wall of the tomb and brought tidings of Elizabeth by return. The connection between the living and the dead, so central to Elizabeth's world view, was felt afresh. The writer of *A World of Love* was now the spirit that corresponds across death's divide by letter.

And Elizabeth's spectral presence would be felt by more people than just Audrey – as the last surviving member of the triangle was about to find out.

Madeline in the garden of 61 Bateman Street, Cambridge

Chapter 17

Cambridge: *A World of Love*

At the beginning of one of my favourite Pedro Almodóvar films, a village of women descends on the local cemetery. It is All Saints' Day – everyone is there, as they should be, to honour their dead. They scrub tombs in a warm wind, arrange their cut flowers, catch up with the neighbours, exchange loud exclamations and kisses.

The same day of the year finds me facing a chilly drizzle in Cambridge City Cemetery. The reception area and chapel are locked. Apart from one man off in the distance, the place is deserted. The only noise is a muted hum of traffic which drifts across the grey rows, their uniform height broken only by a Celtic cross or an elaborate Victorian angel. This is the first time I have visited the grave of my grandparents. It is cold, dreary, and still.

My mother, hearing of my plans to go to Cambridge, is uncharacteristically fretful. About the imagined state of the grave. About not writing interesting enough letters to Madeline from Africa, where my parents lived. About not being in better touch. She asks me to plant small bulbs, which Madeline loved, at the grave. My mother is not known for her sentimentality. I am struck by her request, and so arrive in Cambridge with gardening gloves, packets of bulbs, a trowel and some washing-up liquid.

The directions I have received from the council's bereavement services are good – the grave of my grandparents is in sector 22a, next to a path. The plain headstone carries Humphry's dates and his simple epitaph: 'Man of letters.' Carved beneath this are the words: 'And his wife. Madeline Edith House. 31 Dec 1903 – 21 Feb 1978.' Though worn by the elements, the headstone is still upright. It responds well to a scrub with soapy water.

And then I am on all fours in front of the stone. Digging at my grandparents' grave. Kneeling on plastic bags so as to avoid the worst of the rain. My trowel clicks against the rocky, unyielding ground. I dig with more purpose. As I drop the crocus and snowdrop bulbs into the shallow trench, something tugs at me. A feeling of gratitude for my family, and gladness that I am here in Cambridge, today of all days. Job done, I stand up, stamp the tussocks of grass back into place, and leave.

Back home that evening I call my mother. I tell her about the grave, the rain, the bulbs, the quiet. She confesses she hasn't been back to the cemetery since Madeline's death. We plan to go back to Cambridge together in the spring, when the flowers are in bloom. Return. *Volver.*

1974

The house in Cambridge is still vivid in my memory, like a childhood friend. Opening the enormous, solemn front door you were greeted by a wide staircase. To the left was a bright sitting room. Blessed with afternoon light, it contained a florally painted baby grand piano which was always out of tune. At the front was the dark study, in what was the dining room, looking out over the street with its dense, oozy lime trees. This was the room where Madeline worked on the Dickens letters.

It is also the room I most associate with Linny when we went to visit her as children. And where, in 1974, we celebrated Madeline's literary success. Mrs Fuller, my grandmother's daily helper, brought in a large book-shaped cake for tea. As a greedy ten-year-old, I thought eating the book more important than digesting the reason for the celebration. The icing told the story: the third volume of Dickens's letters was published. Madeline had been working on the correspondence for almost twenty-five years.

As Madeline's frame shrunk, so did her occupancy of the house. A convenient television (black and white) arrived in the study, on which we watched *The Dam Busters* on a rainy afternoon. There was a large cabinet on one wall into which all her scraps of paper, including Embassy cigarette coupons, were cast. We were to check that the coupons from empty or abandoned packets were put safely in the stash and took great relish in telling her that she still needed six thousand more for a lawn mower.

The Cambridge house backed onto the city's Botanic Garden, whose trees were visible over the wall. From the back door you went down a short flight of steps, guarded by two small stone lions, onto the lawn. The grandchildren ran around, played cricket. Here was taken the most beautiful photograph of my mother and grandmother – my taller mother with her arms lovingly and casually draped across my grandmother's chest. My mother wears a fashionable dress and cardigan; my grandmother fixes the camera with a determined smile. Her eyes, now more pronounced because of a thyroid problem, gleam behind her glasses.

Madeline with Helen, the author's mother

The fragments I have of Linny do not make up a full picture. Indeed, they seem as incomplete as a postcard that she sent me when I was nine which I still have. It is a painting of Venice by J. M. W. Turner. The reverse merely says: 'Dear Julia, Isn't it sad to think that Venice is sinking into the water? Love Linny.' It remains the most enigmatic card I have ever received, and the only piece of writing I own of hers that was intended for me.

The dead – those shadowy thirds and demon lovers – are never truly gone in Elizabeth's world. They linger, influence, repossess. As Elizabeth herself said, on hearing news of Humphry's death: 'How people come alive, almost unbearably, when they're suddenly dead.' And so it proved with Elizabeth, her death in 1973 heralding a renewed interest in her life and work. A biography written by Victoria Glendinning was soon under way. Before long, the bones of the affair between Humphry and

Elizabeth were disturbed. What Glendinning needed was to have the story fleshed out. An unexpected letter arrived at the Cambridge house.

By this time, Madeline herself was in her seventies. Though still living independently, she was increasingly frail. Faced with a request for a meeting with Glendinning, Madeline began to search the house for Elizabeth's letters. Likely storage places gave way to unlikely ones, before she eventually brought the missives out of hiding. Elizabeth was removed from the yellowing envelopes. Madeline travelled back forty years to the affair and its aftermath.

She reread of Elizabeth's 'simple, direct' feeling for Humphry, of her weeping in the library at Bowen's Court after Humphry's departure in 1933. Of dinners in Oxford, and her unfulfilled desire for a child. Of Elizabeth's pride in her status as a 'confirmed writer' and her thoughts about the meaning of home. Madeline was reminded of Elizabeth's awful visit to Exeter when Humphry had insisted on thrusting the two women into the same room and sphere. And of other times they shared – in Oxford, at the zoo, and in Ireland. Alone in the dark study she remembered Humphry as a young man, her love for him, the painful infidelities, the nights dancing in Calcutta, and days toiling together over Dickens. His death was a daily blow – the crack in the foundations of the family house would never seal.

Madeline set to work copying out fragments of text that she felt able to share with Glendinning. These notes, in her familiar spidery hand, are on the back of roughly typed scrap pages from the Dickens letters. On one side of the paper was Madeline's professional editing; on the other, her personal. The Dickens letters appear as they were written, in continuous prose, carefully and exactly set down. By way of contrast, the snatches from Elizabeth's letters that Madeline copied are jottings, half-sentences, abbreviations. The punctuation is formed of ellipses, question marks, inverted commas that are opened but not closed. There's a certain breathlessness about them, emotionally and structurally. The pages are palimpsests. Held up to the light, both sides of my grandmother shine through simultaneously.

Reading these letters in the safety of her study, appraising the contents with scholarly rigour, was one thing. Quite another was to entrust this information to someone else, and then to a wider reading public. Madeline realised she needed two things in order to do this successfully. The first was emotional strength. The second was the skills of a storyteller. With Humphry and Elizabeth dead, it remained her narrative to spin.

In preparation for the first meeting with Glendinning, Madeline sought advice from Arthur Calder-Marshall. As a well-known novelist and biographer, Arthur had a wealth of strategies about how to deal with an inquisition, about how to strike the right balance between concealment and revelation.

Arthur Calder-Marshall (ACM) to MH

12 Richmond Bridge Mansions,
Willoughby Rd, Twickenham
2 October [1975]

My dear Madeline,

[…] I'm trying to think as V.G. [Victoria Glendinning] will do, when she comes to see you on Thursday.

As a biographer, I can assure you from experience, she will want to know everything and if there is a suggestion of a cover-up, her curiosity will be whetted and she will try to find from other people what she can't find out from you. So I think you ought to ensure that she leaves you with her curiosity satisfied.

On the other hand, remember that she is really interested in finding out the truth about E.B., her life and her books. She is not interested in Humphry, you, your children and grandchildren as such; but equally, I would guess but this is for you to determine, she would probably not wish to give any of you pain. The important thing from a biographer's point of view is not the name of Humphry House, but the fact that when E.B. married A.C., he was incapable of taking her virginity; that she looked around for someone to do so and she found a brilliant young academic to do so. He was already engaged to be married, but was flattered into acquiescence; and even after he married, she continued the liaison in a ruthless way, until the young man was forced to take an academic appointment abroad. […]

This is what is important to V.G. as a biographer, not the identity of H.H., M.H., the A.C.M.s: and this, I think, you could tell her, provided that no names are named. I think that V.G. would settle for this, provided that you could give her extracts from E.B.'s letters which would substantiate this. I think you should stipulate that nothing should be quoted which identify places and persons, since E.B's emotions etc are the important thing.

Remember that you have the copyright of any letters which Humphry wrote to Elizabeth, and you can refuse to grant her the right to quote from these (supposing they survive, which you should find out before you start talking). She might very well trade anonymity for the right to quote. […]

But, my dear Madeline, you will say, lots of people will guess and even some reviewers will mention who this young academic was. Of course, they will or may. But this information will not be in the book. […]

What is the alternative? That V.G. gets on the scent and starts sniffing around. What would I do, under the circs? Make a bee-line for Isaiah Berlin, that polymathic gossip, whose account would be highly convincing, vastly entertaining, not very true, but since it was concerned with two dead persons, not subject to libel.

[...] Elizabeth might appear as a bitch (which she wasn't, except in veterinary terms, as being 'on heat', poor dear). Humphry might appear as a randy young man, broke and a bit of a snob; as most of us were at that time. You appear as the conquering wife. Amor prevalebit. Which is how it was. [...]

Then there is the next generation. If everything is suppressed (but leaks out) at least some of your grandchildren may think of Humphry in relation to Elizabeth as a sort of Don Juan to be emulated, whereas he behaved, despite his other excellences, as a shit from Sevenoaks on the intellectual ascendant to a room at the academic top. Probably none of them will care much anyway; but better surely for them to love and admire him warts and all, than emulate the warts.

I hope, dear Madeline, this grey letter will make things black and white to you.

Love from us both
Arthur.

Going through a pile of old photographs at the bottom of a cupboard in my aunt's house, I came across a photograph of Arthur Calder-Marshall. A fine Roman nose, hair combed tightly across his large head, a slightly severe countenance lightened by a twinkling gaze. Written across the top of the photo in slightly smudged biro are the words: 'Would you trust this man?' It is a fair question to ask as we read a letter written by someone who knew all three players. His version of events makes his allegiances clear: in his eyes there was something cold and calculated in Elizabeth's pursuit of Humphry – her interest proving so unwelcome that the poor man had no other option than to pick up his skirts and flee to Calcutta. Calder-Marshall correctly identifies the importance of Madeline's trip to India and her recolonising of Humphry's heart there.

Madeline and Arthur Calder-Marshall in younger days

The letter does, however, contain one assertion that is not borne out by the letters themselves. This is Calder-Marshall's statement that Madeline and Humphry were engaged when he met Elizabeth. There is evidence, both in letters and in Madeline's notebook, of their broken engagement at the end of 1932 shortly before Humphry met Elizabeth. But one of Madeline's closest friends appears unaware of this important detail. What this seems to indicate is that Madeline had already begun stitching pleats into the fabric of the past. This way she could lose painful details that made, in her view, no material difference to the central story – the one she told of her love for Humphry and their commitment to one another. His early death may well have prompted this reshaping of memory; it had certainly begun before Elizabeth's biographer arrived at her door.

Over tea, cake, and then sherry, Madeline firmly and unequivocally stated her terms. Victoria Glendinning was given a stark choice. The first option was to name Humphry as a close friend of Elizabeth's at Oxford but not mark their relationship as an affair nor quote from any letters. The second was that she could quote from a limited choice of letters but not disclose to whom they were addressed, except to say that the person involved had formed part of Elizabeth's Oxford life. Glendinning chose the letters, knowing their importance in providing a fuller picture of Elizabeth as a writer and a woman.

Though Madeline dictated the encounter, she found it completely exhausting. She skipped her usual bread and cheese supper, ate a slice of leftover cake from tea and crawled upstairs. The following morning she rose feeling curiously happy, as though a weight had been taken from her shoulders. She wrote immediately to Arthur.

<u>*MH to ACM*</u>

61 Bateman Street, Cambridge
10 October 75

Dearest Arthur (and I know you will let Ara see this letter too),

[…] V.G. must I think be 38. She went to Somerville, Oxf., in 1956 – a year later than Helen [whom she described as "quite a Name in College", though she didn't remember her: different year and different subject]. […] She arrived in one of those leather Afghan coats, blouse and ¾ length skirt below (these details for Ara's sake). Had a pleasant face and a great big nose, and her glasses when she put them on were Enormous [sic].

[…] I asked whether V.G. planned to <u>go into</u> the subject of E's lovers. And she said No no. All she wanted to know was how they influenced E's books. We spoke of Sean O'Faolain, who refused to see her when she wrote to him, but the next time he was in London rang her up and they met. He has a virago of a wife and didn't dare let it be known that he was seeing her. She is <u>NOT</u> going to mention his name in her biog.

So here was my clue for the anonymity for H. – to which she agreed immediately, just on my say-so.

I had, you may be interested to hear, your letter beside me. At no point did I mention your name, but I treated it as if an Elder Stateman's, my Literary Adviser's, every now and then fluttering it about and reading her little bits: e.g. "Remember that V.G. is interested in finding out the truth about E.B., her life and her books. She is not interested in Humphry, you, your children and grandchildren as such;

but… probably would not wish to give any of you pain." -- This went down marvellously well, couldn't have been more in tune with her thinking as – when I told her the story – it developed.

I did tell her the whole story, almost (but leaving out that spot of blood which wasn't necessary). She was, inevitably enthralled, but not at all incredulous: it seemed to fit. I showed her no letters, and she asked to see none. But I read her bits I had copied out of letters, and she did some jotting down. She said (what I already knew) that the whole thing was of immense importance to an understanding of E's life, writing & c. But, all the same, she wouldn't be making <u>much</u> of it.

She will write me a letter promising anonymity. And when it's written, she'll send me a typescript for my checking and vetting.

I <u>think</u> this was all right? and that I wasn't a fool? I hope that my today's happiness is because it <u>was</u> all right, and not just a relief at having the interview behind me.

Any at-all-personal letters that E. left, Spencer Curtis-Brown mad [sic] a great point of returning to their writers. Therefore E. <u>had</u> destroyed H's, as she told you she had.

[…] She also told me that, sometime in the 40s E.B. believed she was pregnant and was delighted [this from Rosamond Lehmann] but it was a false alarm. So perhaps that letter to H. was <u>not</u> false, as I'd thought it.

I think this is all. And planty [sic]. But I thought you'd be interested. Will let you know when I get the letter promising anonymity -- that excellent suggestion which I owe entirely to you. […]

Thank you, dear Arthur, and love to you both,

Madeline

Madeline reveals knowledge of further details of the affair, some of which were contained in letters that no longer survive. These she presumably read and then destroyed. The spot of blood was most likely a mark of the awkward first night Elizabeth and Humphry spent together. The phantom pregnancy that is mentioned belonged to the 1940s when Elizabeth was having the affair with Charles Ritchie. But central to what she writes is the enduring issue of which letters would breathe again in later years, which would live to tell their tales.

Madeline's letter to Arthur contains a bald belief – she was under the impression that Elizabeth had destroyed all of Humphry's letters. That the only original documents that spoke of the affair were the letters she had kept from Elizabeth to Humphry. This shifted the co-ordinates of power considerably in her favour. She could filter what Elizabeth said, especially about her husband and marriage. It protected her, in her own mind, from any sense of betrayal she might feel. As Humphry's words were gone, it meant she was free to sculpt him in any way she chose. It must have made her foot surer and her voice steadier in her interview with Glendinning.

Madeline's ignorance of the existence of Humphry's letters makes my conscience prickle. I not only have Humphry's letters, but am revealing their contents. Once again there is a chafing of family loyalties against historical facts. Yet the words of Calder-Marshall's letter are reassuring. He is conscious that the story will soon be carried forward by a new generation – mine. To Madeline he advocates disclosure. His reason hinges less on truth than emotion. It is concerned with how we, the subsequent House generations (especially the men), will feel about the affair and about Humphry in particular.

If my grandfather was 'a shit from Sevenoaks', he was many other things besides. A brilliant scholar and teacher, remembered fondly by many. Someone who inspired fierce love, loyalty, and devotion. A man beset by vanities and insecurities – the chips on his shoulder enduring. A lover of women who seemed unable fully to appreciate them as equals, despite his painful need for them. As a father, largely absent – his distance from his daughters determined by their gender, and from his son occasioned by his own untimely death. A complex figure, but one I can sense for the first time in my life. His photograph is now on my desk too.

Soon after their meeting, Glendinning wrote to Madeline to recap on the details of their conversation and to thank her for her kindness: 'I am grateful to you for trusting me, if only because half-knowledge is such a dangerous commodity for a biographer.' A few days later Madeline replied:

MH to Victoria Glendinning (VG)

61 Bateman Street, Cambridge
13 October 75

Dear Mrs Glendinning,

Your letter with its admirable recapitulation of what had been agreed while you were here arrived on Saturday. Thank you for it. […] Yes, I had been expecting your visit to be something of an ordeal. But what helped in advance was my decision that – if you did not readily accede to the anonymity request – I would shut up like a clam and tell you virtually nothing! I am so glad that I didn't have to (in fact the idea of anonymity, in relation to the Irishman, came first from you). And after you had gone I felt singularly happy at having placed the EB/HH story in what I was sure were trustworthy hands.

Your sentence "The bond that united Alan and Elizabeth in the first decade of their married life was not principally a physical one" seemed to me, in isolation, good. […] Two things have come into mind since we talked. One is that I rather doubt whether E. and H. slept together often: there weren't so very many opportunities; also it may not have been from her point of view necessary -- though I may be wrong. The other thing that occurred to me is still more speculative much. Is it quite certain that early failures in the marriage were through A's incompetence rather than frigidity on E's part? That later double-bed and the discovery in the bedside drawer made me just wonder.

[…] I think that sometime you would like to read the letters themselves -- but probably rather later on? I imagine it is only the generalizations about herself as a writer (or woman) that you would find relevant to your book. But you are welcome to see them if you wish to. […]

This seems to be all -- except to tell you that the one thing I didn't like about your letter was that it was typed with such an aged ribbon, and extremely hard to read with my slightly groggy sight!

Do come again sometime.

Yours with best wishes for the book,

Madeline House

Madeline's letter to Victoria Glendinning of 13 October marked the start of a friendly correspondence between the two women, which stretched beyond the affair and its shaping in the biography. They discussed Hilaire Belloc, the shabbier parts of north London, and then, inevitably, returned to Elizabeth.

<u>VG to MH</u>

84 Muswell Hill Road, London, N10
16 October 1975

Dear Mrs House,

I went straight out and bought myself a new typewriter ribbon. It's still not as black as yours. I don't know why that is...

I was very glad to get your letter. We have the same thoughts – at least I had thought exactly the same about the early failures in EB's marriage; that the 'difficulty' was probably on E's side. As far as that goes, H probably did the marriage a favour in the long run. Cold comfort for you, and indeed for him. Of course this <u>is</u> speculation, as you say, but it makes sense. Do you have an early collection of her stories called <u>Ann Lee's</u>? Written when they were only married about two years, and not yet in Oxford. There is an extraordinary – and rather good – story in it called "Making Arrangements" that is to me a very strong expression of frustrated or baffled sexuality from the man's point of view, not at all explicit, but far more so than most of what she wrote then or afterwards. Have a look at it if you have it. Not that I want to continue boring you about this side of things – but you are the one person I can discuss it with!

The letter-extracts you sent are very interesting, and very relevant to everything about her. Thank you very much. Of course I would like to see the letters some time; especially if there is more self-analysis of that kind. As you say, that is, for me, their value. [...]

Many thanks for everything. I hope you realise how grateful I am, and under what an obligation to you I feel.

Yours
Victoria

In her letter, Glendinning points Madeline through an early short story of Elizabeth's called 'Making Arrangements' and into the heart of the Cameron marriage. The story tells of a jilted husband, Hewson Blair, who is tasked with packing up his wife's clothes after she leaves him for another man. Hewson gets an erotic thrill touching and then destroying his wife's dresses. Glendinning's letter hints at a similarity between Alan Cameron and Hewson Blair. The protagonist's lack of interest in his wife is described thus: 'His wheels went round without her.'

The homoerotic subtext of the story is given new meaning in Glendinning's biographical reading of it. This connection between the two men, one real and one fictional, proved irresistible to Madeline as well. She wrote soon afterwards to her friend, the literary scholar Kathleen Tillotson: 'The man seems undoubtedly to be Alan C., in – as usual – an imaginary situation. It reveals a side of him which I think she [Elizabeth] may later have regretted revealing.' Though the discussion in both of these letters focuses on Alan, between the lines is another conversation – one about Elizabeth. It speaks of a woman (if we allow the biographical interpretation to stand) who may, early in her marriage, have understood that her husband was more interested in seeing her smartly turned out in fashionable dresses, than in removing them from her shoulders.

Soon after reading the story, Madeline wrote back to Victoria Glendinning.

MH to VG

61 Bateman Street, Cambridge
28 November 1975

Dear Victoria,

[...] I found "Making Arrangements" an electrifying story. How right you were to pick it. But I found "The Secession" (a

subtle title) a very good story too, and in a so-different way a revealing one. [...]

You have no idea with what close attention I am reading, or rereading, EB now -- weighing every word and image. It takes time! Humphry never bought a book of hers, and when he died we only owned four that she had given him (or, in one case, us) though I picked up one or two later. When I read <u>Eva Trout</u>, in someone else's copy, it rather seemed to me that in Henry EB was reverting to HH. [...]

I let a friend of mine who was staying the night here recently, read what EB to HH letters I have got. After Humphry and then me, she was the first person to see them. You will be the next – when you are ready to come. [...]

I don't think you should read the letters simply in search of further passages of self-analysis; but at least as much – for what they show of the sort of woman she was. I wonder if you've managed to see letters to other lovers.

After your last letter to me came -- a letter I liked <u>very much</u>, as I might have said earlier in this one! -- I took into use a "JOLLY JOTTER, Ruled both sides" which one of my grandchildren had given me, in which to JOT passing thoughts that might be of use to you. [...]

Finally, thank you for going straight out and buying a new typewriter ribbon! Why your typing isn't as black as mine is easily explained! You are a typist who uses <u>all</u> your fingers, and the faint letters are where you have used a 4th finger -- while <u>I</u> bash along with a total of one finger from each hand. Humphry used to do the same, and get up a tremendous speed! But your letter was beautifully legible.

Yours

Madeline

Madeline's weighing of every word, image, and figure is not confined to the lives of others. In Glendinning's notes of the meeting between the two women, she mentions their discussion of *The House in Paris*. This was the book which echoed the affair; here was the triangle. Madeline highlighted in their conversation what she saw of Max in Humphry – his brooding countenance, his fidgety behaviour.

As for herself, she willingly took the role, forty years after the affair and the novel, of Naomi Fisher – the listless woman unloved by the hero. This connection with Naomi she explores in more detail in another letter to Kathleen Tillotson, soon after Glendinning's visit: 'I (like Naomi, yes) was a "pillow". I believed, and still believe, that he needed a pillow; needed one all the more, perhaps, when EB erupted into his life! [...] Whether she had added to his capacity for chronic states of anxiety, who can say? – One new anxiety could be, Had he married a nit-wit?'

Madeline can accept the role of Naomi, knowing this is only half the story. She is a pillow, true, but also a survivor – unlike the self-destructive man. Elizabeth's version of Madeline may be unflattering, but it is an acknowledgement of her presence. A gift of a sort. And this is not just about being alive at the end of the book. For Naomi will always enjoy the present tense – she lives on in the novel. Madeline, as much as Elizabeth, knew the power of fiction.

When Glendinning was approaching the end of writing the biography she got back in touch with Madeline. Of this, Madeline wrote to Tillotson: 'She sent me the chapter on the Elizabeth/Humphry affair, asking for comments. Thinking about these and getting my comments on to paper, took a lot of time and thought. In the end I merely sent her a couple of straight corrections, and – more difficult – a rather different interpretation from hers of the whole business.'

Madeline clearly went over, in meticulous detail, what Glendinning had written, and composed pages of corrections and clarifications. There is a summary of key points written in someone else's clear hand on the final page. My grandmother was by this time in poor health and living with my aunt Rachel – it is most likely the latter's handwriting. My aunt's involvement at this point might explain her strong opinions about certain elements of the relationship between Elizabeth and Humphry and her ignorance of others. Furthermore, her role means that every generation of the family has had a hand in writing, typing, and composing the affair.

The notes by her side, Madeline wrote her last letter to Victoria Glendinning. It runs to more than a thousand words. After pages of detailed feedback she concludes: 'I think so much of your EB piece very very good, and hope that any changes you make as a result of this letter won't cause any massive rewriting.' Madeline was determined the treatment of the affair should be brief, and Humphry's identity hidden. The affair was to be all about Elizabeth wanting new experiences as an artist, rather than about attraction.

Glendinning was loyal in her retelling: the version true to Madeline's stipulations and corrections. *Elizabeth Bowen: Portrait of a Writer* was published in 1977 to excellent reviews. A point is made of Elizabeth's virginity and it being lost for 'artistic' purposes. Neither Humphry nor Madeline is mentioned by name.

One of the reviews of the biography did, however, highlight the very gaps Glendinning had been powerless to avoid. It identified 'a distinct whiff of gossip proffered and then hastily withdrawn'. The reviewer goes on: 'One is aware of a reining in of curiosity, a reticence where witnesses have hesitated to inflict wounds on the living or criticise the lately dead.'

Of the death of literary figures and how they should be remembered, Elizabeth was categorical and unsentimental. In a letter she sent Humphry in Calcutta she describes the outcry that greeted an 'article of a debunking nature' about A. E. Housman's verse soon after the poet's death. She writes:

> Once a man is dead he can't be deader: death is an eternity of its own. But there seems to be a feeling he could be deader – just wait till he is, dissentient critic, stay in your hole a little, then pop out cautiously, say what you like. Actually, the death (in body) of a literary figure ought to be incidental: what his work was, it stays.

Elizabeth knew what best would carry her memory. It is there in the final shift of verb tense. The work of the dead writer is what will tell her tale, even if her life story has, for whatever reason, gaps and omissions.

I remember being surprised about the absence of Humphry, incredulous even, the first time I read Glendinning's biography. Little did I know then that this nameless version had my grandmother's fingerprints on it, her seal of approval. Madeline managed not just to hide her husband, but to turn down the volume on Elizabeth – in her own biography.

But the electric connection between the women sent charges in both directions. Madeline marked Elizabeth's death by clipping four obituaries from newspapers, a strange acknowledgement of Elizabeth's place in her life even after death. She did the same with the reviews of the Glendinning biography and popped them carefully inside her copy of *Collected Impressions*. More importantly, Elizabeth's creations haunted and possessed Madeline – her persistent desire was to see these characters as real people. She was Naomi. Humphry was almost every young man that Elizabeth inked in. It was, perhaps, a way of keeping him alive. To subsequent generations Madeline bequeathed this interpretation of the fiction, and particularly of *The House in Paris*. Our oral inheritance included her spin on crucial events. Our heirlooms, the letters she saw fit to preserve. This was the house that Madeline built.

In the last two years of her life, Madeline lived with my aunt Rachel and her husband in a granny flat in the garden of a former manse in Godmanchester. After two strokes she needed extra care, and she had reluctantly given up the house in Cambridge. Like a pirate, she wore a black patch over the injured eye. With the other she continued to proofread the Dickens letters, squinnying over the words right up to her death in 1978.

Though Madeline's health was not strong, the end when it came was sudden. My mother received news of her death in Nigeria where my parents were living. Helen, anguished, came rushing back to England. There is a catch in my mother's voice as she tells me the story.

Madeline's obituary in *The Times* read:

> The sight of her small white-haired figure hunched over the typescripts in her crowded study or poring over a makeshift microfilm reader was a lesson in scholarly and personal devotion. […] Her dedication was matched by a real scholarly penetration, with a nose for the elusive fact and for the irrelevant footnote, which made her contribution to the edition so important.

Driving back from Godmanchester recently with my mother after spending the day with Rachel, the obituary came up in conversation. (My aunt now lives alone in the same annex that Madeline used to occupy.) My mother's voice rose. 'Whenever I read about the little old woman crouched over her papers, I always think she was never like that. She had far too much personality. When anyone says that about me, it'll be time to write me out of the story!'

Unexpected deaths give opportunities. So it was for Madeline. So it has been for me. The death of my dear uncle John delivered me the letters. What I took possession of was both a gift and a responsibility. They arrived, as things do in Elizabeth's world, 'at the hour arranged'. I was free, ready, eager to make use of them. My inner course, as well as my outer trajectory, was set. The jolly jotter filled itself with information. (Surely I was the grandchild who had given it to Madeline?)

The letters themselves, from the first moment, were thrilling: 'The ink, sharp in the candlelight, had not faded.' Now that electric connection between my grandparents, Elizabeth, and myself crackles with even greater life. As I have held the thread from the past in my hand, so my engagement with the present has changed. Unboxing the correspondence has strengthened my relationships with the brilliant House women, my mother and my aunt, and has sharpened my sense of loss about John. In our anxiety to look into the future or disturb the past, we can forget to treasure the lives and stories of those who still surround us.

At the beginning, I felt I knew Elizabeth better than my own family, such are the strange intimacies established by reading and writing. Since then, my appreciation of her has grown enormously; I bring her to class now with added enthusiasm, keen to introduce her to as many young readers as I can. But it is not just Elizabeth as a writer that I have found so compelling. It is her as a woman, a big personality in a time when women were expected to be decorative and obliging. At first glance a woman quite unlike Madeline, a woman who seemed to fit the social mould more successfully. And yet they shared a steely determination to lead literary lives, to value intellect as much as family. Madeline forced her way into the story, thereby making me appreciate both the strength of her character, and the many women's voices of the time that are still unheard.

In an echo of her role in my grandfather's life, Elizabeth acted as the catalyst I needed to begin to write. She then gave me a word in my ear about how to proceed. 'Form is the servant of subject,' she whispered. 'Shape the book in a way that best fits all the material you have.' The guiding hand of Elizabeth and my grandparents about how to approach my task did not stop there. Humphry advised how to craft a book about literary figures without it becoming too intellectual; Madeline provided a model of scholarly brilliance when faced with literary letters; Elizabeth encouraged me to tell the version of my family story that most appealed to me. The inevitable lacunae, she said, lend veracity to the whole. Elizabeth, Humphry, and Madeline were my ghostwriters – their words about the art of writing itself lit my way.

As my relationships with the three protagonists grew, I felt compelled to write letters (on paper, by hand) to each of them. It was a natural part of the rich correspondence I was enjoying with these life-enhancing characters, a conscious crumpling of the envelope that separates the living and the dead. As Elizabeth said, writing to someone is a way of being in their presence. No doubt those letters ended up in the Dead Letter Office, undeliverable. But they made their journey, established a fresh word-road between Elizabeth, my grandparents, and myself. Only now, as I near the end of the page, can I see that my family is the recipient of this, the last and longest letter of them all.

The spirits of the correspondence pushed me not only into writing, but also into motion. Zestfully, I have travelled from Kolkata to Cambridge, Austin to Ireland. Into graveyards, lost homes, hinterlands. I have sensed a sharp place-feeling, like dew, underfoot. But the map I initially carried with me, the one that emerged from the box of letters, is no longer a record of where I have been. The gathered stones speak of so much more than the land from which they came.

On these exhilarating travels – carried by boat, bike, tuk-tuk, and train – I have been accompanied both by my grandparents and by an extraordinary writer obsessed with journeys; the heightened sensibility they bestow, the spells they cast, their dramatic, transformative potential. One of Elizabeth's novels ends with a car crash. Another with a walk along the canal, a triangle of swans winging its way west overhead. And there are taxis everywhere, purring at the kerb, waiting to seal up the story.

In Elizabeth's final novel, a day in Cambridge is rounded off with a taxi ride. The day has not gone quite as Eva hoped, a feeling exacerbated by the vehicle itself. It seems haunted, both by lovers and by the many intellects it has carried. She doesn't look back at the city as she leaves – she cannot bear to.

I do not look back either. And so the taxi drifts past the road of my grandparents' house, past the entrance to the Botanic Garden. Then it is left to the train station, onto the platform, and away.

Someday I'll send you a blank page with 'Love from Elizabeth.'

For the present —
Love from
Elizabeth.

Acknowledgements

I wish to thank first those who have shaped this book most: Tristan Palmer and Robert Crumpton. Their constant encouragement, editorial brilliance, and gentle advice have been the greatest of blessings. Without their support, not to mention endless conversations over bottles of wine, this book would never have happened.

I am indebted to my friends whose thoughtful, perceptive readings of early drafts were so valuable: Maureen Alcorn, Yusef Azad, Lucy Burns, Tracy Collins, Alan Hollinghurst, Fiona Leach, my sister Tiggy Parry, Ann Rossiter, Kate Saunders and Sarah Waters. Doy las gracias por su apoyo moral a Sinéad Agnew, Sarah Atkinson, Mar del Rey Gómez-Morata, Vicky Finlay, Philip Hensher, Jill House, Sally Isaac, Sarah Johnson, Maurey Lancaster, Karen Magnus, Paz Martín García, Roanne Moore, Alba Muñoz, David Parry, Kathryn Purkis, Samira Cheikho, Anmol Sukhwani, Sarah Thurley, Peter Trippi and Cristina Vargas Molina. A huge hug of gratitude to Genevieve Fox for, among so many other things, helping me over the line with her usual panache.

Thank you to my agent Caroline Hardman at Hardman & Swainson for her loyalty, support and steadfast belief in the book. Thank you to everyone at Duckworth Books: to Pete Duncan and especially to my brilliant editor Matt Casbourne, for his forbearance, sharp mind, positive energy and generosity of spirit.

My travels have been filled with the kindness of strangers. Many thanks are due to Patrick and Jane Annesley, Brenda the Good Samaritan from Appleton, Michael Collins, Dan Doolan, Shatna Dutta, Peter Ellis, the Greenslinch sisters, Therese Hallinan, Brenda Hennessy, Michele Pain, the Professor of Bengali at Surendranath College in Kolkata, Rahul and Rumela Tandon, and Dorothea and William Whistler. Not to forget the kind couple whose home I visited in Sussex when I meant to visit the house next door. Thanks to the staff at Clarence Terrace, London; Mount Melleray Abbey, County Waterford, Ireland; the Shakespeare Hotel, Norfolk Square, London; and the Wellington Hotel, Boscastle, Cornwall. Profound thanks to Sajni Mukherji for welcoming me to Kolkata and for all her help with the Indian section of this book.

For practical assistance and/or expertise I wish to thank Norma Aubertin-Potter, Els Boonen, Supriya Chaudhuri, Paul Cleave, Andrew Gray, Brendan Fleming, Marina Garijo Marcos, Darren Marsh, Harriet Moore, Sallie Nicholas, Jenny Savill, Rafal Stachyra, Charlotte Seymour, Isabel Tamurejo García and Gwenda Walters. Thank you to the amiable librarians of the Hyman Kreitman Reading Rooms at Tate Britain where much of this was written and to Ruth, Judith and Francisco who always cheered up my days working there.

I am grateful to various staff and former pupils of Runnymede College in Madrid. Many thanks to my Year 13 English Literature class of 2015 for the practical criticism lesson: Oscar Aston, Eliav Cohen, Sandra Gustafson, Celia Jiménez-Blanco, Nicholas Powell, Diego Rodríguez-Villa, Lara Sevillano, Paloma Tisaire and Isabella Weetch. Thank you to María Fernández-Pita and Elena Monge Imedio for assistance with transcription; to Nigel Bennet for Latin translation; to Pilar Pastor Rosser and Tomás Sánchez de Movellán for help with photography; to Gaye Quinn for proofreading; to Frank Powell; to Paula Hernández Chang for more than one story; to Berit Levy for the stylish website (juliaparry.co.uk); and most especially to Max Long.

For the granting of permissions I am grateful to:

Curtis Brown and the Literary Estate of Elizabeth Bowen for kind permission to quote from Elizabeth Bowen's unpublished correspondence and her published works.

Curtis Brown and the Estate of Sir Isaiah Berlin for permission to quote from the unpublished papers and published correspondence of Sir Isaiah Berlin.

The Carritt family for kind permission to quote from *A Mole in the Crown* (published privately, 1985) by Michael Carritt.

Faber and Faber and the Estate of Seamus Heaney for permission to quote from 'A New Song' in *New and Selected Poems 1966–1987*.

The Society of Authors as the Literary Representative of the Estates of L. P. Hartley and Virginia Woolf for permission to quote from the correspondence of L. P. Hartley and the diary and correspondence of Virginia Woolf.

Judith Robertson and the Estate of Charles Ritchie for kind permission to quote from the diaries of Charles Ritchie.

Wadham College, Oxford, and the Orion Publishing Group for permission to quote from *Memories* (London: Weidenfeld and Nicolson, 1966) by Maurice Bowra.

Curtis Brown and the Estate of Stephen Spender for permission to quote from the works of Stephen Spender.

Extracts from the correspondence of William Plomer are used by kind permission of the William Plomer Estate.

Quotation from the work of May Sarton is reprinted by the permission of Russell & Volkening as agents for May Sarton, copyright ©1976 by Annie Dillard, renewed in 1988.

Quotation from *RAM* magazine (1935) is courtesy of Special Collections, University of Exeter.

Special thanks to Victoria Glendinning for generous permission to quote from her correspondence with Madeline House, and to Anna

Calder-Marshall for her many kindnesses and permission to quote from the unpublished writings of her father Arthur Calder-Marshall.

I am grateful to Wadham College, Oxford, for permission to use the photograph that prefaces Chapter 1. The other photographs were either taken by the author or come from private collections.

Finally, I wish to thank my wonderful family who have supported me throughout the writing of this book. This is for them, and for three people in particular: in loving memory of John, and most especially for Rachel and Helen, the House women. Thank you so much for trusting me to tell my story of your dear parents, for your judicious reading of the manuscript, and for all your care and love. Gracias mil.

Notes

Sources cited in the notes are given in full in the first reference, and thereafter referred to by short title, author's name, or archive name.

All letters, and other unpublished works, are in private collections unless specified.

The following abbreviations are used for people:
EB: Elizabeth Bowen
HH: Humphry House
MC/MH: Madeline Church/House

Abbreviations used in the Notes for works by Elizabeth Bowen

AP: *Afterthought: Pieces About Writing* (London: Longmans, Green and Co., 1968)
BC: *Bowen's Court* (1942; London: Vintage, 1999)
CI: *Collected Impressions* (London: Longmans, Green and Co., 1950)
CS: *Collected Stories* (1980; London: Vintage, 1999)
DOTH: *The Death of the Heart* (1938; London: Vintage, 2012)
EN: *English Novelists* from the 'Britain in Pictures' series (London: Collins, 1942)
ET: *Eva Trout* (1968; London: Penguin, 1987)
FAR: *Friends and Relations* (1931; Chicago: University of Chicago Press, 2012)
TH: *The Hotel* (1927; London: Penguin, 1984)

HIP: *The House in Paris* (1935; London: Penguin, 1976)

HOTD: *The Heat of the Day* (1948; London: Vintage, 1998)

LI: *Listening In: Broadcasts, Speeches, and Interviews*, ed. Allan Hepburn (Edinburgh: Edinburgh University Press, 2010)

LS: *The Last September* (1929; London: Vintage, 1998)

LG: *The Little Girls* (1964; London: Penguin, 1983)

MT: *The Mulberry Tree: Writings of*, ed. Hermione Lee (1986; London: Vintage, 1999)

PC: *Pictures and Conversations* (London: Allen Lane, 1975)

TS: *The Shelbourne* (London: George Harrap, 1951)

TTN: *To the North* (1932; London: Penguin, 1987)

TIR: *A Time in Rome* (London: Longmans, Green and Co., 1960)

WOL: *A World of Love* (1955; London: Vintage, 1999)

Abbreviations used in the Notes for works about Elizabeth Bowen and Charles Ritchie

LCW: *Love's Civil War: Elizabeth Bowen and Charles Ritchie, Letters and Diaries 1941–1973*, ed. Victoria Glendinning with Judith Robertson (2009; London: Pocket Books, 2010)

Oxford: *Encounters*

'*stop worrying … better brain*': letter from EB to HH, 20 January 1936.

'*husks*': *WOL*, p. 34.

'*The ink, sharp in the candlelight, had not faded*': ibid., p. 33.

'*reluctant awe, and some misgiving*': ibid., p. 34.

'*They fell at her feet … rather than she them*': ibid., p. 27.

'*extraordinary power of his illusion*': ibid., p. 97.

'*affecting them, working on them*': ibid.

'*A thread lay dropped on the grass, for Jane to pick up*': ibid., p. 48.

'*electric connection*': ibid., p. 67.

Headington: *The New House*

'*Bowen's novels … on drugs*': Andrew Bennett and Nicholas Royle, *Elizabeth Bowen and the Dissolution of the Novel: Still Lives* (Basingstoke and London: Macmillan, 1994), p. xv.

'*a tough child … or colt*': 'Origins', *PC*, p. 12.

'*I and my friends … Pa's Hands)*': 'The Mulberry Tree', *MT*, p. 17.

'*[I] was extremely keen … genius or gift?*': S133/18/33 Special Collections: Plomley, Roy; Desert Island Discs Scripts, no. 325 – Elizabeth Bowen; Home Service, 11 March 1957, BBC Written Archives Centre, Reading.

'*The fears … her behaviour*': Hannah and Abraham Stone, *A Marriage Manual* (London: The Bodley Head, 1936), p. 26.

'*In cases of frigidity … particular marriage*': ibid., p. 272.

'*latent sexual capacities*': ibid., p. 274.

'*importance of social … in marriage*': ibid., p. 321.

'*The most important … catch*': Jan Struther, 'The Eve of the Shoot', in *Mrs Miniver* (1939; London: Virago, 1989), p. 13.

'*a sort of childish … attachment*': letter from EB to Isaiah Berlin, 8 October 1952, MS. Berlin 245, fol. 146, The Papers of Sir Isaiah Berlin, 1897–1998, Special Collections, Bodleian Library, Oxford.

'*the feeling of being located … sense of reality*': ibid.

'*Of course … my inner life*': 'The Evil that Men Do –', *CS*, p. 85.

'*You must not think* … exterior life': ibid., p. 86.

'*the bricks and wallpaper of a home*': *LS*, p. 129.

'*Lessons given … mundane*': business card of spiritualist Mrs Howarth-Scaling, late 1920s.

'*You have at one … Sacred Cats*': Helen Howarth-Scaling, psychic reading sent to HH, 21 July 1927.

'*wore huge woollen scarves … drank beer*': Isaiah Berlin, *Flourishing: Letters 1928–1946*, ed. Henry Hardy (Cambridge: Cambridge University Press, 2004), p. 17.

'*We were caught … Hopes*': Arthur Calder-Marshall, *God Will Provide a Bit More*, unpublished autobiography, p. 2.

'*the morbid age*': Richard Overy, *The Morbid Age* (2009; London: Penguin, 2010).

'*Money played … University activities*': Stephen Spender, *World Within World* (1951; London: Faber, 1977), pp. 35–36.

'*the future … Stephen Spender*': Arthur Calder-Marshall, *God Will Provide a Bit More*, p. 16.

'*had a poetic gift … private income*': ibid.

'*But to leave … prospect in 1930*': ibid.

'*I felt very strongly … had been*': letter from HH to MH, 24 October 1949.

'*undergraduettes*': John Betjeman, *An Oxford University Chest* (1938; Oxford: Oxford University Press, 1979), p. 39.

'*so thin on the ground … money*': Arthur Calder-Marshall, p. 5.

'*But while he despised me … than I*': ibid, p. 4.

'*this great wave of the talent of my time*': Stephen Spender, p. 167.

'*my kind of prig … year at Oxford*': letter from Isaiah Berlin to EB, [Summer 1936], in *Flourishing: Letters 1928–1946*, p. 181.

'*From the moment … they were inevitable*': 'Places' *PC*, p. 60.

'*the hour arranged*': 'The Demon Lover', *CS*, p. 744.

'*Fate has worked … obsessed by it*': 'The Roving Eye', *MT*, p. 63.

'*in company … the learned*': preface to the 2nd US edition of 'The Last September', *MT*, p. 124.

'*She was handsome … be envious*': Maurice Bowra, *Memories* (London: Weidenfeld and Nicolson, 1966), pp. 190–191.

'*I am not stream-lined for aestheticism*': letter from HH to MC, 11 August 1931.

'*a puny pseudo-Christus … my God*': letter from HH to MC, 2 March 1932.

'*moods wheel … and I want death*': letter from HH to MC, 3 January 1932.

'*Oh thou lord of life, send my roots rain*': Gerard Manley Hopkins, 'Thou are indeed just Lord, if I contend' in *Gerard Manley Hopkins: Poems and Prose* (London: Penguin Classics, 1985), p. 67.

'*foul*': letter from HH to MC, 24 November 1932.

'*marry at Christmas or not at all*': ibid.

'*On receiving … to burn them!*': marginalia by MH, ibid.

Appleton: *The Shadowy Third*

'*Tuesday 14th … awful need*': letter from HH to EB, undated [?July 1933].

'*I wondered … wood wonders*': ibid.

'*the first burst … the palm-tree*': ibid.

'*on Wednesday … Elizabeth Bowen, novelist*': letter from HH to MC, 2 March 1933.

'*mens curva in corpore curvo*': Translation: 'a crooked mind in a crooked body', a description of Alexander Pope, attributed to Bishop Atterbury, in *Alexander Pope and his Critics*, ed. Adam Rounce (London: Routledge, 2004), p. 363.

'*There are phrases … clever*': The letters HH wrote to both EB and MC about Stanton Harcourt were written on Sunday 12 March 1933, the day after his visit to the village.

'*Am I not … is its topography*': 'Places', *PC*, p. 34.

'*dominants*': 'Origins', *PC*, p. 30.

'*Such places are … vicariously me*': 'Out of a Book', *MT*, p. 51.

'*place-feeling*': 'Places', *PC*, p. 44.

'*He does not … non-stop narrative*': ibid., p. 40.

'*I may, too, impart … about railways*': ibid., p. 42.

'*slum quarter*': letter from EB to HH, 23 February 1935.

'*The only sad thing … their presence*': letter from EB to William Plomer, 6 May 1958, GB/0033/PLO/19/8, The William Plomer Manuscripts, Palace Green Library, University of Durham.

'*Never to lie … never wholly alone*': *HIP*, p. 133.

Ireland, County Cork: *Friends and Relations*

'*The country conceals … untravelled roads*': *BC*, p. 5.

'*matriarch*': EB to Charles Ritchie, 12 June 1945, uncatalogued (as of October 2014), Elizabeth Bowen Collection 1923–1975, Harry Ransom Center, University of Texas at Austin, USA.

'*she and those home surroundings … discovery of a lack*': *LS*, p. 166.

'*house-islands*': *BC*, p. 20.

'*river tongues*': Seamus Heaney, 'A New Song', *Opened Ground: Poems 1966–1996* (London: Faber and Faber, 1998), p. 58.

'*with vowelling … staked out in consonants*': ibid.

'*The sense of … country house*': letter from EB to Charles Ritchie, 2 September 1945, *LCW*, p. 60.

'*Really my next of kin is this house*': letter from EB to Isaiah Berlin, 8 October 1952, MS. Berlin 245, fol. 145, Berlin Archive.

'*I speak scarcely … in his shell*': letter from HH to EB, 10 April 1933.

'*I have a fear of blighting your whole stay*': letter from HH to EB, 6 April 1933.

'*pompous & pretentious & imitative & ruined*': Virginia Woolf, diary entry of 30 April 1934, *The Diary of Virginia Woolf Volume Four: 1931–1935*, ed. Anne Olivier Bell (1982; Harmondsworth: Penguin, 1983), p. 210.

'*You have a wonderful gift … from it*': letter from L. P. Hartley to EB, 12 March 1934, Box 11, Folder 5, Bowen Archive.

'villeggiatura *air*': *BC*, p. 26.

'*the sort of expedition … start*': letter from EB to John Hayward, 25 September 1936, GBR/0272/PP/JDH/26/10/2, The Papers of John Davy Hayward, King's College Archive Centre, Cambridge.

'*house's strong* own *life*': *BC*, p. 403.

'*with the superficial … where I was*': letter from EB to HH, 8 November 1934, in the postscript.

'*torn-open ruin*': *BC*, p. 7.

'*I shall not … unexpected*': letter from HH to EB, 22 April 1933.

'*I hope soon … apple trees*': ibid.

'*grim food*': letter from HH to EB, undated [?May 1933].

'*The infinite possibilities … to be told*': 'The Art of Reserve: or the Art of Respecting Boundaries', undated essay, Box 1, Folder 5, Bowen Archive.

'*She must have been one of those women … interested in*': *BC*, p. 387.

'*made me feel I was … hit in the head*': letter from EB to HH, undated [?June 1935].

'*Bath of Ireland*': *BC*, p. 8.

'*irresistibly attractive*': letter from Isaiah Berlin to Maire Gaster, 11 January 1982, Isaiah Berlin, *Affirming: Letters 1975–1997*, ed. Henry Hardy and Mark Pottle, (London: Random House, 2015), p. 181.

'*like a huge, lovelorn dog*': ibid.

'*immensely … put on rouge*': letter from Mary Fisher to her mother Lettice

Fisher, 27 June 1933, in Isaiah Berlin, *Flourishing: Letters 1928–1946*, p. 51.

'*plenty of brute strength … fingers*': letter from EB to William Plomer, 24 September 1945, PLO/19/2, Plomer Archive.

'*tipsy and truculent*': HH to Isaiah Berlin, undated [?June 1933], MS. Berlin 103, fol. 157, Berlin Archive.

'*understand affection*': ibid., fol. 158.

'*incurably intellectual*': ibid., fol. 159.

'*severely rated*': letter from HH to MC, 1 July 1933.

'*It was all very difficult … better than before*': ibid.

'*new contact … intimacy*': HH to Isaiah Berlin, undated [?June 1933], MS. Berlin 103, fol. 159, Berlin Archive.

'*no <u>not</u> what … vulgar*': ibid.

'*It was wretched … Sarah and everyone*': letter from HH to EB, undated, 'Monday' [?July 1933].

'*Then and often … also last week*': letter from HH to EB, undated [?July 1933].

'*I was acutely … hopelessly wrong*': letter from HH to EB, undated, 'Saturday' [?July 1933].

'*For you … for anyone*': ibid.

'*I have very strong … once a month*': ibid.

County Waterford: *The Happy Autumn Fields*

'*I have desired to go … swing of the sea*': Gerard Manley Hopkins, 'Heaven-Haven', *Gerard Manley Hopkins Poems and Prose* (London: Penguin Classics, 1985), p. 5.

'*see what silence does to men*': letter from HH to EB, undated, 'Tuesday' [July/August 1933].

'*awake to Love and Beauty*': Samuel Taylor Coleridge, 'This Lime Tree Bower My Prison', *The Poetical Works of S. T. Coleridge* (1800; London: Frederick Warne & Co, 1890), p. 180.

'*I feel terribly … I wonder*': letter from HH to EB, undated [?August 1933].

'*It might … open susceptibility*': 'The Roving Eye', *MT*, p. 63.

'*Israel = Ireland. Moab = England*': Humphry House, *Ruth*, undated, unpublished novel, p. 2.

'*affable teeth*': ibid., p. 6.

'*awful*': letter from HH to EB, undated, 'Tuesday' [August/September 1933].

'*I will be sending … for typing soon*': letter from HH to MC, 1 July 1933.

'*secretary – hostess*': ibid.

'*An ineffectual rarified … for no salary*': ibid.

'*live with me … the country*': letter from HH to MC, 17 July 1933.

'*I love you … a daily present*': letter from HH to MC, 3 August 1933.

'*very exciting*': letter from HH to MC, 13 August 1933.

'*It is suddenly … stops revolutions!*': ibid.

'*I think even your father … you were happy*': letter from HH to MC, 22 August 1933.

'*He would be … fat bank balance*': ibid.

'*He must be got up to London … should you be there?*': ibid.

'*seem bound for nowhere*': *HIP*, p. 93.

'*Yellow Hat*': ibid., p. 90.

'*highly respectable kind of flashiness*': ibid.

'*hills, houses, trees … become the past*': ibid.

'*You look at places … what did I hope to find?*': ibid.

Exeter, Royal Clarence Hotel: *Recent Photograph*

'*pride, money and opportunity*': letter from HH to MC, 6 October 1933.

'*I used some Keats … not very appositely*': letter from HH to MC, 5 October 1933.

'*Humphry House … which I dread*': letter from Isaiah Berlin to Adam von Trott, 26 October 1933, *Flourishing: Letters 1928–1946*, p. 62.

'*based on complementary … admiration*': letter from HH to EB, 8 October [1933].

'*It will be … support me*': letter from HH to Isaiah Berlin, 18 October 1933, MS. Berlin 103, fol. 124, Berlin Archive.

'*rough and crude*': letter from HH to EB, 23 October 1933.

'*I had begun … no substitute*': ibid.

'*More than half … a toss*': letter from HH to MC, 18 October 1933.

'*In every branch … la Femme*": 'a Suffragette', article entitled 'Votes for Women', *Ram Magazine*, Autumn term issue, volume 1935, p. 15, Special Collections, Old Library, University of Exeter.

'*Today there is a far worse crime … sanity*': Winifred Holtby, *Time and Tide* magazine, 1935, in Juliet Gardiner, *The Thirties: An Intimate Story* (2010; Harper Press: London, 2011) p. 556.

'*had the consciousness … years of danger*': Jane Austen, *Persuasion*, ed. D. W. Harding (1818; London: Penguin Classics, 1980), p. 38.

'*upholstered happiness*': 'The Lover', *CS*, p. 63.

'*appalled at the misapprehension*': *TH*, p. 124.

'*funny law of convenience*': ibid., p. 160.

'*inevitably you will meet her [Elizabeth]*': letter from HH to MC, 22 August 1933.

'*This hotel … I am anxious*': letter from HH to MC, 18 October 1933.

'*Since your letter … one another*': letter from HH to MC, 24 October 1933.

'*I'm glad you're having … behind you*': letter from HH to MC, 8 October 1933.

'*I think the capacity … quite big*': letter from HH to EB, undated, 'Tuesday' [Autumn 1933].

'*She has a strong … the difference*': ibid.

'*confidante*': ibid.

'*Miss Pearn I … run over by a bus*': letter from EB to Isaiah Berlin, 1 December [1936], MS. 245, fols. 80–81, Berlin Archive.

'*remarkably unchanged*': letter from HH to EB, Tuesday, undated [?November 1933].

'*think kindly but not too well of me*': ibid.

'*salmon-coloured in the sunshine*': letter from EB to Isaiah Berlin, 18 December 1933, MS. Berlin 245, fol. 12, Berlin Archive.

'*extreme speed*': ibid., fol. 11.

'*We must just … there it is*': ibid., fol. 14.

'*unsympathetic*': letter from HH to Isaiah Berlin, undated [?November 1933], MS. Berlin 108, fol. 144, Berlin Archive.

'*I am not choosing … you are mistaken*': ibid., fol. 145.

'*Everybody … about it*': letter from MC to her mother Margaret Church, undated [December 1933].

'*England is never … rather Anglophobic*': letter from EB to Isaiah Berlin, 18 December 1933, MS. Berlin 245, fol. 11, Berlin Archive.

'*heart-cloven and split-minded*': Sean O'Faolain, 'A Reading and Remembrance of Elizabeth Bowen', in *London Review of Books*, Volume 4, Number 4, 2 March 1982, pp. 15–16.

'*By the rules … they last met*': *HOTD*, p. 140.

'*Mussolini offers … il duce*': letter from HH to MC, 5 September 1932.

'*chasmal beauty*': Thomas Hardy, 'Beeny Cliff', *Selected Poems* (London: Penguin Classics, 1993) p. 79.

'*opal and sapphire … western sea*': ibid.

'*All winds dropped … from the land*': *BC*, p. 449.

Exeter, Cathedral Close: *Her Table Spread*

'*Their brief irregular meetings … to contemplate*': *TTN*, p. 200.

'*escape from life*': EB to Victor Gollancz, quoted in Victoria Glendinning, *Elizabeth Bowen: Portrait of a Writer* (1977; London: Phoenix, 1993), p. 93.

'*exact a cheque … things we want*': letter from HH to MH, 12 January 1934.

'*disasters to things on our narrow stairs*': letter from HH to EB, 12 January 1934.

'*I think this … getting married*': ibid.

'*How sweet of you … symbol of this*': ibid.

'*Put the meat … bay leaves*': X. Marcel Boulestin, *Simple French Cooking* (New York: Frederick A. Stokes, 1923), p. 71.

'*deplorable taste of soup*': ibid., p. 4.

'*I can imagine … their table*': ibid., p. 1.

'*belongs to the world*': 'New Judgement: Elizabeth Bowen on Jane Austen' *LI*, p. 41.

'*My first solicitude … your world*': ibid.

'*were to be little together they must be calmly apart*': *TTN*, p. 175.

'*I found the Houses … hosts up*': letter from Isaiah Berlin to his mother Marie, 21? March 1934, *Flourishing: Letters 1928–1946*, p. 85.

'*inseeing letters*': letter from HH to EB, undated [February 1934].

'*By far the most … seeing you more*': ibid.

'*Because you can … you read me*': ibid.

'*You demand … rarely reach here*': ibid.

'*Elizabeth Bowen, novelist*': HH to MC, 2 March 1933.

'*I am glad your book is going well*': letter from HH to EB, undated [spring 1934].

'*shy about trying to see known men*': letter from HH to EB, undated [?February 1934].

'*exacting*': letter from EB to HH, 6 June 1934.

'*Remember that you … be like that*': ibid.

'*lack of wholeness*': ibid.

'*the last "serious" letter I shall write you*': ibid.

'*Goodbye for now*': ibid.

'*demonstrative*': HH to EB, June 7–9 1934.

'*diplomatic*': ibid.

'*Have hardly spoken … for weeks*': ibid.

'*great man*': EB to HH, 12 July 1933.

'*clever woman*': ibid.

Greenslinch: *The Man of the Family*

'*serious*': letter from EB to HH, 6 June 1934.

'*snags of joint ownership*': ibid.

'*slave*': https://opendomesday.org/place/SS9603/greenslinch.

'*Elizabeth says … seeing you*': letter from HH to Isaiah Berlin, 24 June 1934, MS. Berlin 103, fol. 219, Berlin Archive.

'*Humphry … have no doubt of*': letter from Isaiah Berlin to EB, [after 6 July 1934], *Flourishing: Letters 1928–1946*, p. 87.

'*proper parents*': *HIP*, p. 206.

'*delightful to meet*': ibid., p. 218.

'*It was understood … uninterrupted and close*': ibid.

'*All contraceptive arrangements … hands*': letter from HH to EB, 23 July 1934.

'*I believe strongly … uncritical eulogist*': Humphry House, 'The Present Art of Biography', *All in Due Time: Collected Essays and Broadcast Talks* (London: Hart-Davis, 1955), p. 261.

'*No one knew … facts of his birth*': *HIP*, p. 219.

'*sureness and delight*': HH to EB, 2 August 1934.

'*spiritual dumbness and numbness*': letter from EB to HH, 8 November 1934.

'*he flowered … charmingly*': letter from EB to Isaiah Berlin, 17 September [1934], MS. Berlin 245, fol. 26, Berlin Archive.

'*I don't know … whole affair*': ibid.

'*a Miss Ursula … B.B.C.*': ibid., fol. 27.

'*I do not know … inauspicious remarks*': ibid.

'*I have enjoyed … gone*': ibid., fol. 28.

'*drivelling schoolmastering*': letter from HH to EB, 1 October 1934.

'*If a son turns up … Humphry*': ibid.

'*I was reading … Balzac's letters*': ibid.

'*whatever went on, goes on, in one form or another*': *TIR*, p. 6.

'*This is Venus*': EB to HH, undated postcard 1 [1934].

'*This is the green bronze door*': EB to HH, undated postcard 2 [1934].

'*my home life and my life with Alan*': EB to HH, 8 November 1934.

Norfolk Square: *Careless Talk*

'*temporary little stale room*': *DOTH*, p. 326.

'*a real grown-up place … leg and texture*': letter from HH to MH, 28 March 1935.

'*necessary lie*': letter from HH to MH, 14 January 1935.

'*great internal change*': ibid.

'*twice as strong … more serious*': ibid.

'*forced up gargles … bad breath*': letter from HH to MH, 17 January 1935.

'*My babe so beautiful … look at thee*': Samuel Taylor Coleridge, 'Frost at Midnight', p. 190.

'*fire in the abstract*': letter from EB to HH, 8 November 1934, in the postscript.

'*Madeline House … falls through?*': letter from EB to Isaiah Berlin, dated Saturday 4 April [1935], archivist correction [?4 May], MS. Berlin 245, fol. 36, Berlin Archive.

'*Have we insisted … disappoint us*': 'Disappointment', essay for *Reader's Digest*, 1954, Box 2, Folder 6, Bowen Archive.

Regent's Park: *The Death of the Heart*

'*He [Plomer] was … than beer*': letter from EB to Isaiah Berlin, 27 September 1935, MS. Berlin 245, fol. 44, Berlin Archive.

'*Humphry left … I feel*': letter from EB to William Plomer, 27 September [1935], PLO/19/31, Plomer Archive.

'*But you and I … break us*': *TTN*, p. 211.

'*There is no comfortable … them*': letter from Gerry Hopkins to EB, 21 August 1935, Box 11, Folder 5, Bowen Archive.

'Physically, *characters … in the novel*': 'Notes on Writing a Novel', *CI*, p. 253.

'*we needn't assume … she wrote it)*': Patricia Craig, *Elizabeth Bowen* (Harmondsworth: Penguin, 1986), p. 70.

'*Elizabeth did seem … version of her*': Victoria Glendinning, p. 95.

'*Naomi Fisher I see … even her clothes*': letter from EB to A. E. Coppard, in Glendinning, p 95.

'*pillow*': letter from MH to Kathleen Tillotson, 21 November 1975.

'*A fatigue … desire of her*': *HIP*, p. 163.

'*Each house seems to … at the gates*': 'The Big House', *MT*, p. 25.

'*the very unhauntedness of "functional" rooms*': 'The Bend Back', *MT*, p. 59.

'*pop-eyed with anxiety the whole time*': EB to William Plomer, 5 June [1938], PLO/19/34, Plomer Archive.

'*Naomi is like furniture … marry her*': *HIP*, p. 146.

'*very nice … from Virginia*': EB to William Plomer, 27 September [1935], PLO/19/31, Plomer Archive.

'*I had the feeling … in hand by a writer*': Virginia Woolf to EB, 26 September [1935].

'*held by someone … of reality*': letter from EB to Isaiah Berlin, 8 October 1952, MS. Berlin 245, fol. 145, Berlin Archive.

'*motherly*': letter from EB to HH, 12 July 1933.

'*Elizabeth lives … Upper Bloomsbury*': letter from Isaiah Berlin to Marion Frankfurter, undated [?early 1936], *Supplementary Letters 1928–1946*, The Isaiah Berlin Virtual Library, http://berlin.wolf.ox.ac.uk/published_works/f/l1supp.pdf.

'*Black Hats*': Victoria Glendinning, p. 105.

'*the fascinating flow … and events*': Charles Ritchie, diary entry, 9 May 1956, *LCW*, p. 230.

'*inevitable*': Maurice Bowra, p. 7.

'*the correct procedure for English families*': ibid.

'*settling and domesticating … I wanted*': HH to EB, 23 July 1934.

'*Humphry … young again*': letter from EB to William Plomer, 20 January 1936, PLO/19/32, Plomer Archive.

'*A fight, soon over … avoid a quarrel*': 'Origins', *PC*, p. 20.

East of Suez: *Gone Away*

'*I don't feel … what matters*': letter from HH to MH, 1 February 1936.

'*I feel already … gone between*': letter from HH to MH, 5 February 1936.

'*So that was over … vanished*': 'The Parrot', *CS*, p. 125.

'*song … unknown bird*': E. M. Forster, *A Passage to India* (1924; London: Penguin, 1966), p. 77.

'*a summary of a happy life*': letter from HH to MH, 5 February 1936.

'*A change there is over … new approaches*': letter from HH to MH, 20 February 1936.

'*In England … even before it*': letter from HH to MH, 3 March 1936.

'*a moving priggish … new life*': letter from EB to Isaiah Berlin, 1 February [1936], MS. Berlin 245, fol. 48, Berlin Archive.

'*The friend becomes a traitor … negation of love*': *DOTH*, p. 163.

'*We still lived … destiny of millions*': Michael Carritt, *A Mole in the Crown* (1985; Hove: published privately), pp. 86–87.

'*If I'm not very careful … mouth shut*': letter from HH to MH, 9 February 1936.

'*Pol: see letter inside*': HH to MH, undated [?March 1936].

'*Will you notice … the top one*': letter from HH to MH, undated [September 1936 postmark].

'*criminal violation … offensive way*': letter from HH to the Deputy Commissioner of Police for Calcutta, 9 August 1937.

'*I trust … in a political context*': letter from HH to MH, 28 June 1937.

'*steam open … four flaps*': letter from HH to MH, undated [September 1936 postmark].

'*thought-read*': *HIP*, p. 59.

'*Getting up and pushing back … he said*': ibid., p. 45.

'"*Oh, you oughtn't … letters to someone else!*"': ibid., p. 59.

'*dishonourable*': ibid.

'*light talks*': letter from P. C. Ghosh to HH, 10 January 1936.

'*They listened like angels … at the back*': letter from HH to MH, 12 March 1936.

'*that particular poet*': letter from EB to HH, 21 May 1936.

'*Yes, I had heard … the dark one*': letter from EB to HH, 28 May 1936.

'*I'm impatient to see them … in a box*': HH to MH, 5 June 1937.

'*the European element … reads trash*': Lionel Fielden to HH, 26 August 1937.

'*I am loving being … do enjoy speed*': letter from EB to HH, 6 May 1936.

'*She combines … washerwomen have*': letter from Arthur Calder-Marshall to HH, 13 May 1936.

'*Of the British … liked him*': Andrew Robinson, *Satyajit Ray: The Inner Eye* (London: André Deutsch, 1989), pp. 43–44.

'*a clattery steel hedge … half my faculties*': letter from EB to HH, 28 May 1936.

'*Silences don't matter, but their quality does*': ibid.

'*is … like being in the sun*': ibid.

'*savage*': ibid.

'*terrible row*': letter from EB to William Plomer, 20 January 1936, PLO/19/32, Plomer Archive.

'*Very good luck … all your undertakings*': letter from EB to HH, 28 May 1936.

'*Nothing arrives … at all*': *DOTH*, p. 7.

'*suspicious as a Scotsman … may be picked*': letter from EB to HH, 12 June 1936.

'*mean and muddled … own nature*': ibid.

'*not a bulliable person*': ibid.

'*Humility is … both of us*': ibid.

'*I see now that … never turned off*': letter from EB to HH, 28 May 1936.

'*This is no country … can be left*': letter from HH to MH, undated [March 1936].

Calcutta: *The Heat of the Day*

'*almost erotic fondling of the pen*': letter from EB to HH, 29 June 1936.

'*A sentence … astringent about it*': ibid.

'*no more … paper screen*': letter from EB to Isaiah Berlin, 23 September 1936, MS. Berlin 245, fol. 62, Berlin Archive.

'*we Irish are squeamish … for her*': ibid.

'*crashed across … everyone else*': ibid., fol. 63.

'*This is no house … outraged something*': ibid.

'*pro-Indian feelings*': letter from HH to MH, 23 August 1936.

'*He is a man … absolute trust*': letter from HH to MH, 31 August 1936.

'*I am rather lost … both camps*': letter from HH to MH, 12 March 1936.

'*He's off bathing … won't join*': letter from HH to MH, 31 August 1936.

'*mission house in the slums*': letter from HH to MH, 23 October 1936.

'*The street outside … cows of course*': ibid.

'*cinema apparatus*': letter from MH to Margaret Church, 28 October 1936.

'*great flopsy bunny of a woman*': ibid.

'*I have done … Government official*': letter from MH to Margaret Church, 21 December [1936].

'*unbalanced as a schoolboy … first infatuation*': letter from Sudhin Datta to MH, 25 March 1937.

'*emphasized your goodness … as a writer*': ibid.

'*On whom H. had a great crush, 1937*': accretion by MH to a programme of *Savitri* presented by the Calcutta Art Players, 1 May 1937.

'*this extraordinary woman*': May Sarton, *A World of Light* (1976; London: The Women's Press, 1996), p. 196.

'*I understood … period was over*': ibid., p. 195.

'*It took me years … their stream*': ibid., p. 196.

'*looked out … in the moonlight*': ibid., p. 197.

'*sudden irrational attachments*': ibid., p. 196.

'*the truth*': ibid., p. 197.

'*despatched … May Sarton*': letter from Virginia Woolf to EB, 9 October [1937], Box 12, Folder 4, Bowen Archive.

'*By the way … questions about*': HH to MH, 8 July 1937.

'*You have given me … water over me*': HH to MH, 11 March 1938.

'*so glad*': letter from EB to Isaiah Berlin, undated [Jan 1937], MS. Berlin 245, fol. 93, Berlin Archive.

'*G. M. H. fills me with horror … "inscape"?*': ibid., fol. 92.

'*You won our … a friend*': valediction from Presidency College students to HH, 30 April 1937.

'*the other thing …* "I": letter from HH to MH, 31 August 1936.

'*brilliant*': review in *Amrita Bazar Patrika*, 24 October 1937.

'*modern little classic*': ibid.

'*In Rome I wondered … creates distance*': *TIR*, p. 6.

Ashdown Forest: *The Last September*

'*The struggle … in modern society*': Stephen Spender, from the introduction to *Poems for Spain* (1938), in Gayle Rogers, *Modernism and the New Spain: Britain, Cosmopolitan Europe, and Literary History* (Oxford: Oxford University Press, 2012), p. 180.

'*vehemence*': 'Panorama of the Novel', *LI*, p. 143.

'*The obvious absence … in England*': ibid.

'*Younger writers … hands of women*': ibid., p. 141.

'*horrible trap*': *DOTH*, p. 115.

'*It is an exact … the make-up*': Charles Ritchie, diary entry, 18 October 1941, *LCW*, p. 25.

'*I am rather worried … to apply*': letter from HH to MH, 22 January 1938.

'*damn the debts*': letter from HH to MH, 17 January 1939.

'*Elizabeth wrote me … deaf ear*': letter from HH to Alan Cameron, 15 May 1938, RCONT1 file Humphry House: 'Talks' File 1 (1938–1951), BBC Written Archives Centre, Reading.

'*it should be … intellectual*': letter from William Plomer to EB, 31 May [1938], Box 11, Folder 8, Bowen Archive.

'*I don't make much … feels uneasy*': ibid.

'*I'm interested … I suppose*': letter from EB to William Plomer, Sunday [5 June 1938], PLO/19/34, Plomer Archive.

'*that queer … rabbit hutch*': letter from EB to William Plomer, 3 August 1938, PLO/19/18, Plomer Archive.

'*I felt … you again*': ibid.

'*Yes, this place … the library*': letter from HH to Isaiah Berlin, 22 September 1938, MS. Berlin 106, fol. 89, Berlin Archive.

'*teaching in England … Heart indeed*': ibid.

'*at history from the literary end*': letter from HH to MH, 17 January 1939.

'*absolute mediocrity*': EB to William Plomer, 17 August 1936, PLO 19/33, Plomer Archive.

'*His linked senses of threat … houses and streets*': *EN*, p. 31.

'*I hadn't realized … book out*': letter from EB to Charles Ritchie, 6 May 1950, *LCW*, p. 169.

'*Short of there … and me*': letter from EB to Charles Ritchie, 17 June 1948, *LCW*, p. 124.

'*plain blond babies*': letter from EB to William Plomer, 3 August 1938, PLO/19/18, Plomer Archive.

'*The Dickens books … in a day*': letter from HH to MH, 5 April 1939.

'*London yesterday … reactions at all*': letter from EB to IB, Friday [30 September 1938], MS. Berlin 245, fol. 133, Berlin Archive.

'*nothing but eat … hair shampooed*': ibid.

'*it seemed to me ... to evaluate*': *BC*, ibid.

'*Inside this frame ... outlines in*': ibid., p. 452.

'*My family ... they were its agents*': ibid., p. 453.

'*Like all stories ... appeals to me*': ibid., p. 67.

'*We went into ... those bushes*": EB to William Plomer, 7 August [1939], PLO/19/26, Plomer Archive.

'*war-fears*': ibid.

'*I would rather ... Unknown Soldier*': Humphry House, unpublished essay, August 1939.

'*fixed, close, narrow, unbroken routine*': letter from HH to MH, 23 October 1940.

'*the atmosphere ... deeply changed*': letter from HH to MH, 11 October 1940.

Old Forge Lane: *A Day in the Dark*

'*It is a fine morning ... deserted palace*': 'London, 1940', *CI*, pp. 218–220.

'*Elizabeth "Espionage" Bowen*': http://www.aubanehistoricalsociety.org.

'*spies*': *LCW*, from the editor's introduction, p. 5.

'*lucid abnormality*': preface to 1st US edition of 'The Demon Lover and Other Stories', *CI*, p. 48.

'*the hour arranged*': 'The Demon Lover', *CS*, p. 745.

'*insisted on forcing their own way out*': *WOL*, p. 35.

'*You've read ... recovered now*': letter from MH to HH, 21 April 1941.

'*Darling, the hens ... troubles begin*': letter from MH to HH, 30 June 1941.

'*geography, history, and nature-study*': HH to MH, 23 January 1941.

'*And today ... how they go*': letter from MH to HH, 6 March 1942.

'*Never I ween … Archbishop of Rheims!*': Thomas Ingoldsby, 'The Jackdaw of Rheims' in *Ingoldsby Legends, or Mirth and Marvels* (London: Richard Bentley, 1840), p. 171.

'*I was trying … mutual esteem*': letter from MH to HH, 20 January 1941.

'*You know when you write … with furniture!*': letter from MH to HH, 16 March 1941.

'*setting*': letter from EB to HH, 8 November 1934.

'*like furniture or the dark*': *HIP*, p. 146.

'*spat on and polished … battle dress*': letter from HH to MH, 2 January 1941.

'*I am not a soldier … work again*': letter from HH to MH, 6 November 1941.

'*Only Jane Austen … nasty week*': letter from HH to MH, 6 August 1941.

'*appalling chaos*': letter from HH to MH, 18 May 1941.

'*great delight*': letter from HH to MH, 9 March 1942.

'*I think it would be best … I mustn't*': ibid.

'*Saturday and Sunday … I do need*': letter from HH to MH, 17 March 1942.

'*She is a really … seven days' leave*': ibid.

'*spiritual dumbness and numbness*': letter from EB to HH, 8 November 1934.

'*Last night too … in those old ways*': letter from MH to HH, undated [?April/May 1942].

'*bloody week*': ibid.

'*your desperate gloom … the question)*': ibid.

'*Often I've met … my fears*': ibid.

'*stern little cottage*': letter from MH to HH, undated [August 1944].

'*We look across … friendly*': ibid.

'*an incredible little tough … exhibitionist*': ibid.

Pendine: *The Disinherited*

'*I am really excited … let you see*': letter from HH to MH, 30 April 1945.

'*a bit difficult … MS etc*': letter from HH to L. C. Martin, 25 August 1946.

'*we got on … been made earlier*': ibid.

'*the house might contain untold treasure*': ibid.

'*in a very superficial … music yet known*': ibid.

'*sort of literary advisers*': ibid.

'*Very like* The Aspern Papers': ibid.

'*I do honestly think … have been asleep*': ibid.

'*I want it to be … won't be scared*': ibid.

'*I am truly feeling … cigarettes*': letter from HH to Maurice Bowra, 28 June 1946.

'*If it hadn't … lecturing technique*': ibid.

'*deformity*': letter from EB to Charles Ritchie, 24 October 1949, *LCW*, p. 141.

'*In some cases … the reader*': letter from EB to Daniel George, 2 June 1948, Box 10, Folder 4, Bowen Archive.

'*the exact psychological impact*': ibid.

'*particularly the long stay … to rest*': letter from HH to MH, 10 July [1948].

'*I made myself … respects I am*': ibid.

'*It is a* sine qua *… the century*': 'A New Edition of Dickens's Letters', *All in Due Time*, pp. 225–226.

'*I feel I am getting … I could do*': letter from MH to HH, 1 May 1951.

'*£3 a week to offset housekeeper expenses*': letter from MH to HH, 14 March 1954.

'*a firm understanding*': ibid.

'*beauty*': letter from MH to HH, 5 December 1953.

'*they pay handsomely*': letter from EB to HH, 29 June 1936.

'*not only the anchorage ... good in it*': letter from EB to Isaiah Berlin, 8 October 1952, MS. Berlin 245, fol. 145, Berlin Archive.

'*really the feeling ... winds that blow*': ibid.

'*Darling, it was ... another curve!*': letter from MH to HH, 8 May 1950.

'*The love of my family ... sweet and fair*': letter from HH to MH, 31 January 1949.

'*Death ... last two years*': HH, fragment, 30 December 1950.

'*done in*': letter from HH to MH, undated [Spring 1951].

'*I hate the idea ... get used to it*': ibid.

'*The only thing ... character*': letter from EB to Charles Ritchie, 25 February 1955, *LCW*, p. 205.

'*Humphry's death ... with them*': letter from Maurice Bowra to EB, 24 February 1955, Box 10, Folder 6, Bowen Archive.

'*dear*': the will of Arthur Humphry House, 8 January 1936.

'*My dear Isaiah ... Madeline*': letter from MH to Isaiah Berlin, 22 February 1955, MS. Berlin 140, fols. 276–277, Berlin Archive.

'*For Humphrey ... where you lie*': Stephen Spender, 'Eleven Bagatelles: VI, For Humphrey House' in *The Generous Days* (David R. Godine: 1969), p. 16.

Hythe: *Requiescat*

'*Why then fear ... experience more*': EB, 'The Beauty of Being Your Age', undated essay, Box 1, Folder 5, Bowen Archive.

'*For women ... unforeseen treasure*': ibid.

'*Form is the servant ... itself*': EB, lecture notes on the short story, Vassar College [?1960], Box 7, Folder 3, Bowen Archive.

'*a unique expression*': ibid.

'*What would Chekhov ... or unconscious?*': ibid.

'*When we were … die and rot*': letter from EB to Charles Ritchie, 8 July 1962, *LCW*, p. 392.

'*She was now in a state … works, and letters*': *ET*, p. 110.

'*with a climate … its own*': letter from EB to Isaiah Berlin, 8 October 1952, MS Berlin 245, fol. 145, Berlin Archive.

'*Don't rack your heart … you were*': letter from Arthur Calder-Marshall to MH, undated [?1955].

'*capacity for interest … quite big*': letter from HH to EB, undated [Autumn 1933].

'*Gratters, old girl … way it happened*': letter from Arthur Calder-Marshall to MH, 12 June [1965].

'*In memory of … her home*': plaque on the wall of Farahy Church, County Cork, Ireland.

'*The news is not only good … we always did*': Audrey Fiennes to Rosamond Lehmann, 19 November [1975], GBR/0272/PP/RNL 2/185/1, The Papers of Rosamond Nina Lehmann, King's College Archive Centre, Cambridge.

Cambridge: *A World of Love*

'*Dear Julia … Love Linny*': postcard from MH to Julia Parry, 1973.

'*How people come … dead*': letter from EB to Charles Ritchie, 25 February 1955, *LCR*, p. 205.

'*simple, direct*': letter from EB to HH, undated [?May 1935].

'*confirmed writer*': letter from EB to HH, 6 June 1934.

'*shit from Sevenoaks*': letter from Arthur Calder-Marshall to MH, 2 October [1975].

'*I am grateful … for a biographer*': letter from Victoria Glendinning to MH, 10 October 1975.

'*His wheels went round without her*': 'Making Arrangements', *CS*, p. 183.

'*The man seems … revealing*': letter from MH to Kathleen Tillotson, 21 November 1975.

'*I (like Naomi, yes) … a nit-wit?*': ibid.

'*She sent me … whole business*': letter from MH to Kathleen Tillotson, undated [November 1976].

'*I think so … massive rewriting*': letter from MH to Victoria Glendinning, 12 November 1976.

'*a distinct whiff of gossip … withdrawn*': Claire Tomalin, review of *Elizabeth Bowen: Portrait of a Writer*, in *The Sunday Times*, 9 October 1977.

'*One is aware … the lately dead*': ibid.

'*article of a debunking nature*': EB to HH, 28 May 1936.

'*Once a man is dead … it stays*': ibid.

'*The sight of her small … important*': obituary of Madeline House, in *The Times*, 7 March 1978, p. 18.

'*the hour arranged*': 'The Demon Lover', *CS*, p. 744.

'*The ink, sharp in candlelight, had not faded*': *WOL*, p. 33.

Select Bibliography

Baker, Deborah, *The Last Englishmen: Love, War and the End of Empire* (London: Chatto & Windus, 2018)

Berlin, Isaiah, *Affirming: Letters 1975–1997*, eds. Henry Hardy and Mark Pottle (London: Random House, 2015)

Berlin, Isaiah, *Flourishing: Letters 1928–1946*, ed. Henry Hardy (Cambridge: Cambridge University Press, 2004)

Bennett, Andrew, and Nicholas Royle, *Elizabeth Bowen and the Dissolution of the Novel: Still Lives* (Basingstoke and London: Macmillan, 1994)

Betjeman, John, *An Oxford University Chest* (1938; Oxford: OUP, 1979)

Boulestin, X. Marcel, *Simple French Cooking* (New York: Frederick A. Stokes, 1923)

Bowen, Elizabeth, *Afterthought: Pieces About Writing* (London: Longmans, Green and Co., 1962)

Bowen, Elizabeth, *A Time in Rome* (London: Longmans, Green and Co., 1960)

Bowen, Elizabeth, *A World of Love* (1955; London: Vintage, 1999)

Bowen, Elizabeth, *Bowen's Court* (1942; London: Vintage, 1999)

Bowen, Elizabeth, *Collected Impressions* (London: Longmans, Green and Co., 1950)

Bowen, Elizabeth, *Collected Stories* (1980; London: Vintage, 1999)

Bowen, Elizabeth, *English Novelists* from the 'Britain in Pictures' series (London: Collins, 1942)

Bowen, Elizabeth, *Eva Trout* (1968; London: Penguin, 1987)

Bowen, Elizabeth, *Friends and Relations* (1931; Chicago: University of Chicago Press, 2012)

Bowen, Elizabeth, *Listening In: Broadcasts, Speeches, and Interviews*, ed. Allan Hepburn (Edinburgh: Edinburgh University Press, 2010)

Bowen, Elizabeth, *Pictures and Conversations* (London: Allen Lane, 1975)

Bowen, Elizabeth, *The Death of the Heart* (1938; London: Vintage, 2012)

Bowen, Elizabeth, *The Hotel* (1927; London: Penguin, 1984)

Bowen, Elizabeth, *The House in Paris* (1935; London: Penguin, 1976)

Bowen, Elizabeth, *The Heat of the Day* (1948; London: Vintage, 1998)

Bowen, Elizabeth, *The Last September* (1929; London: Vintage, 1998)

Bowen, Elizabeth, *The Little Girls* (1964; London: Penguin, 1983)

Bowen, Elizabeth, *The Mulberry Tree: Writings of*, ed. Hermione Lee (1986; London: Vintage, 1999)

Bowen, Elizabeth, *The Shelbourne* (London: George Harrap, 1951)

Bowen, Elizabeth, *To the North* (1932; London: Penguin, 1987)

Bowra, Maurice, *Memories* (London: Weidenfeld and Nicolson, 1966)

Calder-Marshall, Arthur, *God Will Provide a Bit More*, unpublished autobiography

Calder-Marshall, Arthur, *The Magic of My Youth* (London: Hart-Davis, 1951)

Carritt, Michael, *A Mole in the Crown: Memories of a British Official in India who worked with the Communist Underground in the 1930s* (Sussex: published privately, 1985)

Clapp, B. W., *The University of Exeter: A History* (Exeter: University Press, 1982)

Craig, Patricia, *Elizabeth Bowen* (Harmondsworth: Penguin Books, 1986)

Dickens, Charles, *The Letters of Charles Dickens: Volume 1, 1820–1839*, The

Pilgrim Edition, ed. Madeline House and Graham Storey, (Oxford: The Clarendon Press, 1965)

Dutta, Krishna, *Calcutta: A Cultural and Literary History* (Oxford: Signal Books, 2003)

Forster, E. M., *A Passage to India* (1924; London: Penguin, 1966)

Gardiner, Juliet, *The Thirties: An Intimate Story* (2010; Harper Press: London, 2011)

Gilmour, David, *The British in India: Three Centuries of Ambition and Experience* (2018; London: Penguin, 2019)

Glendinning, Victoria, *Elizabeth Bowen: Portrait of a Writer* (1977; London: Phoenix, 1993)

Graves, Robert and Alan Hodge, *The Long Weekend: A Social History of Great Britain 1918–1939* (London: Faber and Faber, 1940)

Hall, Lesley A., *Hidden Anxieties: Male Sexuality, 1900–1950* (Cambridge: Polity Press, 1991)

House, Humphry, *All in Due Time: Collected Essays and Broadcast Talks* (London: Rupert Hart-Davis, 1955)

House, Humphry, *Aristotle's Poetics*, (London: Hart-Davis, 1956)

House, Humphry, *Coleridge: The Clark Lectures* (London: Hart-Davis, 1953)

House, Humphry, *The Dickens World* (Oxford: OUP, 1941)

House, Humphry, *I Spy With My Little Eye* (Calcutta: published privately, 1937). *https://jadunivpress.com/2019/04/10/i-spy-with-my-little-eye-2/*?

House, Humphry, *The Note-books and Papers of Gerard Manley Hopkins*, ed. (London & New York: Oxford University Press, 1937)

Kiberd, Declan, *Inventing Ireland: The Literature of the Modern Nation* (1995; London: Vintage, 1996)

Lassner, Phyllis, *Elizabeth Bowen* (London: Macmillan, 1990)

Lee, Hermione, *Elizabeth Bowen* (1981; London: Vintage, 1999)

Marsh, Darren, *Exeter's Royal Clarence Hotel* (Exeter: The Devon and Exeter Institution, 2017)

Moorhouse, Geoffrey, *Calcutta* (1971; London: Phoenix, 1998)

Nicholson, Virginia, *Among the Bohemians: Experiments in Living 1900–1939* (2002; London: Viking, 2003)

Overy, Richard, *The Morbid Age* (2009; London: Penguin, 2010)

Peters, Margot, *May Sarton: A Biography* (New York: Knopf, 1997)

Pugh, Martin, *We Danced All Night: A Social History of Britain Between the Wars* (London: The Bodley Head, 2008)

Robinson, Andrew, *Satyajit Ray: The Inner Eye* (London: André Deutsch, 1989)

Rogers, Gayle, *Modernism and the New Spain: Britain, Cosmopolitan Europe and Literary History* (Oxford: Oxford University Press, 2012)

Rees, Goronwy, *A Bundle of Sensations: Sketches in Autobiography* (London: Chatto & Windus, 1972).

Sarton, May, *A World of Light* (1976; London: The Women's Press, 1996)

Spender, Stephen, *World Within World* (1951; London: Faber, 1977)

Stone, Abraham and Hannah, *A Marriage Manual: A Practical Guide-book to Sex and Marriage* (London: Gollancz & The Bodley Head, 1936)

Struther, Jan, *Mrs Miniver* (1939; London: Virago, 1989)

Szreter, Simon and Kate Fisher, *Sex Before the Sexual Revolution: Intimate Life in England 1918–1963* (Cambridge: CUP, 2010)

Walshe, Eibhear, (ed.) *Elizabeth Bowen – Visions and Revisions: Irish Writers in their Time* (Dublin: Irish Academic Press, 2009)

Williams, Terry Tempest, *When Women Were Birds: Fifty-Four Variations on Voice* (New York: Farrar, Straus and Giroux, 2012)

Wilson, A.N., *After the Victorians: 1901–1953* (London: Hutchinson, 2005)

Woolf, Virginia, *The Diary of Virginia Woolf Volume Four: 1931–1935*, ed. Anne Olivier Bell (1982; Harmondsworth: Penguin, 1983)